ALAMO - - -
THE PRICE OF FREEDOM

A HISTORY
OF
TEXAS

2nd Edition

ISBN 0-924307-00-5
Library of Congress Card 88-141628

Printed and Distributed By
Docutex, Inc.
P. O. Box 101050
San Antonio, Texas 78201

FORWARD

If this forward reads similarly to the one I wrote in *A Time to Love--A Time to Die*, it's because I intend it to be. With fervor I repeat the opening phrase in that forward --rarely is a book or story the independent effort of one person (and certainly not a history book).

I am deeply indebted to a host of people--some very close to me, but mostly strangers who are fellow authors. The latter group is shown in my bibliography, representing several generations of noted historians. I hope I have listed all who have contributed to my research and trust that I have not misrepresented or misused their distinguished works. If I have done so, it was unintentional and inadvertent.

Focusing on those who are friends and have helped me is like focusing a kaleidoscope--many faces come into my mind. But two in particular stand out sharply: Doris Menke, my faithful, indefatigable secretary, who has so unselfishly given much of her own time to this project and words alone cannot express my gratitude. Nor can mere words convey my appreciation to Bernice Strong, Archivist of the DRT Research Library at the Alamo. She has strived to keep me on the straight and narrow (though not always successfully) when my mind and pen wanted to stray. A mere "thank you" seems so insufficient. My feelings in regard to these two ladies parallel those of Sam Houston for his old friend, General Andrew Jackson, when in moments of despair, Houston's behavior caused the General great pain. Houston wanted to atone for this period of delinquency by doing something grand--to capture an empire and lay it at his old chieftain's feet. Alas, I'm afraid the world is out of empires to capture, but at least the three of us share the dream of a new estremadura.

Next, my beloved wife of forty-four years, Lavonia--only an understanding woman can tolerate the selfish demands of a writer--always in a hurry; no time for parties, Sunday afternoon drives, movies or dining out. A heartfelt thank you is but a token of my appreciation.

Others, mostly associated with the Alamo, have been so helpful in this endeavor--their names, alphabetically listed: June Barth, Chapel Hostess at the Alamo; Steve Beck, Curator at the Alamo; Sharon R. Crutchfield, Director of the DRT Library at the Alamo; Ed Gearke, Assistant Curator at the Alamo; and Charles J. Long, Curator Emeritus at the Alamo.

Because the final chapter of this book spawned the IMAX movie, "Alamo...The Price of Freedom," I must also thank Kieth Merrill, the director, and all of the cast--particularly the "re-enactors" who, in my opinion, made the movie. The book and movie are definitely intertwined. I am proud to have conceived both, and thank God I have lived to see a twelve-year dream become a reality. The movie and this book carry a message--my legacy to future generations-- that freedom rests finally upon those willing to die for it.

ALAMO ... THE PRICE OF FREEDOM

TABLE OF CONTENTS

List of Pictures and Illustrations

TEXAS--A Synopsis

Sired in 1521 when Hernando Cortez of Spain conquered the Aztec nation of Mexico and claimed it for his King; gestated in the womb of a virgin continent for three hundred years and born in the bottomlands of the Brazos River in 1821 when Stephen F. Austin brought the first of the "Old 300."

A half-loved, half-hated, and ill-treated child of Mexico, but suckled and kept alive by every suffering pioneer mother; then miraculously transfused with the blood from one hundred eighty-nine heterogeneous men from seven countries and twenty-one states who died at the Alamo on that immortal day, March 6, 1836.

Finally after San Jacinto, it stood proud and tall on the wobbly legs of a new Republic, weak and in need of nourishment, but with a hybrid vigor that guaranteed it would grow to become the giant it is today.

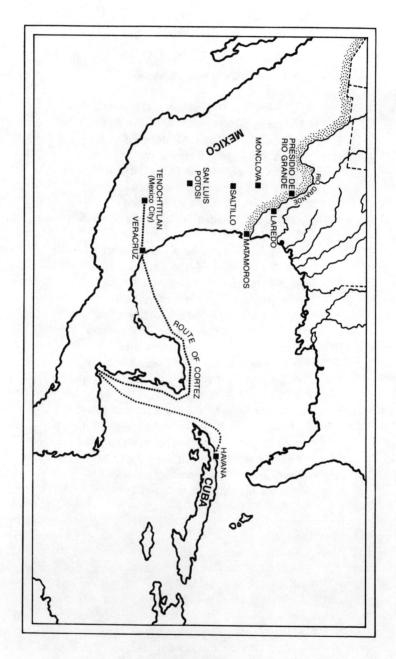

CORTEZ'S ROUTE

CHAPTER 1

GENESIS

Soon after Columbus discovered the New World, the Spanish king, influenced by stories from various adventurers, believed there was great wealth in the West Indies and Mexico. The crown decided to extend its tentacles of empire. In 1518 Captain Hernando Cortez was sent out with about seven hundred men and eleven small ships to explore the mainland (now Mexico) west of Cuba.

In the early spring of 1519 Cortez anchored at the port of San Juan de Ulloa on the east coast of present Honduras, then proceeded north along the coast, found a suitable harbor, and founded Vera Cruz--City of the True Cross. It was from here he decided to invade the interior (without official sanction). First, he burned all of his ships except one. He did this so none of his men would be able to desert and return to Spain. The one vessel he saved would be used to carry messages back to Spain.

Cortez left a few soldiers to guard Vera Cruz. He led the remainder overland toward what is now Mexico City, then called Tenochtitlan, the capital of the Aztec nation. The Spaniards arrived on November 8, 1519, and were graciously received by Montezuma, the Aztec emperor. But Cortez rejected the friendly hand of Montezuma and advised him that he came as a conqueror, not a guest. The Aztecs plotted to drive out the Spaniards, but Cortez learned of the scheme, seized Montezuma and forced the emperor to deliver to him great quantities of gold and precious jewels.

Soon the Aztec people revolted against both Montezuma and Cortez. In the course of the uprising, Montezuma was killed; and Cortez and his soldiers retreated from Mexico City. The Spaniards were pursued for six days and finally overtaken. A great battle was fought on the plain of Otumba; the Aztecs were defeated. Cortez claimed the entire country of Mexico for Spain on July 7, 1520. Reinforcing his army with men from the local Indian tribes who hated the Aztecs, he recaptured Mexico City the following year on August 13, 1521, after a siege of several months. (It would be three hundred years before Mexico would throw off the Spanish yoke.)

Cortez sent his one remaining ship back to Spain with word of his conquest. King Charles was so pleased he made him governor of Mexico. In 1528, after seven years, Cortez returned to Spain, content that the Spanish crown was firmly entrenched in the New

World. And so it was. He had divided Mexico into several provinces, each with a governor. One such governor was Francisco Vasquez de Coronado, who ruled the state of Nueva Galicia, sprawled across the central part of Mexico. We will learn more about Coronado later.

PONCE DE LEON
Other adventurers of the Spanish crown were exploring the New World. In 1513 Ponce de Leon, searching for a fountain of youth of Indian legend, discovered and partially charted the coast of Florida, which he thought to be an island. He was wounded by an Indian arrow and returned to Cuba where he died.

ALONZO ALVAREZ DE PINEDA - FIRST SPANIARD IN TEXAS
These early explorers believed that all of the West Indies were really outlying islands of the Asian mainland through which they could find a water route to the Far East. In 1519 the Spanish governor of Jamaica sent a navigator to the west coast of Florida to follow up Ponce de Leon's exploration. He was to sail westward to chart the coast of any other islands and find a possible route westward. This navigator was Alonzo Alvarez de Pineda, who would become the first European to set foot on Texas soil.

Pineda sailed up the west coast of Florida and discovered to his surprise it was not an island. He continued west and made the first, albeit inaccurate, chart of the shores of the Gulf of Mexico all the way from Florida to Vera Cruz. On the way he made several stops along the Texas coast, probably the first on Galveston Island. When he returned to Jamaica, he gave a glowing report of this new land and recommended that a colony be established at what is believed to be the mouth of the present Colorado River.

INDEFATIGABLE CABEZA DE VACA
No action was taken on Pineda's recommendation for a colony, but shortly another Spaniard would set foot in Texas due entirely to an unfortunate accident. His name was Alvar Nunez Cabeza de Vaca, member of a large expedition commanded by Panfilo de Narvaez, sent to conquer Florida. In 1520 Narvaez first landed on Florida's northwest coast. His plan was to send his ships northward to a rendezvous point up the coast; he would then lead his soldiers overland to the rendezvous. From the beginning his force was plagued by mosquitoes, hostile Indians, snaky swamps, hurricane winds, and extreme heat. The land party slowly worked

its way northward to the rendezvous point, but when they arrived there were no ships to be seen. The captain of the ships, after waiting more than twice the agreed upon time, sailed back down the coast looking for his lost commander. Failing to find Narvaez, he returned to Cuba. In desperation, Narvaez ordered rafts and boats built from trees. Loading what provisions they could find, they launched themselves to the mercy of the sea. By the needle, he headed southwest toward Mexico. A great hurricane blew across their course and swamped most of their crafts. But two boats, each with about thirty dying men, washed ashore many days later on a sandy beach which is now Galveston Island on the Texas coast. A band of Indians nurtured them back to health and then enslaved them. Many of the decimated men died that winter; and by the spring of 1529, only fifteen were alive. Among the survivors was a strong Negro by the name of Estevanico and a hardy nobleman named Cabeza de Vaca, who would turn out to be one of the most resourceful adventurers in recorded history.

TREK ACROSS HALF A CONTINENT

De Vaca escaped from the first tribe only to be captured by another. Each time he learned more about Indian culture. He enhanced his status by posing as a medicine man, and his movements became less restrictive. De Vaca planned an escape at the first opportunity; it came in 1535. With the Negro, Estevanico, and two other Spaniards, he set out for Mexico. He knew only that the Spanish colonies lay somewhere to the southwest. Without a compass and only the sun and stars to guide him, he headed west across Texas. This amazing man walked across nearly half the continent, but his exact course is not known. However, it is very likely that he passed in the vicinity of present San Antonio and then south across the Rio Grande, then west again, finally reaching the Pacific coast of Mexico. Luckily he encountered a detachment of Spanish troops on an expedition looking for Indians to enslave. They could hardly believe that the tattered, gaunt, incoherent men who ran up shouting and crying were actually fellow Spaniards. Only their dark beards and garbled Spanish saved them from being killed as crazed Indians. When the soldiers were finally convinced of their identity, De Vaca and his companions were escorted to Mexico City. Here he was greeted as one who had returned from the dead, and every word he uttered was accepted with wonder and amazement.

CITY OF GOLD

Of the many stories he told, one in particular had great appeal. De Vaca related an Indian legend he had heard about a golden city somewhere to the northwest of his route where riches were greater than the treasures found in Mexico City. Almost immediately every adventurer in Mexico volunteered to be a part of a new conquest. Some knew firsthand of the fantastic fortunes that had been acquired by the men who served with Cortez. Wasn't it just as likely that even greater wealth could be had by looting and plundering this legendary city to the north?

CORONADO'S DREAM OF WEALTH

This dream of wealth appealed particularly to the governor of Nueva Galicia, the heretofore-mentioned, Francisco Vasquez de Coronado. Though very interested in De Vaca's tale of wealth, he prudently decided to send a reconnaissance party to determine the strength of the defenders and the exact location of this purported city of gold before ordering out a large expedition. In 1539 the Negro, Estevanico, was sent out with a Franciscan monk, Father Marcus de Niza, and a small band of friendly Indians. The party crossed into the present United States in the vicinity of eastern Arizona where Estevanico was murdered by hostile Indians. Father Marcus promptly headed back to the safety of Mexico City. But the padre was a man of remarkable imagination, and he reported that he had seen the fabulous city from a high hill and that its walls were, indeed, made with gold bricks and its gates studded with jewels. Even its very streets were paved with silver. Coronado listened with great interest. He yearned to own this wealth which was beyond his wildest dreams. He decided to find this magnificent city.

Coronado had no trouble enlisting hundreds of soldiers and many Indians on this, the grandest and most promising entrada yet spawned in the New World. In 1540 with more than a thousand men, at least 1,500 horses and mules, herds of sheep and cattle, more than a dozen priests, and scores of women who were carried along as cooks and laundresses, Coronado and his group headed out with dreams of wealth spurring them northward.

GRAND CANYON DISCOVERED

Coronado crossed into what is now the United States somewhere in present Arizona and found the Zuni pueblo city called Hawikuh near the current border of Arizona and New Mexico. The Spaniards, upon entering the city, were dejected to find only sun-dried bricks of clay and worthless Indian pottery. Now Coronado split his force, sending one group westward— under the command of his army master, Don Lopez de Cardenas. Cardenas did not find the legendary golden city, but he did discover one of the seven wonders of the world. He became the first European to gaze upon the splendor of the Grand Canyon and was awe-struck by its beauty and grandeur.

Coronado's group headed eastward, but he decided to set up winter headquarters at the pueblo village called Tiguex on the Rio Grande. When spring came, he listened to a new guide, an Indian called "El Turco." El Turco promised he could guide him to the city of gold, so Coronado marched eastward into Texas. Unfortunately his route is no better known than that of De Vaca's, but the consensus of historians suggest that he entered the Texas Panhandle west of the present city of Lubbock. He crossed the high plains which the Spaniards named the Llano Estacado (a name it still carries.) Then his course took him northward, and he probably discovered the Palo Duro Canyon near present Amarillo. From the canyon he continued northward to a land that he named Quivera. Quivera could be in what is now Oklahoma somewhere near the Canadian River or perhaps even further north on the Arkansas River in the current state of Kansas (the latter is believed more likely.) But the only thing Coronado found that even remotely resembled gold were the millions of acres of gold-crested Indian grass waving on the prairies. Coronado was disillusioned and realized that El Turco had led him for many months on a vain search. He ordered the Indian beheaded and turned southwestward toward New Mexico, spending the winter again at Tiguex. The following spring in 1542 he returned to Mexico, claiming all the land he traversed for Spain. The only purpose the expedition served was to prove there was no gold in the north for the avaricious Spaniards to seek. To a significant extent this delayed the development of Texas because in the minds of the Spaniards, there was nothing north of the Rio Grande worthy of their attention. Yet the legend of the golden city grew and even became intertwined in myth of the Seven Cities of Cibola.

Coronado had no way of knowing as he rode across the grassy plains of Texas in the summer of 1541 that yet another party of Spaniards led by Hernando de Soto was struggling westward, likely through present Oklahoma; and the two parties were probably at one time no more than two hundred miles apart. How did De Soto happen to be in Oklahoma? His expedition had landed in Florida in 1539 and headed westward. He had been wandering across the continent for over two years; but after traveling some distance into Oklahoma, he decided to return to the Mississippi River. There De Soto died and his command passed to Luis de Moscoso, but Moscoso and his men had enough of wandering and decided to return to Mexico City. They marched southwestward and entered Texas in the vicinity of the present city of Texarkana during the summer of 1542. Continuing westward only a short distance, they decided to return to the Mississippi, where they built rafts which they alternately sailed, rowed, and drifted to the mouth of the Mississippi and then crept along the coast of Texas and finally reached the mouth of the Panuco River in Mexico.

TENTACLES OF EMPIRE - NEW MEXICO

Moscoso's report on Texas was only slightly more favorable than that of Coronado. His findings, combined with Coronado's, further convinced the Spaniards that there was nothing north of the Rio Grande worth searching for. But memories are short and new generations are born. Other adventurers wanted to emulate the conquest of those who had gone before; and thinking themselves perhaps a little smarter or luckier, they knew they could find wealth by following the needle northward. Some of these trekked the Rio Grande into New Mexico. Their forays caused missions to be built in Mexico's northern states of Chihuahua, Coahuila, and Nuevo Leon and wealthy Spaniards established large estates in the north central valleys of Mexico. Large ranches needed workers and this meant slaving parties that captured peaceful Indians in New Mexico and either brought them back to serve in peonage on the large ranches or put them to work in the silver mines. Toward the end of the century, the tentacles of the Spanish empire were definitely reaching into the heart of New Mexico territory.

With these tentacles of empire came soldiers and priests, the latter interested in the salvation of souls of the Pueblo Indians. But the vision of a city of gold just over the next mountain still danced in the minds of every adventurer.

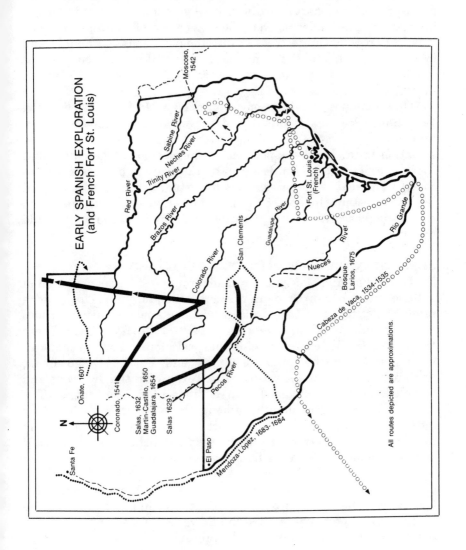

EARLY SPANISH EXPLORATION
(and French Fort St. Louis)

Moscoso, 1542

Sabine River

Neches River

Trinity River

Red River

Brazos River

Colorado River

San Clements

Guadalupe River

Fort St. Louis (French)

Nueces River

Rio Grande

Bosque-Larios, 1675

Cabeza de Vaca, 1534-1535

All routes depicted are approximations.

N

Santa Fe

Oñate, 1601

Coronado, 1541

Salas, 1632
Martin-Castillo, 1650
Guadalajara, 1654

Salas 1629

Pecos River

El Paso

Mendoza-Lopez, 1683-1684

EARLY SPANISH EXPLORATION

9

GENESIS

SANTA FE, EL PASO DEL NORTE, AND ALBUQUERQUE ESTABLISHED

In 1598 the viceroy commissioned Juan de Onate to establish a permanent settlement on the upper reaches of the Rio Grande. He followed the river northward and finally established headquarters in 1600 just a few miles north of the present city of Santa Fe. In 1601 it is known that Onate crossed into today's Texas Panhandle and followed the course of the Canadian River until he reached the land of Quivera like his predecessor, Coronado; but also like Coronado he found no riches.

Onate did not remain as governor of New Mexico after 1609, the year Santa Fe was founded and served as the capital of New Mexico. Priests came, along with troops, seeking to bring salvation to the heathens populating the Pueblo villages (now that these heathens had been declared by the Pope to possess a soul to save.) The zeal of the priests was important because, in essence, it led to the establishment of the province of New Mexico; and from this springboard further exploration of Texas from the west would occur.

JUMANO INDIANS - WEST TEXAS EXPLORED

In 1629 a band of Jumano Indians from West Texas appeared at a little mission church near present Albuquerque. They told a remarkable story of a Lady in Blue who had appeared several times at their village telling them the story of Christianity. These Indians actually came seeking her religion. Two Franciscan missionaries, Father Juande Salas and Father Diego Leon, intrigued by their story, returned to Texas with the Jumanos and traveled inland about one hundred miles to the southeast. The padres spent several months among these Indians, distributing gifts and baptizing them. The exact location of the Jumano camp has never been determined; but the reported distance would place it somewhere along the Pecos River, where it crosses Interstate 10 in west Texas. In 1632 Father Salas with another priest, Father Juan de Ortego, and a few soldiers went back to the Jumano area. This time they penetrated into Texas about two hundred miles to the southeast and probably reached the Edwards Plateau at the junction of the three Concho Rivers near the present city of San Angelo.

For the next twenty years, there was sporadic trade between the Jumanos of Texas and the Spaniards in New Mexico. The Spaniards occasionally visited Jumano country, and the Jumanos traded buffalo hides for tools and weapons. These Spaniards discovered and named the Nueces River (the River of Nuts, referring to the pecan). It was also from the Jumanos that the Spanish first learned of the Tejas Indians, who inhabited the woodlands of Texas some four hundred fifty miles to the east. It is interesting to note that it was on one of these entradas to the junction of the three Conchos that the Spanish discovered what the Indians already knew. Fresh water pearls, found in mussels, were abundant in the clear waters of the Conchos. The mussels multiplied prolifically on the sandy beds of these rivers. Although of poor quality, these pearls were used by the Indians in trade and served to stimulate further exploration of the area.

In 1654 a second expedition led by Diego de Guadalajara left Santa Fe with about thirty soldiers and over two hundred friendly Indians. The Spanish again gathered pearls from the mussel beds of the Concho and attempted to reach the land of the Tejas. They marched eastward some two hundred miles and were attacked by a band of Indians they called Cuitaos. They defeated the Indians but turned back without really getting close to Tejas country which lay in extreme eastern Texas. After this entrada Spanish interest in Texas waned considerably.

CHIEF SABEATA

It was not until 1683 that another official expedition was sent into West Texas. Had it been successful, it would have changed the course of Texas history--and perhaps western history as well. This expedition, commanded by Juan Domingo de Mendoza, was sent at the plea of a wily Jumano Indian chief named Juan Sabeata. Sabeata had good reason for wanting Spanish help. The Apache Indians from the north (the low hills of eastern Colorado) were migrating southward, riding on multi-colored Spanish horses that had either strayed or been stolen. They were the first Plains Indians to have mounts. On the backs of these swift ponies, they became the masters of the hunt and the fiercest of warriors until the Comanche also became mounted and began moving southward, sweeping all tribes in their path aside. But they were still years away. The Apache, for now, was king.

Chief Sabeata was desperate to protect his people from the Apache. He knew he must ask the Spanish to establish a permanent settlement in his country with guns and soldiers to deter this aggressor. But Sabeata was wise and also knew the Spaniards would not come without purpose. He would give them a reason by asking that a mission be built in his country. This would mean padres, and padres meant soldiers. The Spanish governor was hesitant, therefore, Sabeata would use a ploy. He told the Spaniards that he had seen a cross appear in the sky over his camp many times and that the Jumano wanted to change from their pagan ways. The idea of bringing Christianity to an entire tribe interested Father Nicolas Lopez, and he persuaded Juan Dominguez de Mendoza to lead an expedition.

Due to Chief Sabeata's pleas, the expedition of 1683 led by Mendoza and Father Lopez and guided by Sabeata proceeded beyond the Trans-Pecos by way of present Fort Stockton to the Pecos River, near today's West Texas city of McCamey, then eastward to the junctions of the three Conchos where San Angelo is now located. Thence, the entrada continued generally southeastward to a river which Mendoza called the San Clemente, (very likely the San Saba), where a mission was built, probably somewhere between the present Texas towns of Menard and Ft. McKavett.

THE APACHE

The Apache fiercely resisted this intrusion into their hunting grounds. Attacking the Spaniards three different times, they inflicted many casualties. Mendoza had enough and retreated to Mexico to appeal for help. He pleaded for 200 soldiers so he could conquer western Texas for the crown and also asked for a permanent mission. But government officials were not listening to his plea, for their eyes and ears were on southeast Texas where the French were rumored to have established a fort on the Gulf Coast.

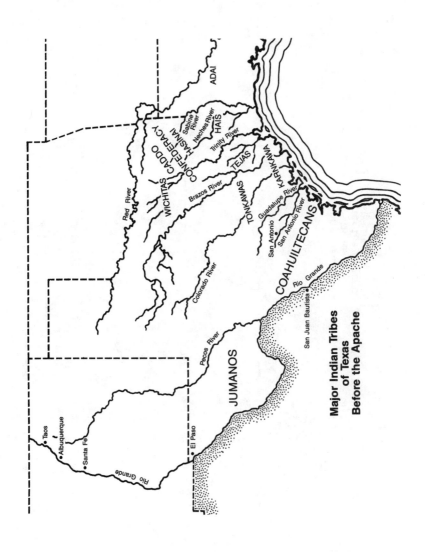

Major Indian Tribes
of Texas
Before the Apache

MAJOR INDIAN TRIBES IN TEXAS BEFORE THE APACHE

GENESIS

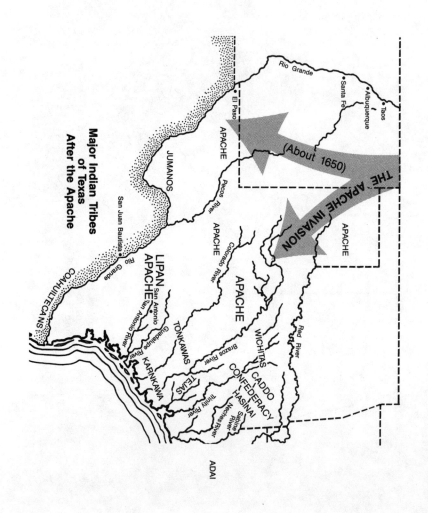

Major Indian Tribes
of Texas
After the Apache

(About 1650)

THE APACHE INVASION

MAJOR INDIAN TRIBES OF TEXAS AFTER THE APACHE

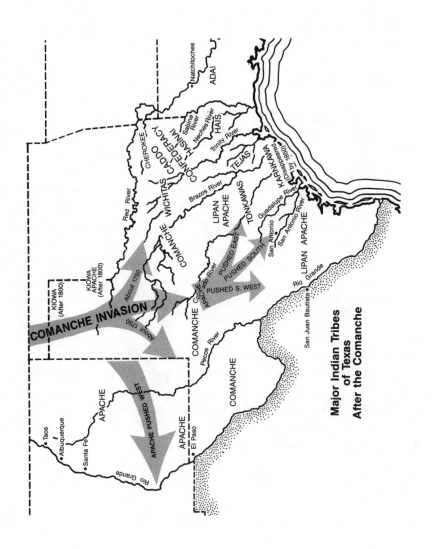

MAJOR INDIAN TRIBES OF TEXAS AFTER THE COMANCHE

GENESIS

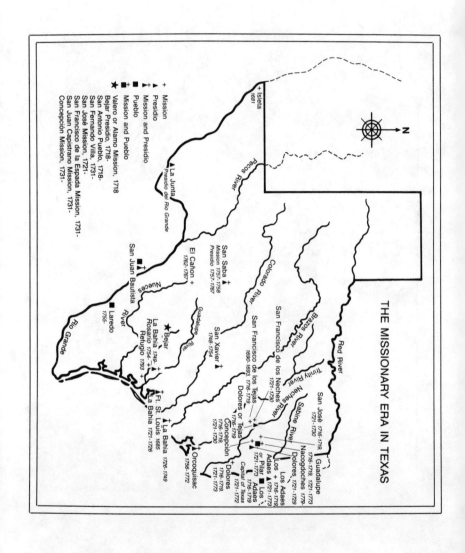

THE MISSIONARY ERA IN TEXAS

CHAPTER 2

THE GESTATION

THE FRENCH IN TEXAS

The rumor the Spanish government in Mexico City had heard was true. In 1685 a French explorer by the name of Rene Robert Cavalier, Sieur de La Salle, planted upon the soil of Texas the second of six flags that would fly against her azure skies. He landed in Matagorda Bay at the mouth of the Lavaca River, where he established Fort St. Louis, giving France a claim to Texas. King Louis XIV of France was determined not to abide by the Pope's decision that divided all of the unknown world between Spain and Portugal. He refused to let France be excluded from these riches and launched his own explorers and settlers into the New World.

France concentrated its attention initially in what is now Canada, entering the interior through the St. Lawrence River. The French set up trading posts in Quebec and Montreal and on all of the Great Lakes. Two of their priests, on an overland portage from the Fox to the Wisconsin Rivers, discovered the upper Mississippi. Shortly thereafter a young man in the service of his king, Rene Robert Cavalier, established Fort Frontenac at Niagara and began such a lucrative fur trade with the Indians that he gained a title, Sieur de La Salle.

LA SALLE AND FORT ST. LOUIS

Known simply as La Salle, this man at age 40 portaged from the Illinois River, drifted down the Mississippi to its mouth and in 1682 laid claim for France to all the lands drained by the mighty river and its tributaries. (He was perhaps trying to match the audacity of Balboa, when he crossed the Isthmus of Panama in 1513 and claimed all of the land touched by the Pacific Ocean for the king of Spain.) La Salle returned to Canada and then back to France where he received permission to colonize the mouth of the Mississippi.

He left France in the summer of 1684 with four ships and over two hundred settlers, but the expedition was beset with bad luck from the beginning. A storm in the Gulf of Mexico destroyed a ship carrying most of the supplies. La Salle became ill and quarrels developed between himself and his principal ship commander. Sailing past the mouth of the Mississippi, the expedition landed in Matagorda Bay at the mouth of the Lavaca River in Texas. Another storm sank two other ships, and the remaining ship and its crew sailed back to France, leaving the colonists to whatever fate was in store. Though not recovered from his illness, La Salle was eager to begin the construction of a fort. He marched several miles up the Lavaca River and established Fort St. Louis in 1685.

La Salle, over the next two years, made forays westward ostensibly looking for the Mississippi, but it is hard to believe that this experienced explorer was not aware that the Mississippi lay to the east. There is some evidence that he never intended to colonize at the mouth of the Mississippi but was more interested in Spanish silver mines in northern Mexico. By now his supplies were running low and his charges were becoming disobedient. Although some of his colonists wanted to stay at Fort St. Louis, other colonists and all of the soldiers wanted to return to Canada. In March 1687, leaving much of the food, ammunition and other essentials with those who stayed, La Salle headed for Canada. Unfortunately, he was assassinated one night somewhere in east Texas, possibly near the present city of Navasota.

Back at fledgling Fort St. Louis on Matagorda Bay, the colonists ran low on provisions and waited desperately for La Salle's return. Winter caught them entirely without food and with little ammunition to kill game. Many of them died of sickness, starvation or at the hands of the Indians. Those still alive found refuge with a friendly band of Indians (probably Tejas) and abandoned Fort St. Louis altogether. Thus, the first French colony in Texas ended in abject failure, but it had given France a vague but important claim to Texas. Although temporary, the establishment of Fort St. Louis had a very significant immediate effect.

ALONSO DE LEON AND FATHER MASSANET
FIND FORT ST. LOUIS

When the Spaniards heard of this French intrusion, they began a campaign to strengthen their hold on Texas. Their concerted effort to build missions and forts in East Texas as a buffer to the French certainly diverted the Spanish attention from the Edwards Plateau and the Concho country of West Texas which they were not to re-enter for almost three-quarters of a century.

But they had not found Fort St. Louis; and to that end, Alonso de Leon, accompanied by Father Damian Massanet, left Mexico in the spring of 1689. They finally found the ruins of Fort St. Louis, and Father Massanet burned the remnants to the ground, hoping to forever erase any trace of France in Texas. But the French would be back.

FIRST MISSION WAVE IN TEXAS

Now Father Massanet turned his attention to establishing a mission. The Spaniards had recognized the Tejas (one of several tribes of the Caddo nation) as the most civilized and advanced Indians in the territory. They lived off their farms and gardens and did some hunting but were not aggressive. Furthermore, some had expressed a desire to become Christians; this fact aroused the zeal of Father Massanet even more. In May 1690 De Leon helped him select a mission site on a small creek west of the Neches River near a Tejas village. They named the Mission San Francisco de los Tejas. De Leon and Father Massanet returned to Mexico in July, convinced that the little outpost would be successful.

Because of their favorable reports, the government ordered the establishment of six more missions in the province north of the Rio Grande (sometimes called Rio Del Norte or Rio Bravo). Father Massanet returned to Texas with an expedition under the command of Domingo Teran de los Rios. Teran had been appointed governor of this new province in Texas and was to explore the entire east Texas area. Father Massanet brought nine additional padres with him and assigned them at his discretion.

TEXAS IS NAMED

For the new province, the Governor selected the name Nuevo Reyno de la Montana de Santandero y Santillana, but even the Spaniards had trouble with this cumbersome appellation. In time it was replaced in favor of the name Tejas (pronounced Tay-has in Spanish) thus Texas got its name. In 1691 and 1692 Teran's explorations took him through eastern Texas and western Louisiana where he visited several villages of the Caddo Indians who inhabited the area. (Note: The Caddo confederacy included the Tejas, Hasinai, and many others.) In April 1691 he returned to Vera Cruz, leaving Father Massanet in Texas.

The Father was discouraged with what he found at Mission San Francisco. While he was gone, one of the priests, without permission, had established a second little mission a few miles away on the Neches River; but an epidemic struck and a number of Indians who had visited the new chapel became sick and died. They blamed the padre for this evil spirit which came upon them. (Many ills such as measles, smallpox, and cholera were brought to the Indians by Europeans.) Then in January 1692, bad luck struck again; and the mission was wiped out when the Neches River flooded the area. Back at the San Francisco Mission, the Indians were becoming openly hostile. They refused to work or help in establishing more missions.

Provisions were running low and Father Massanet sent six of the priests back to Mexico to get supplies. Teran then sent Captain Gregorio de Salinas Varona to Mission San Francisco with provisions, but when he returned his report was so unfavorable that the government decided to abandon the area. But before this word reached Massanet, the priest had already made the same decision in view of increasing hostility from the once-friendly Tejas. The choice was bitter for him but necessary. On October 25, 1693, Father Massanet, with the three remaining padres, left for Mexico. It would be 25 years before Spain re-established missions in East Texas, and when they did it would be because the French were again attempting to gain a foothold.

FRENCH INADVERTENTLY INVITED TO TEXAS

For years the Louisiana French harbored a desire to establish commerce, not only with the East Texas Indians, but also with the Spanish colonies in Mexico along the Rio Grande. But this was out of the question as Spain's empire had closed its door to foreign trade. Spain's colonies, outside of Mexico itself, were far flung and generally followed the Rio Grande northwestward. They were located in Albuquerque, Santa Fe, El Paso, and San Juan Bautista, the latter just across the river from the present site of Eagle Pass. But the French knew that these outposts had to be supplied and wanted to be that supplier. To their surprise, they were aided in achieving their goal by a Franciscan priest, Father Francisco Hidalgo. Father Hidalgo had begged the Spanish government to reopen the missions in East Texas or to at least authorize him to return and minister to the Indians. All of his pleas were rejected. Finally in despair, he wrote a letter in 1792 to the governor of Louisiana, Lamothe Cadillac. He reasoned that since the French were also Catholic, they would be pleased to send a priest to East Texas to tend to the souls of his erstwhile charges. Both the French and the Father were equally surprised.

ST. DENIS

The French governor was delighted to have an excuse to intervene in Texas and immediately responded to Father

Hidalgo's request by sending a young Frenchman by the name of Louis Juchereau de St. Denis to San Juan Bautista. Although St. Denis was not a priest, the governor could not have sent a better envoy. St. Denis spoke Spanish, as well as French, and several Indian dialects. En route to San Juan Bautista, he stopped at the Indian village of Nachitoches on the Red River. He had previously established a good relationship with the chief there and had, apparently, stored a large supply of trade goods in the village. Then during the summer of 1714 he crossed Texas to San Juan Bautista, where he was given a warm welcome in the home of the commandant, Diego Ramon. St. Denis was a very handsome man and soon won the heart of Ramon's granddaughter, Manuela Sanchez; but in doing so, he became the enemy of another admirer whose jealousy caused St. Denis to be arrested and sent immediately to Mexico City. Again this amazing Frenchman, with his glib tongue and winning personality, had a remarkable good fortune. Instead of being executed, St. Denis was unbelievably named co-commander of an expedition to establish a French settlement in East Texas! He had succeeded where the pleas of Fathers Massanet and Hidalgo had failed. Six missions and a presidio (fort) were ordered to be founded in East Texas.

SECOND MISSION WAVE CO-LED BY ST. DENIS

St. Denis returned to San Juan Bautista and married Ramon's granddaughter in the spring of 1716. Then accompanied by Father Hidalgo and with a force of twenty-five mounted soldiers, thirty settlers, and nine priests, all commanded by the uncle of St. Denis' wife, Domingo Ramon, he headed for East Texas, generally along the route that would later be known as the Old San Antonio Road (see map on page 104.) Two months later his entourage including chickens, sheep, goats, and horses arrived at the Neches River. Presents were quickly distributed among the Indians who again seemed friendly and welcomed them. They helped rebuild Mission San Francisco de la Tejas. Father Hidalgo was left in charge and St. Denis and Ramon traveled a few miles eastward to establish a second mission they named Nuestra de Senora de la Purisma Concepcion near a Hasinai Indian village. Then they went to the Nacogdoches Indian village (which would become the site of the present city of Nacogdoches) and established a third mission called Nuestra Senora de Guadalupe. Yet a fourth mission named San Jose de los Nazonis was built just a few miles further north at the

Nazoni Indian village. (Note: All of these tribes belonged to the Caddo confederacy.)

By this time St. Denis had almost forgotten he was a Frenchman. He had a Spanish wife and had been living with Spaniards for months; but suddenly he remembered his true allegiance and led the expedition to the Natchitoches Indian village on the Red River, where he opened his stored merchandise and immediately established a trading post that would endure for years. It is amazing that the sudden reversal to his true French colors cost him neither his Spanish bride nor his good standing with her countrymen. On the contrary, he continued to assist the Spaniards and established two more missions in East Texas. One was called San Miguel de Linares at the Adaes (Caddo) Indian village located about twenty-five miles southwest of Natchitoches on the Red River in present western Louisiana; the other, Nuestra Senora de las Dolores at the Ais (Caddo) Indian village located near the present city of San Augustine, Texas. Before leaving East Texas, Ramon built a presidio named Nuestra Senora de las Dolores de las Tejas on the Neches River near the San Francisco Mission. The settlers they had brought were divided between the San Francisco Mission and the San Miguel Mission in present western Louisiana. This latter mission became the most important settlement in East Texas, probably because of its proximity to the trading post at Natchitoches.

St. Denis had done a remarkable job for his governor, his king and the Spaniards as well. He had created not only a Spanish market for French goods but had been able to bring the Spaniards to within twenty miles of the Natchitoches trading post which he owned. This new relationship with the French seemed to be an ideal "marriage" from the Spanish point of view. So much so, the viceroy in Mexico City decided to establish a half-way station on the route to East Texas and ordered the Governor of Coahuila, Martin de Alarcon, along with Father Antonio Olivares, to establish San Antonio, which would become the most important and lasting settlement in Texas.

FOUNDING OF SAN ANTONIO

Governor Alarcon acted almost immediately and in April 1718 led an expedition across the Rio Grande and selected a site for the so-called "half-way station" on the San Antonio River. The location was well known and said to be one of the most beautiful camp sites in Texas. The road from San Juan Bautista to the East

Texas missions would later be known as the Old San Antonio Road and would play a very important role in Texas history. San Antonio, though it was only one-third of the way from San Juan Bautista on the Rio Grande to Mission San Francisco on the Neches, would become the hub of Spanish Texas and would be center-stage in the coming drama of Texas history.

On May 1, 1718, almost two hundred years after Cortez landed on the coast of Mexico, Father Olivares formally dedicated the Mission San Antonio de Valero; just four days later Captain Alarcon established the presidio of San Antonio de Bejar, less than one-half mile away (later San Antonio would be commonly called Bejar. In this book, these names are used interchangeably). The chapel of San Antonio de Valero, which was built several years later, was destined to become world famous as the Alamo, deriving its name from a troop of Spanish soldiers who were later quartered there and came from Alamo del Parras in the Mexican state of Coahuila.

The founding of the Texas missions in 1716 and 1718 was prima-facie evidence that Spain planned to make good her claim to this territory. But France was doing some founding of her own. The city of New Orleans was also founded in 1718. The Spanish were quite aware of the significance of this new port city near the mouth of the Mississippi, and again the specter of French encroachment into Texas loomed ominous.

The Spanish found their missions in East Texas were weak even though Domingo Ramon, with fifty soldiers, remained at the presidio near the Dolores Mission. The frailty of Spanish hold on East Texas became evident in 1719 when France declared war on Spain. A French force out of Natchitoches sent by St. Denis advanced westward and captured the Mission Los Adaes. This created such terror and fear among the Spanish settlers and padres that they fled to the safety of the Dolores Mission and its presidio. But its commander, Ramon, knew that the Indians favored the French. He decided their position was untenable and sent word to all East Texas missions to retreat to the safety of the new missions in San Antonio. A withdrawal in near panic resulted, but the frightened Spaniards reached San Antonio safely in October 1719.

Strangely, the French made no attempt to follow up their success. But when word of the rout reached Mexico City, the viceroy was furious and swore that Spanish honor would be vindicated. He immediately appointed the Marquis de San Miguel de Aguayo to lead a large force back to East Texas to re-establish Spanish control so emphatically it would never again be doubted.

THIRD MISSION WAVE AND SAN MIGUEL DE AGUAYO

Aguayo, himself wealthy, married wealth. He would underwrite the cost of the reoccupation of Texas. He was rewarded by the viceroy who made him governor of the provinces of Coahuila and Texas. On March 20, 1721, he crossed the Rio Grande leading a force of five hundred men, the largest to date sent to Texas. He went up the now well-marked road to San Antonio and immediately dispatched Domingo Ramon to found the presidio, Mission La Bahia del Espiritu Santo, close to the site of old Fort St. Louis at the mouth of the Lavaca River. The ghost of La Salle still stalked the coast of Texas, or so the Spanish believed.

After Aguayo had ensconced himself in San Antonio, he was informed that a mission he had earlier sanctioned five miles downriver from Mission Valero had been completed and named San Jose y San Miguel de Aguayo in his honor. San Jose would become the most successful Spanish mission. It had a chapel that could accommodate 2,000 people; quarters and offices for a large number of padres; a granary; carpenter shop; mill; spinning and weaving rooms, and a large dining area. San Jose has been authentically restored and is now a National Historical Monument. Aguayo's main concern, however, was to re-establish the East Texas missions and presidios. Soon he marched eastward--again on the Old San Antonio Road accompanied by most of the padres and colonists who had fled to San Antonio earlier. Upon reaching East Texas, they were surprised to find no sign of the French.

First, Aguayo relocated Mission San Francisco a few miles away and renamed it San Francisco de los Neches. He distributed priests and supplies at each of the other five missions and always with a show of Spanish force to impress the Indians. He built a new and stronger presidio at Los Adaes named Nuestra Senora del Pilar, where he stationed one hundred troops along with six cannon.

Aguayo then went visiting, going to the French post at Natchitoches, where he learned what St. Denis had known for a long time--their mother countries were no longer at war. The loquacious St. Denis assured Aguayo of his friendship and agreed to limit his trading activities to the east side of the Red River. But Aguayo left only half convinced of St. Denis' good intentions and vowed to keep the French out of Texas. He re-established the presidio at Dolores on the Angelina River near Mission Concepcion and manned it with one hundred soldiers.

In January 1722 Marquis Aguayo returned to San Antonio. In March of that year he visited La Bahia, where Ramon had established the presidio Nuestra Senora de Loreto on the coast at the very site of old Fort St. Louis. A short distance away, the priests founded Mission Nuestra Senor del Espiritu Santo de Zuniga. Both the presidio and the mission were commonly called La Bahia, even after being moved a hundred miles inland in 1749 to present Goliad.

Now Aguayo felt that he could return to Coahuila, his goal of a strong Spanish Texas evident. However, in his report to the viceroy, he strongly recommended that two hundred settlers be brought in from Cuba or the Canary Islands. He recognized it was next to impossible to get Spanish colonists to go where great fortunes could not be easily made and life itself was insecure at best.

The typical Spanish citizens in Mexico were not ready for the hardships of the frontier. The Apache, still moving into Texas from the north and west, made travel and work in the fields impossible except in large parties. Even military expeditions against them met with little success. They would simply vanish into the wilderness and pick their own moment to fight. They could live off the land for days, weeks, or months which the Spanish soldier could not do. The Apache lurked on all roads leading from the Rio Grande to Los Adaes and La Bahia, waiting for the unprepared traveler.

LA VILLITA AND THE CANARY ISLANDERS

The Spanish crown took Aguayo's advice on colonization, but then as now, bureaucracy moves slowly. It was not until 1731 that fifteen families (totaling fifty-six people) arrived in San Antonio from the Canary Islands. Each family head was granted a town lot around today's Main Plaza (known then as Plaza de las Islas) and a farm in the country. Shortly, the Islanders organized their community which was the first in Texas to have legal status as a villa with some degree of self government. Their village, San Fernando, was named in honor of the king's son, Ferdinand VI. As time passed they built homes and a parish church of stone that later became known as San Fernando Cathedral. Aguayo hoped that other Islanders would settle in East Texas as more colonists were needed there.

THE GESTATION

DILEMMAS OF GOVERNMENT - INDIANS AND MONEY

The government in Mexico City became concerned about the cost of operating its vast frontier territory and ordered Colonel Pedro de Rivera y Villalonto inspect the northern frontier in 1724 to make recommendations for reducing costs. Colonel Rivera spent four years traveling some 8,000 miles through northern Mexico, present New Mexico, and Texas. It was probably the most thorough reconnaissance that had been done to date. He visited each frontier post from La Bahia to the Sabine Pass and made extensive and elaborate notes on all the Indian tribes that crossed his path. His report when finally submitted included three important recommendations that affected Texas. 1) Consolidate all of the East Texas missions. 2) Transfer the mission and presidio of La Bahia to the Medina River near San Antonio. 3) Begin immediately a war of suppression against the Apache. Fortunately, or unfortunately, none of the colonel's recommendations were adopted. It can be said that he recognized the need to deal with the Indian problem. The government, however, would only recognize the Indians posed a problem after another mission wave.

SENO MEXICANO - THE STRATEGIC COASTLINE

At the beginning of the final era of Spanish expansion, it is important to understand just where the frontier lay in 1750. Generally, it wound through the wilderness north of the valley of Mexico and through isolated areas that barely met the definition of civilization. Then the line extended to the more substantial cities of Monclova, Saltillo, and Monterrey--on up to northern New Mexico following the Rio Grande. Settlements on the Rio Grande-- Santa Fe, El Paso and San Juan Bautista--were few and far between. In Texas, settlements were generally grouped in three areas--San Antonio, La Bahia, and East Texas, anchored by Los Adias. San Antonio and Los Adias were connected by the Old San Antonio Road. Even San Antonio was considered a frontier post at the time, though it offered more safety than most towns. Significantly, on the Texas coast there was not a single Spanish settlement from Tampico Bay on the east coast of Mexico to Louisiana. Even the strategic coastal region between Tampico and Matagorda Bay, then known as Seno Mexicano, was unsettled.

Spain and Great Britain were at war, with the former becoming painfully aware of the great power of the British navy. This forced the Spanish to take a hard look at the Texas coast. The viceroy of Mexico City ordered Jose de Escandon, an efficient career officer of the Spanish army, to lead an expedition to settle this area. He left with a large force in January 1747 and spent the next year and a half in intensive study of the lower Rio Grande, and surprisingly to a much less extent the Seno Mexicano. His plan of colonization for the lower Rio Grande was approved in 1748, and due to his careful organization and leadership, one of the most successful and enduring Spanish ventures on the northern frontier came into fruition.

Escandon, with seven hundred fifty soldiers and a score or more of priests, led a caravan of 2,500 settlers into the southern Rio Grande region and in the next seven years founded twenty-three towns and fifteen missions. The first two were Camargo and Reynosa, established on the south bank in 1749. The next year he built the town of Dolores in present Zapata County. Then came the town of Mier in 1753 on the south side of the river and Laredo in 1755 on the north side. All of the area which he explored was named Nueva Santander, with its northern boundary set at the Nueces River. While Escandon was building along the southern Rio Grande, the so-called western mission fields were being established.

THE FOURTH AND LAST MISSIONARY MOVEMENT

The fourth and last missionary wave was divided into three parts: 1) San Gabriel, 2) San Saba, and 3) El Canon. The first, San Gabriel, was located in Tonkawa Indian country near the town of Cameron in Milam County. The Tonkawas were a rather fierce and war-like band who sometimes practiced cannibalism and were definitely less civilized than tribes in the Caddo confederacy. They were not as troublesome to the Spanish as the Apache, their natural enemy.

In 1745 four Tonkawas came to San Antonio and asked that a mission be established at their rancheria. Franciscan Father Mariano Francisco de los Dolores y Viana, who had visited the Tonkawas earlier, established Mission San Xavier for them on Brushy Creek in 1748. Two more missions were established in 1749 in the area--San Ildefonso, and Nuestra Senora de la Candelaria. In 1752 the presidio, San Francisco Xavier, was built about two miles from Mission San Gabriel, and a compliment of fifty soldiers was stationed there.

For decades there had been an ongoing and deteriorating state of antagonism between priests and military, and this flared into a bitter quarrel at San Gabriel between the captain of the presidio, Felipe de Rabago y Teran, and Father Juan Jose Ganzabal. As a result the captain killed the friar in 1752. He was removed from his command but was never tried and was returned to duty at another station. This had a devastating effect on the morale of the padres, and all but one deserted and returned to San Antonio. The remaining priest, Father Anda y Altamirano, kept Mission San Francisco Xavier open but with only a handful of Indians and a few soldiers at the presidio. The officials knew that San Gabriel, as located, was doomed and in 1755 ordered the mission and presidio moved about one hundred miles to the southwest near present San Marcos, Texas, and an affiliated presidio established on the Guadalupe River near present New Braunfels. Perhaps they were too close to San Antonio, for the San Gabriel Mission and presidio were soon closed. Their inventories would be assigned later to a new project.

THE COMANCHE - TERROR OF TEXAS!

The Franciscan padres were persistent and dedicated to the task of Christianizing Indians. Their next missionary effort was centered in Apache country in what is now Menard County. The reader must remember that the Spanish missions and presidios can be related to the chicken and egg theory; one begot the other. Inasmuch as presidios were directly controlled by the government, it was government that decided where missions would be located. Rumors drifted back to Mexico City that silver deposits in great quantities had been found along the San Saba River in present Menard County. That was enough to get the government's attention. Also, the government was finally becoming aware that a new and even more hostile Indian force from the north was driving the heretofore dominant Apache south, east and west. This force was the Shoshone-speaking Comanche who had lived for generations in the foothills of the Rockies along the Platte and Yellowstone Rivers. Around the beginning of the eighteenth century, their lifestyle changed drastically with the acquisition of the Spanish horse.

Not even the Apache mastered the horse like the Comanche. Where their ancestors were content to eat grubs, roots, nuts, and small game, the new Comanche liked the taste of buffalo meat and venison and dared to take the hunting grounds of any tribe, including the Apache, where these animals abounded. In just two or three decades, they swept all other tribes out of a large area of Texas, establishing undisputed domain over the south plains from the Red River to the Rio Grande and from the mountains of New Mexico to the hill country of Texas. The Comanche and the Apache posed a far greater detriment to Spanish dominance in Texas than the French ever would.

In 1757 the Mission San Saba de la Santa Cruz was founded by Father Alonzo Guraldo de Terreros on the south bank of the San Saba River near present Menard. Two miles upstream and across the river, Colonel Diego Ortiz de Parilla, with one hundred troops and nine Christianized Indian families, built a massive stone presidio called San Luis de las Amarillas. The remaining troops from the now defunct San Gabriel presidio (near present Cameron, Texas) were assigned to it, and other friendly Indians came into the mission to give a total population for both presidio and mission of nearly four hundred persons. They were now ready to Christianize the Lipan Apache, but these nomadic Indians had no intention of adopting civilized life inside the mission. They came to the vicinity of the mission in large numbers but chose to camp nearby and came inside only to trade. Sometimes their numbers would be 3,000 or greater; but just as suddenly as they came, they would often all disappear to hunt and then return at a later date. On one of their visits, they brought rumors of a planned attack on the mission by the Comanche. The padres did not believe the fickle Apache and refused Colonel Parilla's urging to seek safety in his presidio.

Early in the morning of March 16, 1758, a large war party of over 2,000 Comanche suddenly appeared and surrounded the mission. They told the trusting padres they only wanted to trade, and the unsuspecting Father Terreros opened the gate of the wooden stockade. Once inside the Comanche began a horrible massacre-- slashing, burning, and killing all except nine men who had barricaded themselves in one room and were luckily overlooked. Then the Comanche proceeded to attack the presidio but were driven off. Later the soldiers went to the smoking ruins of the mission and rescued the hidden men, but only four were now alive. The others had died from wounds.

In this first encounter with the Comanche, the Spanish were shocked at their treacherous savagery. After a council of war in San Antonio, it was decided that the Comanche must be punished. An expedition led by Colonel Parilla with a force of over five hundred men left San Antonio in the summer of 1759. Parilla went north and chased a small band of Comanches to the Red River. Here to his amazement stood a fortified town flying a French flag. He began a bombardment of the palisades surrounding the town, but even his small cannon were ineffective and he decided to charge the fort. The Comanches turned back their charge, and the Spaniards had to flee for their lives, abandoning all of their supplies and cannon. To add insult to injury, Apache Indians accompanying the troops stole all of their horses one night, leaving them to walk the rest of the way back to San Antonio. Spain would never again mount a military operation against the Comanches.

The Indian village that Parilla had attacked on the Red River was the center of Indian commerce for French traders from Louisiana and the Plains Indians from the buffalo hunting grounds. It was from the French that they received their guns and ammunition. Many years after it was abandoned, settlers coming through from the East inappropriately named the ruins "Spanish Fort." Obviously, they knew nothing of its history.

When Parilla retreated, he stopped at the presidio on the San Saba. He left his troops and continued on to San Antonio to make a report and receive treatment for a wound. This presidio, under pressure from frequent Comanche raids, was abandoned in 1768. The soldiers were withdrawn to a mission on the upper Nueces River in present Edwards County. Two small missions were located here--San Lorenzo de la Santa Cruz and Nuestra Senora de la Candelaria del Canon. Both were abandoned in 1771, being dismally unsuccessful in converting the Lipan Apache to Christianity. The closing of these two missions marked the end of the Spanish effort to Christianize the Plains Indians. It was becoming clear to government in Mexico City that the Comanche menace was a grave threat to Spanish civilization in Texas. Even San Antonio was not safe. But in spite of hostile Indians, the brave (or foolhardy) still traveled the Old San Antonio Road; and in 1779 a man by the name of Antonio Gil Ybarbo founded the present city of Nacogdoches where the Trinity River crosses the Old San Antonio Road. Though lacking official sanction, it would become the most important settlement in east Texas for the next fifty years.

THE COASTAL MISSIONARY ACTIVITY - NOT A MOVEMENT

Seno Mexicano and the rest of the Texas coast were sadly in need of missions. In 1749 the only coastal mission, Nuestra Senora del Espiritu Santo de Zuniga at La Bahi along with its presidio were moved one hundred miles inland to a permanent site on the San Antonio River at the present city of Goliad (but it would still be called La Bahia for almost another century.) The main reason for this move was to place the operation under control of the governor-general of Nueva Santander, Jose de Escandon. Efforts to bring the coastal Karankawa Indians into mission life was unsuccessful. Moreover, the Karankawas persuaded the other Indian converts already in the mission to run away.

But neither the padres or Escandon were ready to give up on the Karankawas. A related mission, Nuestra Senora del Rosari, was established only four miles away in 1754. Basically it was to free the parent mission from the nuisance of the fickle Karankawas. Rosario was small but resolute, clinging to a fragile existence (except for the period from 1781 to 1789) until 1830-1831 when both it and its parent, Nuestra Senora del Espiritu Santa de Zuniga, were secularized.

Spain finally decided to establish a mission just off Galveston Bay near Anahuac in present Chambers County. In 1756 they built both the Mission Senora de la Luz and a presidio, San Augustin de Ahumada (known collectively as Orcoquisac, named after a local Indian tribe). They were erected as a result of finding a French trader in the area the year before. But missions, presidios, and problems seemed to be synonymous. The presidio was destroyed by a storm in 1766, and though rebuilt, it was hardly worth the effort. Five years later there were only three soldiers at the presidio and two priests at the mission. The following year it was abandoned. The Texas coast would be bare of missions until Refugio (the last of the Spanish missions was established in 1793).

THE WORLD-WIDE POLITICAL PICTURE

Now it's time to take a quick look at the world-wide political picture. The French in 1754 began a war with the British in western Pennsylvania known as the French and Indian War. The fighting became international in 1756 when Spain was pulled into the fight by a treaty with France. But the eighteenth century British navy was invincible and easily occupied the vital Spanish ports of Havana in Cuba and Manila in the Philippines, shutting off a major source of Spanish commerce.

It became obvious to both France and Spain that the British would prevail. France knew she would lose her colonial possessions. Spain realized that she would have to give up some territory to Britain in order to break their blockade of Havana and Manila. A conference was called in 1763 to work out details for the Treaty of Paris which would end the war. But just before the treaty was signed, Spain and France came up with a territorial treaty of their own. France ceded western Louisiana to Spain which included all of the territory west of the Mississippi River. In the Treaty of Paris, Great Britain agreed to this transaction but demanded that Spain transfer its claim to Florida in exchange for the ports of Havana and Manila. It was a large price to pay, but the Spanish agreed.

The Treaty of Paris in 1763 was the final chapter in the long drama of empire rivalry between Spain and France. Spain lost France as a neighbor but now faced Britain along the length of the Mississippi. The British wasted no time in showing their muscle in the New World, quickly establishing territorial government in Canada. But seeds of discontent were being sown among her colonists along the Atlantic seaboard. Only two years later, with the Stamp Act of 1765, Britain took the first step in alienating the colonists and setting them on the road to revolution. Indeed, policy changes brought about by the Treaty of Paris would ultimately cost Britain her Atlantic colonies. But Spain did not suffer such immediate drastic consequences. Not only was France no longer a threat in East Texas, the French in Louisiana became Spanish citizens and many were eager to serve their new monarch. Spain's chief concern now was to strengthen Louisiana as a buffer against a far stronger potential enemy--the British. But Spain never guessed that the eventual independence of Britain's thirteen American colonies would play a major role in the demise of Spanish influence in the New World and the emergence of Texas as a Republic.

END OF THE MISSION ERA AND ITS EFFECT

When the last Spanish mission was founded at Refugio in 1793, a century had elapsed since De Leon and Father Massanet established the first mission named San Francisco de las Tejas in May 1690. In that one hundred years, more than two dozen missions had been established (see map on page 16). These missions were designed as instruments of both church and state. The padres, while bringing Christianity to the Indians, were expected to instruct them in becoming peaceful and productive Spanish citizens. In its original concept, however, the missionary effort in Texas can be termed a failure. The Caddos in East Texas and the Apache, Comanche and other wild tribes in West Texas never embraced the Spaniard's religion nor his civilization.

The presidios, designed to protect the missions, also fared badly. Soldiers were poorly paid and equipped and sometimes of low character. The padres often preferred to labor without the assistance of military personnel.

To their everlasting credit, the Franciscan missionaries left an enduring legacy to the future of Texas. They labored above and beyond the call of duty in remote areas where others dared not go. First to explore much of this vast territory, they established permanent settlements in South Texas, on the Rio Grande, and along the Gulf coast.

THE AMERICAN REVOLUTION LINKED TO THE TEXAS LONGHORN THROUGH BERNARDO GALVEZ

Another important legacy left to Texas by the Spaniards and still flourishing today is cattle and ranching. South Texas was very suitable for the Spanish cattle, particularly the land between the San Antonio River on the west to the Guadalupe River on the east and stretching all the way to the Gulf of Mexico. Most of this land was owned by the missions, and on it grazed tens of thousands of Texas Longhorns, spawned by the few Spanish cattle brought originally Alarcon and Aguyo. Each generation grew longer horns, leaner bodies, and shorter tempers. Today, thanks to many stories, and movies like John Wayne's "Red River," people all over the world recognize the Texas Longhorn and know about the great cattle drives to the railheads of Kansas in the years following the Civil War. But few are aware that great cattle drives started in Texas almost 100 years earlier. Even fewer know that it was the Texas Longhorn and a Spaniard by the name of Bernardo Galvez, governor of Spanish Louisiana, who provided the link connecting Texas to the American Revolution via a cattle trail from San Antonio to New Orleans. Time and space precludes me from telling the full story about this interesting man and his enormous contribution to the defeat of Great Britain. It is shameful that we do not honor him on a pedestal equal to that of Lafayette, for his contributions were equally as important. True, a great Texas city – Galveston – perpetuates his name. But it was Spanish surveyors in 1785 that named the site which would later become the city.

He was the fist son born to one of the most distinguished families in Spain and was a soldier by age 16. He was fighting Apaches on the plains of Texas at age 25. Years later he would remember the hardy Texas Longhorn that roamed like buffalo. Galvez was appointed Governor of Louisiana by King Carlos in 1776. He sympathized with the colonists and for two and half years prior to Spain's entry (in 1799) into America's fight for independence did all he could to aid the colonists. This included a $300,000 loan, 2,000 barrels of gunpowder, large quantities of lead, and thousands of blankets. Also, he permitted America's ships of war and commerce to seek safe haven in the port of New Orleans. But most importantly, he agreed to attack the British strong points in The Floridas (there were two then, East and West) and along the Mississippi. To do this he would need food for his soldiers and remembered the Texas Longhorn – a traveling commissary. In 1779 he sent a letter to the Governor of Texas requesting to buy up to 2,000 head. This resulted in the first cattle drive out of Texas. Vaqueros braved Indians, mosquitoes, fever, and hurricanes to deliver them to New Orleans. By the time Cornwallis surrendered to George Washington at Yorktown on October 19, 1781, more than 9,000 head of Texas Longhorns had followed the blazed trail to New Orleans. They would feed the hungry soldiers of Galvez as he kept 10,000 British regulars busy in The Floridas that otherwise could have been used against the colonists. It's possible these soldiers would have turned the tide for Britain and changed history. Bernardo de Galvez, truly a faithful and zealous American, died of cholera in Mexico City at the age of 38 in 1786.

TEXAS AT THE DAWN OF THE NINETEENTH CENTURY

At the end of the eighteenth century there were less than 5,000 people in Texas, counting soldiers and civilized Indians. There were only three major centers of population, San Antonio, La Bahia and Nacogdoches. San Antonio was without a doubt the center of Spanish culture. It had five secularized missions; Villa San Fernando with its church; Presidio San Antonio de Bejar with a governor's palace; and a pueblo (La Villita) next to Mission Valero. The total population was about 2,500 (half of the total population of Texas). La Bahia had three missions, a presidio, and the pueblo town with a population of over 1,000 that eventually became the present city of Goliad. Nacogdoches had a church, school, a small military garrison, and a population of less than 500. Obviously Spain had failed to populate Texas due in large measure to the fierce Comanche and Apache Indians. This failure to populate contributed greatly to Mexico's ultimate loss of Texas.

THREE SIGNIFICANT EVENTS

In a span of fifty years, beginning in 1776, three major independent factors changed the destiny of Texas. The first of these was the success of the American colonist in their revolt against Britain (which will not be detailed here). The second was the acquisition of Louisiana by the United States, and the third was the successful war of independence by Mexico against Spain.

Louisiana had become French territory in 1682, when La Salle laid claim to the entire Mississippi Valley for his king. But in 1763 France ceded Louisiana to Spain and the area prospered under Spanish rule. However, the secret treaty of San Ildefonso in 1800 engineered by Napoleon Bonaparte, forced Spain to return Louisiana to France, although Spain continued to govern Louisiana.

Thomas Jefferson, newly inaugurated as President of the United States in 1801, was anxious to obtain New Orleans, and hopefully all of Louisiana from France so that trade all through the Mississippi Valley could be assured for all the states that touched it. He decided, however, to concentrate initially on acquiring the port of New Orleans. To that end he sent James Monroe and Robert R. Livingston to negotiate with Napoleon. The negotiations went on for months, seemingly unproductive. For some reason known only to himself, in April 1803 Bonaparte had his ministers inquire what price the United States would pay for all of Louisiana. Monroe and Livingston, though unauthorized, quickly negotiated a treaty for the purchase of Louisiana for sixty million francs (about $15,000,000 at the time). President Jefferson overcame his constitutional questions about the agreement and lobbied successfully for its ratification in the Senate. On December 20, 1803, Louisiana officially became a territory of the United States. The Louisiana Purchase placed Spain in a worse situation than it had previously been in with France. Now the young and aggressive United States was its neighbor along an undefined boundary that touched most of its colonial empire.

SANTA ANNA AND FATHER MIGUEL HIDALGO

Many unrelated events seemed to happen just at the end of the eighteenth century and the beginning of the nineteenth century that would affect the future of Texas. One of these was the birth of

Antonio Lopez de Santa Anna on February 21, 1794. On the day of his birth, George Washington had just been inaugurated for his second term as President of the United States, and France was gripped in revolution. Blood ran in the gutters of Paris, perhaps an omen of the blood that would flow both in Mexico and Texas at the hands of this man.

Santa Anna was of Spanish descent with almost no formal education. His father, a mortgage broker, wanted young Antonio to become a businessman like himself; but the strong-willed youngster had only one desire and that was to become a soldier. In 1810 when barely sixteen, he lied about his age and entered the Spanish army as a cadet. At that time Mexico was still a Spanish province. Its war of independence would begin that same year, set off by the "Grito de Dolores" issued by Father Miguel Hidalgo, a priest in a little village church in Dolores, north of Mexico City in Coahuila. This document exhorted his followers to rise up and throw off the oppressive yoke of Spain. Father Hidalgo had great sympathy for the hopeless plight of the lower order (the caste system will be explained later) in Mexico and the treatment they received from their wealthy Spanish overlords. He was a forceful champion of the ideals of democracy. Father Hidalgo organized a conspiracy to overthrow the Spanish government, but his plan for insurrection was short-lived. He was captured and executed in Chihuahua in March 1811.

The Father never reached Texas, but some of his followers carrying his ideas did. On January 22, 1811, Juan Bautista de las Casas, with a small band of insurgents, took the Royalist (Spanish) military headquarters in San Antonio. He imprisoned Governor Manuel de Salcedo and proclaimed himself the revolutionary governor of Texas. He immediately sent insurgents to La Bahia and Nacogdoches and easily replaced the Royalist officials with revolutionaries; but his triumph was brief. On March 2 counterattacks led by Juan Zambrano, a native Mexican-Texan (Tejano), wealthy land owner and rancher, and ex-army officer, quickly disposed of Las Casas. Then Zambrano organized resistance with the aid of such other prominent Tejanos as Juan Veramendi, Erasmo Seguin and Francisco Ruiz. Just as easily, they now defeated the insurgents at La Bahia and Nacogdoches. Zambrano promptly turned the government back to civil authorities on July 22, 1811, and Texas was back in the Royalist fold. This revolutionary foray was only a preview of events to come.

GUTIERREZ-MAGEE EXPEDITION TO TEXAS

One of Hidalgo's proponents a landowner and merchant named Bernardo Gutierrez de Lara, had met Father Hidalgo in Saltillo before his capture and they plotted to take over Gutierrez's native province of Nueva Santander (present Tamaulipas). Gutierrez escaped and made his way to Nachitoches, Louisiana, where he set up a base of operations.

Gutierrez believed, as did Las Casas, that Texas could be made the focal point for Mexican independence. By geography it was far removed from Mexico City many of its residents were liberals, plus it was very close to the United States which could be a source for volunteers. Gutierrez immediately went to Washington D.C. where he had friends. Soon he returned to Louisiana with letters of introduction to Governor W. C. C. Claiborne and William Shaler, a consul agent in Natchitoches. Shaler became a very close confidant to Gutierrez, and together they persuaded a young United States Army lieutenant, Augustus William Magee, to resign his commission and command an expedition to free Texas. Magee was interested because he was disappointed that the United States Army had failed to promote him properly. He jumped at this opportunity for fame and fortune--and an instant promotion to colonel.

Magee set up headquarters at Natchitoches and was able to quickly gather scores of eager volunteers. Among them were Americans, French, and many Mexican revolutionaries. The combined force totaled initially about one hundred fifty men. They crossed the Sabine on August 8, 1812, and easily took over the Spanish post at Nacogdoches. Now Mexican and American volunteers poured in and their force grew to about seven hundred.

Magee's army continued into Texas and proceeded to the old presidio of La Bahia, where they easily overwhelmed the token Spanish guard on November 7, 1812. The re-installed Loyalist governor, Manuel Maria Salcedo, besieged La Bahia and sporadic fighting went on for the next four months. Particulars are not known, but Magee died on February 6, 1813, and Samuel Kemper assumed leadership. Under Kemper the insurgents counterattacked Salcedo, defeated him, and occupied San Antonio.

GENERAL ARREDONDO - SANTA ANNA'S MENTOR

Gutierrez to this point had remained in the background, but with the capture of San Antonio, he asserted himself. After their victory on April 1813, the American volunteers had issued a "Declaration of Independence of the State of Texas" based on the American Declaration of Independence, reflecting liberties contained therein. Gutierrez and his group demanded control and drew up their own document which Kemper and his followers regarded as being far from liberal as it gave Gutierrez dictatorial powers.

The Anglos' disenchantment with Gutierrez changed to outrage when he executed Governor Salcedo and thirteen other Spanish leaders by cutting their throats. Kemper and one hundred of the men abandoned the expedition and returned to the United States. Gutierrez now organized a military junta to govern Texas. But his rule was short-lived, because in early August another insurgent arrived who would take his place. Colonel Jose Alvarez de Toledo ousted Gutierrez with the backing of Shaler. Toledo was now in command of the insurgency.

Gutierrez returned to Nachitoches downcast, although Toledo had actually saved his life. On the very day Gutierrez left San Antonio, a Royalist army of 3,000 strong under General Joaquin de Arredondo was barely thirty miles from San Antonio. Arredondo was known for his cruelty, and he would live up to this reputation of butchery for all insurgents. It is interesting to note that with General Arredondo was a 21-year-old first lieutenant by the name of Antonio Lopez de Santa Anna.

On August 15, 1813, Arredondo's force reached the Medina River and Toledo and his army came out to meet them. Santa Anna got a first-hand lesson in Napoleonic military tactics as Arredondo overwhelmed Toledo's army at the Battle of Medina. He also got a lesson in cruelty, as many of the survivors were executed, including several citizens of San Antonio whom Arredondo believed collaborated with Gutierrez. Arredondo then turned his troops loose upon the town's people to pillage, torture, and rape. This was Santa Anna's first trip to San Antonio, but it would not be his last.

SANTA ANNA AND ITURBIDE AND THE PLAN DE IGUALA

By 1821 Antonio Lopez de Santa Anna was twenty-seven years old and a captain in the Royal Spanish Army. The young captain had already earned the reputation of being "an opportunist" and stood waiting in the wings. He would shortly play a leading role in dramatic events that would occur over the next fifteen years.

The fires of revolution which had been started in 1811 by Father Hidalgo, were banked but smoldering. Hidalgo's disciples continued to carry on a guerrilla rebellion in many parts of the interior, however their cause lacked support of the wealthy and powerful criollos (Spaniards born in Mexico). By 1820 the revolution, seemingly, had lost much of its force. But the criollos still feared the Hidalgistas, who touted social reforms that would undermine their wealth and power. This concern magnified when the Spanish crown in 1820 was forced by the Hidalgistas to establish a liberal constitution. The criollos felt that their position of wealth and authority (and the caste system) could only be preserved under an independent monarch of Mexico. They reasoned that they must throw off the reins of Spanish government and establish such a monarch. The criollos found their champion in a brilliant and ambitious army officer, Colonel Augustin de Iturbide. Interestingly, Santa Anna, though presently fighting for the Spanish crown, kept one eye upon the situation and was keenly aware that the criollos might be successful now that they were apparently backing Iturbide.

The viceroy had just ordered Iturbide to eliminate the last of the Hidalgo forces led by Vincente Guerrero. But Iturbide, like Santa Anna, was a chameleon when it came to changing colors and loyalties for personal benefit. He betrayed the Loyalist government and made a pack with Guerrero to join forces and fight for the independence of Mexico (this, of course, met the approval of the criollos.) On February 24, 1821, Iturbide and Guerrero secretly drew up the Plan de Iguala, which basically provided for the establishment of a limited monarchy in Mexico, apart from Spain. Although Santa Anna now felt, for the first time, the revolution had a real chance of success, he did not think it opportune to join Iturbide.

In early September 1821, Santa Anna led his troops against the rebels in a morning battle. His Royalist soldiers killed many of the insurgents and captured many more. Santa Anna had plainly won the engagement and was pondering where his loyalty should be when, in the middle of the afternoon, strong rebel reinforcements arrived to continue the battle. Santa Anna, learning early to be an opportunist, saw an opportunity now. Guessing correctly that Iturbide would be successful, he felt he must do something to demonstrate his loyalty. Santa Anna deserted the Royalists and went over to the insurgents and offered his services in return for a promotion to major.

This would be only the first in a long series of volte-face manuevers (about-face) for Santa Anna. In the future he would demonstrate many times a shallow loyalty and would betray causes and friends whenever it would benefit him personally, with no qualms whatsoever. The same day of his defection, the Spanish viceroy, upon hearing of Santa Anna's defeat of the rebels and being unaware that he had defected, sent him a promotion to lieutenant colonel. Santa Anna immediately demanded and received from the insurgents the rank of full colonel in the rebel army. It was a timely and fortuitous switch of allegiance. He must have smiled when news came that Iturbide and Guerrero had combined forces and overwhelmed the Royalists.

TREATY OF CORDOBA - MEXICO WINS FREEDOM FROM SPAIN

Augustin de Iturbide in many ways was like Santa Anna. They were both opportunists. As a colonel in the Spanish army, he had distinguished himself by his ferocity in slaughtering the insurgents. Now, encouraged by his criollo friends, he believed he could be the ruler of an independent Mexico. It was with this goal in mind that he had made a pact with Vincente Guerrero. This pact outlined the major facets of the Treaty of Cordoba, which would be forcibly signed just a few months later (on September 27, 1821) by the last representative of the Spanish crown. Among other provisions, the Treaty provided that Mexico would be independent of Spain. Its government would be a constitutional monarchy, and its religion would remain Roman Catholic; but the criollos had won only a limited victory, because the treaty also provided for the end of the distinction between social classes which the Spanish had rigidly maintained (the royal-blooded Spaniard being at the top, the wealthy criollos [Spaniards born in Mexico] second, the Mestizos [mixed-blood Spaniards] third, and the Indians last). All Mexicans would be equal under the new law. The criollos resented this, but for the moment there was nothing they could do. The crown of this new sovereignty would be offered to a member of the Spanish royal family in Europe (to the dismay of Iturbide). In the meantime a provisional military junta would govern until a monarch could be selected.

Iturbide called for a provisional congress to meet in Mexico City in February 1822 to draw up the laws of a new government which would be patterned after the constitution of the United States; but immediately there was discord as the political heirs of Father Hidalgo wanted to form a republic, not a limited monarchy. This, of course, was not what Iturbide wanted. Worse, his criollo friends split over whether to back him as the new monarch or to invite a Bourbon prince from Europe.

All of this, given time and in the normal course of events, would have had a long-term effect on Texas. But unknown to Iturbide, the dream of one man--an American--would have a dramatic and immediate effect on Texas. At that very moment, he was riding to San Antonio from St. Louis, Missouri, to present his dream to the governor of Texas. Dreams have often influenced the course of world events, but this man's dream would even change history. His name was Moses Austin.

MOSES AUSTIN
(NOTE: There is no substantive proof that this is indeed Moses
Austin, even though there is a likeness to known portraits of the
Austin family and to written descriptions of the man. Missouri
Historical Society.)

STEPHEN F. AUSTIN
(Courtesy of the DRT Research Library at the Alamo)

CHAPTER 3

BIRTH OF TEXAS

MOSES AUSTIN

The dream of colonizing Spanish Texas with Anglo Americans was born in the mind of the enterprising Moses Austin in 1820. He was now fifty-nine years old and had just lost all of the family fortune in lead-mining ventures in southeastern Missouri and the failure of a bank he had started in St. Louis. Austin believed opportunity came in many disguises, and the successful entrepreneur must recognize it regardless of the guise it wore when crossing his path. He was confident that Texas was his opportunity, perhaps his last, to recoup the family prestige and fortune.

Moses Austin had prior contact with the Spanish government due to his mining ventures. In 1798 he had obtained from the Spanish crown the grant of a league of land for his Missouri lead mine. He had built smelting furnaces and established a general store which later became the town of Potosi. His business initially enjoyed only minor success, then mushroomed after the United States acquired the territory in 1803. But with the War of 1812 his business suffered. His fortunes totally disappeared and he was virtually wiped out when he helped found the Bank of St. Louis in 1816 only to see it fail in 1819 along with most others in the bank panic of that year. It was during this period of stress that Austin formulated his idea to settle colonists in Spanish Texas.

As he rode to Texas, Austin probably reviewed the reasons why his plan should succeed. First of all, he knew about recruiting and leading others--an experience he had with his miners. A second reason was that he knew how to deal with Spanish bureaucracy, having worked with high officials when obtaining his land grant for the lead mines. The third factor in his favor was timing. Many people had lost all they had in the Panic of 1819 and would welcome an opportunity to start over, albeit in a foreign land. He must have been convinced that his dream to colonize Texas would be met with praise by the Spaniards; and with these thoughts in mind, he no doubt approached his destination with high hopes.

In December 1820 Moses Austin arrived in San Antonio and went immediately to see the governor, Antonio Martinez. Martinez, suspicious of all Americans, flatly refused to listen to his plan and ordered him out of Texas. Austin must have been utterly dejected. At fifty-nine years of age, this might be his last chance to succeed, but luck was on his side. He accidentally encountered an old friend and acquaintance, Baron de Bastrop. Austin had first met the Baron in Louisiana when Moses visited that territory and Bastrop was involved there in land speculation. Bastrop was not a Spaniard but spoke fluent Castillian with an accent. He seemed a man of mystery, and there was much speculation about his background and his wealth. (On his death in 1827, his will gave his true name as Felipe Enrique Neri and his birthplace as Holland. Recent research has disclosed that there he had been a tax collector until he suddenly disappeared with all of the tax revenues.) In any event, Bastrop, who was very influential with Governor Martinez, intervened in Austin's behalf. Perhaps history can be kind concerning the Baron's past indiscretions; for without his chance meeting with Moses Austin that cold day in December of 1820, the Texas of today may never have been born.

Bastrop promptly persuaded his friend, Governor Martinez, to see Austin again. Subsequent to the conference, Martinez forwarded Austin's petition to General Joaquin de Arredondo, then commandant of the eastern provinces at Monterrey (the same Arredondo who defeated and massacred the 700 Americans and Mexicans remnants of the Gutierrez-Magee expedition in 1813). Had Moses Austin known about Arredondo's record, he would have held little hope for approval of the application; but the same luck that brought the paths of Moses Austin and Baron de Bastrop together in San Antonio still held. Unexplainable and illogical as it seems, Arredondo approved Austin's proposal and on January 17, 1821, signed a decree that gave Moses Austin permission to move three hundred Anglo families into an area of 200,000 acres in Texas. The instrument did not specify the location of these acres nor give any details as to how the colonies would be administered. Austin would have reason to believe that he himself had received the grant of 200,000 acres, although transfer of title was not stipulated in the agreement.

Moses Austin spent January and February in San Antonio and did not learn of his good fortune until March 1821. When the news was received, he was no doubt overjoyed and anxious to get home to Potosi and start the project!

STEPHEN F. AUSTIN

The specter of death rode double with Moses Austin on the long trip home that spring in 1821. Now nearly 60, he traveled relentlessly through cold rains and winds. The hard journey sapped the aging man's energies, and he contracted a bad cold which turned to pneumonia. He died on June 10, 1821. Perhaps Austin had a premonition of his fate, for he had persuaded his eldest son, Stephen Fuller Austin, to join him in his Texas venture. Young Stephen, then 27 years old, had only recently arrived in New Orleans to beginstudying law when he received his father's pleading letter. As a faithful son, he agreed to be a part of the colonization plan, not knowing the severity of his father's illness and had arranged to meet him in Natchitoches. He was there waiting when he learned of Moses Austin's death. After much soul-searching, he decided to proceed with colonization if the Spanish government would recognize him as his father's successor. In the company of Erasmo Seguin and Juan Veramendi, who had been sent to Natchitoches to receive his father, Stephen F. Austin rode to San Antonio in the summer of 1821.

Governor quickly gave Stephen F. Austin permission to take over his father's grant and supplied details to the contract. Austin would offer land to the perspective colonists for a fee of 12 1/2 cents per acre to be retained for his services. Each family head would receive 640 acres and an additional 320 acres for each family member, plus 80 acres for each slave. Austin would assume responsibility for the conduct of each colonist and act as an agent for the governor in administrating government for the colony. Further, he must organize a militia for protection from Indians as Martinez would not provide troops. The only question remaining was where the colony would be located. The Governor authorized Austin to explore the coastal plains between the San Antonio and Brazos Rivers and make the site selection himself. On his return to New Orleans, he made a careful study of the Texas terrain, exploring each river valley that he crossed. Finally he decided to settle his colonists on the rich bottomlands of the Colorado and Brazos Rivers.

Upon arriving at New Orleans, Austin immediately placed advertisements in various newspapers and received hundreds of inquiries from perspective colonists. With funds borrowed from his friend and law partner, Joseph H. Hawkins, Austin bought needed supplies and chartered a ship, *The Lively* to carry the first colonists and supplies from New Orleans to the mouth of the

December 1821 he proceeded overland to meet other settlers who had agreed to come. When he arrived several families were already there anxious to get settled. Some were located at present Columbus on the Colorado, others at the present site of Washington-on-the-Brazos.

By March of 1822 one hundred fifty perspective colonists had arrived to pick out their land tracts. The project seemed to be going very well, but bad fortune intervened. First, *The Lively* did not arrive as scheduled. Austin waited for several days and then gave up and rode to San Antonio to seek the advice of Governor Martinez. There he received the second disappointing news. Martinez advised him that Mexico had overthrown Spanish rule and was now being run by a provisional government in Mexico City. He further advised Austin that the provisional officials at Monterrey did not recognize Austin's grant because the agreement had been struck with Spain. He felt it was probable the new government would be interested in colonization; but until the provisional congress passed a general colonization law, the colonists would have to leave Texas or move to San Antonio. Austin asked for a delay in enforcing this regulation, giving him time to go to Mexico City and make a plea to the new government to confirm his grant. Martinez agreed and Austin expressed his appreciation. After a quick trip back to the colonists to give them the bad news, a dejected Austin left for Mexico City at the end of March 1822.

THE CALDRON
Mexico City was a caldron of political instability in the aftermath of revolution. Stephen F. Austin arrived there on April 29, 1822. He had been on the road for some seven weeks. Many times he had disguised himself as a beggar, for robbers and thieves were everywhere and law and order had virtually disappeared.

Austin had acquired a little Spanish by this time, and he personally submitted his petition for a colony to the revolutionary congress. His diplomacy, natural courtesy, and tact won him instant friends in the provisional congress. However, the consensus was that a general colonization law was needed, not just a one-time agreement with a single man. But their opinion really didn't matter much, as events that followed left them without power.

Just three weeks later on May 18, Augustin de Iturbide staged a coup by his army troops with a well-rehearsed chant, "Augustin I, Augustin I--" initiated by one of his trusted sergeants and picked up by a throng that had gathered in the city. Iturbide, with tongue in cheek, graciously accepted the demands of the people. Now with the army and apparently the citizens solidly behind him, Augustin Iturbide proclaimed himself Augustin I, Emperor of Mexico. As a reward for his help, Santa Anna was made a brigadier general by the Emperor to whom he made this pledge, "I will be your loyal subject and defender until death." (In less than six months, Santa Anna would be plotting to dethrone Iturbide.) In the meanwhile, he attempted to gain favor with the Emperor by proposing marriage to his 60-year-old sister, a proposal Iturbide rejected with a sneer.

But Augustin Iturbide and Antonio Lopez de Santa Anna had more in common than being opportunists. Both men were unprincipled and ruthless; each, however, had great personal charm and magnetism with the ability to incite crowds and bend them to their way of thinking. Both were greatly attracted to the opposite sex, but Santa Anna's reputation as a womanizer far exceeded that of his Emperor, who knew that his young brigadier was ambitious and growing alarmingly popular. He acted to blunt this by having Santa Anna transferred to Vera Cruz. But Santa Anna recognized what Iturbide was attempting and vowed he would watch for the opportunity to unseat his Emperor whose throne had wobbly legs.

Meanwhile Stephen Austin's petition was ignored in the subsequent bickering that arose between the provisional congress and Iturbide. Iturbide made matters worse by dismissing the congress and replacing it with his own junta of five members (of which he was one). Austin reacted swiftly and submitted his petition to the junta, while at the same time cultivating influential men in the imperial court of justice where he thought the petition might ultimately be decided.

Much to Austin's dismay, the junta (like the liberal provisional congress), favored a general colonization law. Austin was also surprised to learn he was not alone in his zeal to speculate in the vast lands of Texas. A growing number of men from America, Europe, and Mexico were well aware of the opportunities a general colonization law would bring. One prominent Mexican leader, Lorenzo de Zavala, enthusiastically embraced the idea. Others were Green DeWitt, an American from Missouri; General Arthur Wavell, an English mercenary who was now a brigadier general in the Mexican army; General James Wilkinson, a former commandant of Louisiana; and a German merchant by the name of Joseph Vehlein.

The junta bowed to the pressure exerted by these men, and on January 4, 1823, passed a general colonization law which received the approval of Iturbide on February 18, 1823. The act permitted Austin to continue his colony, but it also allowed these men and others to enter into colonization contracts with the imperial government.

Stephen F. Austin, always the astute leader and endowed with an analytical outlook, feared that the law would be short-lived and delayed his departure home. It proved to be a wise decision, as only one month later, on March 19, 1823, Iturbide was forced to abdicate his throne. (Exiled to France, he returned to Mexico the next year and was killed.)

Congress reconvened and quickly nullified all of the acts of the imperial government which, of course, included the newly enacted colonization law. Austin promptly resubmitted his petition to the congress where he had many friends. Congress now made a special exception and authorized a contract with him in accordance with the recently annulled law. This contract was officially signed on April 11, 1823, by the acting president of Mexico.

The congress then proceeded to draft a constitution patterned on the United States Constitution, which Austin had helped translate for them. It was an excellent document which provided for three branches of government--executive, legislative, and judicial; guaranteed the rights of its citizens; and in short, was a democratic philosophy within a republican framework. It became known in Texas and Mexico as the Constitution of 1824.

Austin headed back for Texas in a state of elation. The contract was much more generous than he could have expected. It offered a league of land (4,428 acres) and a labor (177 acres) of land to all heads of families who settled in Austin's colony and subsequently engaged in farming or stock raising, provided (1) they would agree to become Roman Catholics and (2) become citizens of Mexico. Single men had to agree to the same terms but would receive only one-third of the land. As empresario (land agent), Austin was granted 100,000 acres if he were successful in bringing three hundred families to Texas. Further incentive for the colonists was that nearly all duties and taxes would be waived for six years.

It must have been a happy Austin who rode back with the good news for the colonists he had brought and settled in the rich bottomlands on the Brazos and Colorado Rivers. But when he arrived he found that many of them had left, discouraged by his long absence and the continued rumors that his grant would not be validated by the Mexican government. The loss of supplies on *The Lively* further discouraged them, not to mention the fact that the Karankawa Indians had stolen most of their livestock.

BIRTH OF TEXAS - THE "OLD 300"

Austin, however, was not one to give up easily, particularly when he was this close to envisioned success. He had brought with him his father's old friend, the Baron de Bastrop, who had been named land commissioner by the Mexicans. Austin, together with Bastrop, began issuing titles just as quickly as his surveyor, Horatio Chriesman, could survey the land. News of Austin's return with a favorable contract raced through Louisiana and overtook many of the original settlers who returned post haste to claim their land.

By August 1824, Austin had issued 272 of the alloted 300 land grants. Within another year almost all of the original land grants were issued, and these first settlers would become known in history as the "Old 300,"--the pioneers who gave birth to Anglo-American Texas. They went about the task of clearing fields, planting crops, and building homes with such energy and eagerness that it amazed the officials in San Antonio who were accustomed to the easy-going ways of the native Hispanic population. But the colonists were just beginning; they established grist mills, brought in a cotton gin (the gin had just been invented in America in 1793), and even started a town a short way up the Brazos, named San Felipe de Austin. They formed a militia to ward off the fierce Karankawas. In the years that followed, the gentle stream of immigrants from the east became a flood of Anglo Americans sweeping into Texas. The early admiration of the Mexican officials in Texas now turned to grave concern.

GROWTH OF THE COLONIES

Though sizeable in 1827, the migration increased in 1828 and 1829 to several hundred families each year. A number of these were so happy with their new homes in Texas and the prospects for their future that they sent for friends and families. Some even ran stories about opportunities in Texas in their hometown newspapers. Stephen F. Austin's colonies were the most publicized and popular. This influx increased the population of his colonies to over 4,000 by 1830.

Some of the immigrants came to Texas on their own, settling wherever the landscape appealed to them. They established homesites where there were no colonies and no official land grants--in other words they were squatters who looked forward to a bright future. Many of them settled north of Galveston Bay in an area that is now the town of Liberty. Ben Milam, who would later die at the Battle of Bexar, brought in several families to Arthur Wavell's grant on the Red River.

It was obvious even to the casual observer that Texas under Anglo-American influence was looking more like a civilized state. Towns with schools and churches were established; roads were built; ferries were running at major river crossings; several cotton gins and grist mills were now operating. Some colonists who came to Texas with wealth built elegant homes. Due to slave labor, their plantations functioned effectively and profitably.

But regardless of appearances, Texas was still a frontier; and real luxuries were scare at best and non-existent generally. Hard cash was rare, and most fees were paid in barter with goods of one kind for another. Corn was the commodity used for most trading, as it suited many requirements quite well. It could be grown abundantly, be eaten before maturity as roasting ears, or after maturity ground into meal and baked, distilled into liquor, or held in the V-shaped and slatted corncribs as feed for livestock during the winter months, and finally regenerating the cycle through its seed. Cotton was the money crop, although getting it to market sometime proved difficult. All in all, life went on and growth continued in nearly all the colonies.

HOW THE COLONISTS LIVED

The typical frontier Texas home consisted of two rooms, separated by a "dogrun" (breezeway). The breezeway was a cool place to sit or sleep during the summer. It had a particular appeal for the family dogs; thus the breezeway was colloquially called the "dog run." Generally, the homes had no windows but all had a fireplace for cooking and heating. Sometimes chimneys and fireplaces were made of mud and sticks when stone or rocks were not available. Almost every home had an attic where the children slept on pallets, particularly in the winter months when the attic was warm. Schools with regular teachers were rare but existed in a few towns like Nacogdoches and San Felipe. Of course, the wealthy plantation owners brought in tutors from the East.

But if education was scarce, religion was more so. Because most of the colonists had Protestant affiliations (though they were required by law to become Roman Catholics), some of the settlements had illegal Protestant churches. However, must of the colonists were not much concerned with religion, and Monterrey did not even bother to send a priest to East Texas until 1831. Then came a jovial Irishman by the name of Father Michael Muldoon. If a colonist had not already taken his vows to the Catholic church, Father Muldoon would provide the rites with as little ceremony as possible. His converts became known as "Muldoon Catholics." It is said that he took a special delight in marrying couples who had been living together by common law and following the marriage ceremony, baptizing the children of the couple.

SLAVERY IN TEXAS

As stated earlier, cotton was the money crop and this meant slaves. It is thought that over one-third of the total population was black; but it must be said that these slaves were concentrated on the larger plantations, as the ordinary colonists could not afford to own more than one or two, if any. Further, the question of slaves in Texas was complicated by the laws of the state constitution of Coahuila y Texas, which made it illegal to import slaves and also stated that any child born of slave parents would be free. However, this law was nullified by a 1828 decree which permitted life-time work contracts which, in effect, gave the government's blessing to slavery. In 1829 slavery was abolished in Mexico by President Vincente Guerrero, who had become president after Iturbide's forced abdication. Although, the law was never enforced in Texas, some of the empresarios considered the decree an attempt by Guerrero to slow down the influx of Anglo Americans. This seems to have been the intent, for in 1830 further importation of slaves into Texas was forbidden; and in 1832 labor contracts were limited to ten years.

TERAN'S REPORT ON TEXAS

The Mexican officials who in 1824 had been amazed at the energy of the first Austin colonists, were completely stunned and bewildered with what had transpired in less than five years. From the reports they received, it seemed that Texas was rapidly becoming Americanized. This caused the Mexican government real concern, and they decided to send their own envoy to make an official inspection and report. Their agent was named Manuel de

Mier y Teran. He came to Texas in early 1828, stopping first at San Antonio and then traveling through all the settlements, terminating his inspection at Nacogdoches.

Teran wrote to his superiors that the demise of Mexican influence as he moved northeast was quite evident and was almost non-existent in Nacogdoches. What few Hispanics were there were of the lowest classes and outnumbered thirty to one by Anglos. He also reported that in Nacogdoches, there was an English-speaking school and perhaps a protestant church. His report further stated that the Anglos knew more about constitutional government than most native Mexicans, and some had come to Texas with the United States Constitution memorized.

The sum and substance of Teran's report stated that "Texas could throw the whole nation into revolution unless timely measures are taken." But he modified this rather strong statement by saying that he was not opposed to American immigration but wanted to balance the Anglos with Mexican colonists of better quality. His warning that "Texas could throw Mexico into revolution" was absurd since Mexico had been in a constant state of revolution from 1810 to 1821. In the eight years hence, it had only already been ruled by one emperor and four presidents. At the very moment Teran was making his recommendations, another revolution was building in Mexico City. But the government took his recommendations more seriously than he ever intended; and an impressive edict known as the Law of April 6, 1830, was issued only after two successive coups had placed the centralist element in Mexico in control of government, albeit illegal.

TURMOIL IN MEXICO - GUERRERO AND PEDRAZA

Ever since the abdication of Iturbide, the conservative criollos were fearful of the popular clamor for liberal doctrines such as election of public officials, human rights, and a totally democratic government. Knowing they were too few in number to win a national election with their own candidate, the criollos reasoned their best hope would be to throw their support behind the more conservative candidate of the opposition party. This they did in the national elections of 1828. Their man was Gomez Pedraza while the liberals supported Vincente Guerrero. True to form the election turned into utter chaos with Pedraza appearing to win by electoral votes; but the liberals claiming that the vote count was fraudulent and that Guerrero had won the popular vote.

To enforce their claim, the liberals (Federalists) took up arms and insisted that Guerrero be inaugurated; but before an inauguration could be held, Centralist troops chased them out of Mexico City, and the Federalists then retreated to the mountains. But if two bears fight over a fish that one has just taken from the river; an otter is likely to steal it while they are fighting. This happened while the two groups were away from the capitol fighting. Another Federalist group illegally and unconstitutionally inaugurated Guerrero as president. Sadly, in the first national election after the establishment of the Republic of Mexico, the party representing itself as defending the concept of constitutional government rejected the results of the public election and resorted to armed force. The country's political instability continued and from 1821 to 1830, Mexico would have an emperor and eleven presidents--one a self-styled dictator. It would be more than a century and many more revolutions before the people of Mexico finally realized that accepting the results of elections is essential to a democracy.

THE REPRESSIVE LAW OF APRIL 6, 1830

Action and counteraction by Centralists and Federalists made all of Mexico an armed camp during June, July, and August of 1829. But an event over which President Guerrero had absolutely no control would mean not only the end of his presidency but also his life. He heard that Spanish troops, determined to reconquer Mexico for the crown, had landed at Vera Cruz. Guerrero sent his army to repulse the invaders, and this was the opportunity the Centralists had been waiting for. Their army, several thousand strong, stormed Mexico City under the cover of darkness, captured Guerrero and executed him. The leader of this Centralist coup was Anastacio Bustamente, who immediately installed himself and assumed the role of dictator.

But the Spanish invasion produced a hero for the Federalists-- the cunning and capable Antonio Lopez de Santa Anna. He easily repelled the Spaniards, becoming the "darling" of the Federalists. From the winter of 1829 until 1833 (when Santa Anna would assume the presidency), fighting continued almost unabated, making Teran's statement that "Texas might throw the whole nation into revolution" seem ridiculous indeed.

However, Teran's recommendations regarding Texas had fallen into the hands of the Centralist government who feared the talk of a separate state and democratic government for Texas.

Vowing to stop further Anglo-American immigration, they drafted the Law of April 6, 1830, whose chief architect was Lucas Alaman, the real master-mind of the Centralists and the power behind Bustamente. The law did not reflect Teran's actual recommendations; it was far too harsh. Its contents as formulated by the Centralists were generally as follows: 1) It forbade all foreigners to cross northern borders without a passport from the Mexican government. 2) It forbade all further immigration of Anglo Americans into Texas and cancelled all existing empresario contracts. 3) It established military garrisons in Texas, and worse, specified manning them with convict soldiers who would be allowed to settle in Texas when their duty was finished. 4) It created a special commissioner of colonization to enforce the law and regulate the colonists. The only good and positive portions of the law permitted an open port on the coast to promote trade with Tampico and Vera Cruz; and the law encouraged, via government subsidies, more Mexican families to come to Texas.

THE GARRISONING OF TEXAS

Teran now found himself in an uncomfortable position. He was not an avowed Centralist, but he was a personal friend of Bustamente, who promptly named him to the newly created post of Commissioner of Colonization. Due to his appointment, most Texans looked upon him as a minion of Bustamente, whom they had learned to hate. But Stephen F. Austin had met Teran while in Mexico and believed him to be reasonable person. Austin and Teran immediately began corresponding and established a friendly relationship. In fact, Teran once wrote Austin, "The affairs of Texas are understood by only you and me, and we alone are able to regulate them."

Due to his admiration of Austin, Teran probably overlooked some facets of the Law of April 6, 1830. For example, he interpreted the suspension of empresario contracts to apply only to those who had brought in fewer than one hundred settlers. This interpretation, of course, permitted Austin and DeWitt to continue as in the past. Furthermore, Teran ordered all garrison commanders in Texas to restrain their soldiers from aggravating the settlers. He also showed leniency in other ways. Nevertheless, garrisons were built where they did not exist before and manned with convict soldiers and all Anglo immigration was officially stopped. Worse, an "open" port of ingress and egress was never implemented. The Americans in Texas bristled at the idea of being cut off from friends, surrounded by military garrisons, and not having a free port for shipment of their goods. There is little doubt that the Law of April 6, 1830, marked the beginning of wide sentiment in the colonies for independence. Nevertheless, the majority of colonists still believed in Austin who counseled patience and peace.

THE DESPISED COLONEL JUAN DAVIS BRADBURN

Though friendly with Austin, Teran still carried out his assigned duty and appointed officials for custom houses on the coast and military garrisons to guard them. Anahuac, on Trinity Bay, was the most important port of entry for East Texas. In accordance with the Law of April 6, 1830, a customs house and military garrison were built there; and Colonel Juan Davis Bradburn, a Kentuckian in the Mexican army, was appointed to command the fort. George Fisher, a Serbian immigrant, was designated customs collector.

Bradburn had been a mercenary in the ill-fated Mina expedition to La Marina on the Tamaulipan coast in 1817. Just when he entered the service of the Mexican government is not exactly known; but records show that by some brave act during the Battle of Iguala, he secured a promotion in the Mexican army. In the early part of 1830, he was sent by the Mexican government to New Orleans, very likely as a spy to ascertain if the United States was going to establish an outpost on the Sabine River and to learn something of the attitudes of the incoming settlers to East Texas. Just after Bradburn's return from his mission to New Orleans, he was ordered to Galveston Bay; and from the day he got there, he began to antagonize the citizens with his overbearing ways. The colonists had a dual dislike for Bradburn: (1) for being a turncoat to the United States and (2) for accepting a position of authority from the Mexican government to administer an unjust law to his own countrymen. The fact that most of Bradburn's soldiers were former convicts was another source of resentment. Then Bradburn heaped insult upon injury by granting clemency to a citizen of Anahuac accused of murdering his wife if he would enlist in the Mexican army. The colonists were shocked, but this was only a mild beginning.

Shortly before Bradburn came to Anahuac, the Mexican governor of Coahuila y Texas had been petitioned to issue land titles to the people who were settled east of the San Jacinto River.

The government complied and commissioned Francisco Madero, a citizen of Monclova, to issue the titles. Madero arrived in January 1831 at the settlement on the Trinity, held a meeting of the settlers, and selected a name for the town as Villa de la Santisima Trinidad de la Libertad, which was later abbreviated to simply Liberty. Madero installed the ayuntamiento and began issuing land titles. Bradburn interpreted the act as a violation of the Law of April 6, 1830, and ordered the arrest of Madero. He proceeded to dissolve their ayuntamiento on December 10, 1831, in spite of the fact the congress of the state of Coahuila y Texas declared the action of Madero legal the following January 2, 1832. Bradburn intervened to prevent an election to re-establish the ayuntamiento by threatening to employ military force if they proceeded. Then he began a program to confiscate the land grants of the colonists, taking personal possession of any land he wanted.

In the fall of 1831 Bradburn closed all the ports of Texas except Galveston. The irate citizens of Brazoria met on December 16, 1831, to protest this harsh measure. They took their complaint to Austin, who appealed to Teran. Teran asked Bradburn to make an exception of that port, and Bradburn had no choice except to comply.

But his compromise was short-lived. Within a few days he declared the "whole country lying within ten leagues of the coast to be under marshal law and threatened all civil authorities with exemplary punishment if they should dare to assert a rival jurisdiction."

WILLIAM BARRET TRAVIS
©Lajos Markos, 1984

WILLIAM BARRET TRAVIS 58

CHAPTER 4

WILLIAM BARRET TRAVIS

THE RED-HEADED STRANGER

As the fires of dissatisfaction smoldered in Anahuac, a tall red-haired stranger from Alabama rode into the town on an evening in May 1831. While the arrival of William Barret Travis on the scene in Texas was not particularly conspicuous, his departure in death at the Alamo less than five years later would be so gallant and inspiring that his name will always be remembered as a "paladin extraordinary" for the cause of liberty and justice. The reader should pause now and look at the early life of this impetuous and sensitive young man who believed he had a date with destiny, but "fortune favored the brave."

William Barret Travis was born in South Carolina in August 1809, on the family farm near the village of Redbank Church, a few miles south of Saluda in Edgeville County, later to be renamed Saluda County. Only five miles to the northwest of the Travis farm was the plantation of the wealthy parents of James Butler Bonham.

Among the many unanswered questions concerning the men of the Alamo, is the extent of the boyhood association of "Buck" Travis and Jim Bonham. Ruby Mixon, an early Travis biographer (Mixon, Ruby. "William Barret Travis: His Life and Letters," Master's Thesis, The University of Texas at Austin, 1930), maintained the boys were close friends who attended the same Oldfield school, hunted, fished, and rode together. Later writers, including Walter Lord (Lord, Walter. "Myths and Realities of the Alamo," The *Republic of Texas*, 1968), hold that a close boyhood friendship was unlikely due to the differing social backgrounds of the families; the fact that Bonham was two years older than Travis; the young age that Travis left South Carolina for Alabama; and that no documentation exists to support the close friendship theory. It cannot be disputed, however, that the life of these two men were closely intertwined--they sprang from the same soil, and though separated for most of their years, came together again in an old mission compound on whose soil they shed their life's blood for a cause that would enshrine their names forever in the hearts and minds of freedom-loving people all over the world.

About the time Buck Travis had reached his ninth birthday in 1818, his family joined other migrating Americans traveling an old Indian trail known as the Federal Road from the Piedmont region of the Carolinas, and headed for the fertile agricultural coastland north of the Gulf of Mexico. The Mark Travis family settled in Alabama on a farm near Sparta, located in Conecuh County. His father purchased 82 1/2 acres there for $1.25 an acre. The location undoubtedly had already been picked by a brother of young Travis' father, a Baptist missionary by the name of Alexander Travis, who had preceded the family there in 1817 and founded the town of Evergreen, also located in Conecuh County and only ten miles from Sparta. Young Travis' father was an astute businessman, hard worker, and the family prospered in their new home. At the time of Mark Travis' death in September 1836, the records show he had accumulated considerable substance including several hundred acres of land, a dozen slaves, and several hundred head of cattle.

Alabama had not been admitted to the Union when the family settled there, but so many people were migrating that its population increased rapidly. Alabama was admitted to statehood in 1819. This was the same year that Florida was secured from Spain by the Adams-Onis Treaty. In the same treaty a boundary was established between the Louisiana Territory and Texas which is still valid (See map on page 117). The eastern boundary of Texas was defined as follows: From the mouth of the Sabine River, up the west bank of the Sabine to the 32nd parallel, thence directly north to the Red River and up it to the 100th meridian, then up that line to the Arkansas River and up its south bank to the headwaters, thence directly north to the 42nd parallel, and thence along the 42nd parallel to the Pacific.

Following the admission of Alabama to statehood came substantial economic and cultural improvements. By 1819 the state had six newspapers, and both public and private schools were operating in the larger cities. Eight academies had been chartered by 1824, one of which was located at Sparta with the Reverend Alexander Travis, brother of Mark Travis, as a superintendent. Cotton was the money crop throughout the state. This, of course, meant an increasing slave population in Conecuh County where the Travis family lived.

Buck Travis demonstrated his ability and desire to learn while attending school near his father's farm, so his mother enrolled him in the academy of Professor McCurdy in Monroe County, possibly located at Claiborne, the largest town in the county. Records do not indicate his status there but do show that he graduated from Sparta Academy and is listed today as "its most famous graduate." The school offered higher mathematics, Latin, and Greek; but the subjects Travis studied are not known. Other records reveal that he was enrolled also in Evergreen Academy in Conecuh County, but again details are not known.

It was at these schools where Travis demonstrated an interest and aptitude for the written word. He enjoyed poetry and oral expressions, some of which, like "Victory or Death," would be a part of his personality in Texas. It is also probable that during these formative academic years, he acquired a taste for reading Sir Walter Scott and other classics of literature which would influence his moving and compassionate letters written from the Alamo. It is said both he and Bonham admired South Carolina's own Francis Marion, the "Swamp Fox" of the American Revolution, whose motto was "Victory or Death."

There is no doubt that the academic excellence of William Barret Travis caught the eye of one of the best criminal lawyers in the state of Alabama, Judge James Dellett of Claiborne; for he elected to tutor Travis in the intricacies of law. While serving as an apprentice to Judge Dellett, Travis also taught school to support himself, and doing this before he reached his twentieth birthday. It is reasonable to believe that young Travis' relationship with Judge Dellett helped to mold his character and gave him the courage of conviction that he demonstrated so forcefully at the Alamo. Travis learned the social graces while working with Judge Dellett and on one occasion assisted in entertaining the French general, the Marquis de Lafayette. Lafayette, of course, was the champion of liberty and justice who helped George Washington defeat the British. (It is interesting to note that Lafayette also visited the college in South Carolina where Jim Bonham was enrolled. It is quite possible both young men met Lafayette.)

Travis was admitted to the bar in Monroeville, Alabama, and practiced both in Claiborne and Clarksville before he reached his twenty-first birthday. An indication to the respect his peers and elders had for this young man was his installation in the Masonic Order of Claiborne, Alabama Lodge No. 3, in 1829. Perhaps even more important was the award of a commission in the Alabama

Militia on January 3, 1830, by Brigadier General John W. Moore. Travis served as the adjutant of the 26th Regiment, Eighth Brigade, 4th Division of the Alabama Militia. This is significant in that it revealed that Travis had military experience before coming to Texas and with the duties as adjutant, took care of correspondence and other paperwork related to military administration.

Travis fell in love and married one of his pupils, Rosanna E. Cato, who was the daughter of a very successful farmer of Monroe County, William M. Cato. They were married October 26, 1828 (Travis was nineteen) and to this bond, two children were born--a son, Charles Edward Travis, whom Travis dearly loved, and a daughter, Susan Isabella Travis, whom he would not see until she was about five years old.

For reasons not known, the marriage was unhappy; and in early 1831, Will Travis suddenly left his pregnant wife and his two-year-old son to go to Texas. Why did a promising young attorney and protege of one of the most successful judges in the state toss all this away and leave? It is an intriguing question and one whose only answers are found in half-truths and myths.

Some of the legends and myths that have sprung up concerning Travis' reasons for leaving Alabama are ridiculous. One involves the location of the county seat of Clark County, which was being moved from Clarksville to another town. Travis had aligned himself with the group opposing the move; and when they lost, he supposedly left for Texas, disgruntled and frustrated, commenting he would not live in a state where people were so stupid. Another tale, even more ludicrous, is that he made a business trip to Andalusia, Alabama, and while he was transacting business there, some local ruffian sheared off the tail of his horse as a joke. Travis, disgusted at the outrage and embarrassment, vowed not to live in a state where such acts were committed. It is difficult for the author to believe that a man who would lay down his life so courageously a mere five years later would let any ruffian run him out of a bar, much less a state and his home, leaving a pregnant wife and little son.

One of the most persistent and widespread rumors involved a Negro slave of Judge Dellett who was the defendant in a murder case, with Travis as his appointed counsel. The slave supposedly discovered the body of a prominent citizen (whom he was known to dislike) as he went about his daily chores. Asserting from the witness stand that he had found the body sprawled face down on property adjoining his master's, he was immediately suspected of committing the crime. Shortly, he was arrested and brought to trial, vehemently protesting his innocence. Judge Dellett himself supposedly presided at the trial and selected Travis to defend his servant. It became obvious to Travis as the trial progressed, he would lose the case in spite of the fact that only circumstantial evidence could be brought against the Negro. The jury returned a verdict of guilty and assessed a penalty of death by hanging. Travis made an impassioned plea for a stay of execution so that he could file an appeal. The Judge granted 24 hours, and Travis assured him that by the next day, he could produce proof of the slave's innocence.

Late that night young Travis paid a visit to the Judge and, as a fellow Mason, indulged his confidence. He confessed that he had killed the man he had reason to believe was Rosanna's lover. Judge Dellett was astounded and outlined three choices for his young friend: 1) he could keep his admission of guilt quiet and let the slave hang. 2) he could confess the crime and take his own chance with the gallows or 3) he could leave Alabama immediately. Travis found the first two unacceptable. Before dawn he swam his horse across the Alabama River and headed for Texas. This story, with variations, is most often given as the reason for Travis' sudden departure.

We should be reminded, however, that no history is without myth and many myths are anchored in history. But let it be understood that there is no positive proof that Travis killed a man over his wife. There is nothing in the county records of Monroe County, Clark County, or Conecuh County to indicate a murder involving the name of William Barret Travis.

THE COMMON DENOMINATOR - A NEW START, NEW HOPE

While the exact reason for his sudden departure from Alabama to Texas must forever remain a secret, it is a matter of record that William Barret Travis left a troubled marriage. He had disavowed Rosanna completely. This is borne out by his land grant application on which he boldly wrote his marital status-- "Single."

Like Travis, many of the men who came to this raw and newly settled Mexican territory, left problems behind--business failures, disappointed love affairs, unhappy marriages, or in some cases-- the death of a loving wife. But most came for the sheer adventure and a new start, the thrill of the unknown. This was probably the common denominator for most--a new start--new hope. While their reasons were diverse, their goal was the same--Texas! Even the name was magnetic!

The anticipation of this untamed land was an analgesic for most men as they laid their travel-weary heads upon a blanket roll for a night's sleep after scratching "G.T.T." (Gone to Texas) on the doors they left behind.

THE HETEROGENEOUS MEN OF TEXAS

Many of these men in their own way contributed significantly to Texas and to its ultimate independence. Of course, there were the well-known names such as Travis, Crockett, Bowie, Bonham, and Houston. But there were others not so well-known--one was John Hubbard Forsythe, whose wife had died on Christmas day in 1828 at his home in Avon, New York. It was a personal tragedy from which he sought escape, and Texas seemed to be the cure. Then there was the pint-sized Henry Warnell, a jockey from Arkansas who talked tall, drank hard, and could spit tobacco juice three times his shadow length at four in the afternoon. He left Arkansas to get away from a nagging wife and the responsibility of fatherhood. There was Dr. Amos Pollard, also of New York, whose medical practice was unsuccessful, causing him to look for a new place to hang his shingle where his skills might be in demand. Making his way to Texas was the tall and chisel-boned country boy from North Carolina, also Dalton Floyd, who just plain got tired of the monotony of his plow and staring a mule in the rear for ten hours a day; Daniel Cloud, the young lawyer was from Kentucky; and there was a cobbler, Marcus Sewell; an ex-sailor, William Jackson; and another doctor, John Sutherland of Alabama; a merchant from Falmouth, Massachusetts, Nat Lewis, who founded a store in San Antonio on Main Plaza in 1832; and a stalwart by the name of John W. Smith from Missouri, a wondrous jack-of-all-trades who excelled as a carpenter, businessman, engineer, and part-time tavern keeper; Micajah Autry came--a man of many talents--musical, artistic, and literary; none of which ever made him any money. He left a lovely wife to seek his fortune in Texas; and wrote saying, "I am determined to provide for you a home or perish;" and, of course, the inimitable Sam Houston, who built a record of public service that will probably never be equaled in the annals of American history--Congressman twice from Tennessee, Governor of that state, Ambassador to the Congress of the United States from the Cherokee nation, Commander-in-Chief of the army of the Republic of Texas, twice the president of the Republic of

Texas, led the effort to get Texas admitted to the Union on December 29, 1845; served as the state's first senator from 1846 to 1859, and finally served as governor until 1861. The city of Houston honors the name of this man who never darkened the door of a schoolroom but who was so articulate that his prose and poetry can be favorably compared to some of the masters. His memory was such that he could quote most of the twenty-four books of Alexander Pope's translation of Homer's *Illiad*. Sam Houston was a man whose life was truly a kaleidoscope, ranging from the darkness of despair to the euphoria of almost touching the heavens.

The list of contributors of early Texas history is almost endless: young attorney, Patrick C. Jack, born in Georgia but practiced law in Alabama with his older brother, William H. Jack; the gregarious R. M. "Three-Legged Willie" Williamson, a brilliant lawyer and dynamic man, whose idol was the English poet, Lord Byron, and who like Williamson, was handsome but a cripple. Williamson suffered from a childhood illness (probably polio) and his right leg was drawn backward at the knee, causing him to use a wooden appendage and walk with a cane. But he was a fastidious dresser and had his trousers tailor-made to accommodate the "three legs," wearing a shoe on his useless right foot. The name of Gail Borden stands out--an excellent surveyor and part-time entrepreneur--ever looking for evasive success until he accidentally invented evaporated milk and subsequently founded the Borden Milk Company. The county of Borden in Texas and the little city of Gail, its county seat, are named in his honor. There were many other stalwarts like William H. Wharton and his brother, John A. Wharton; David G. Burnett; Ben Milam; Francis W. Johnson; Luke Lesassier; Mirabeau B. Lamar; James "Brit" Bailey; Erastus "Deaf" Smith; John Austin; James Allen; Jesse Badgett; Mosely Baker; John J. Baugh; William Blazeby; Andrew Briscoe and Sam Maverick.

Many Tejanos (Texans of Spanish and Mexican blood) played a major role in the Texas Revolution. Among them was that wonderful patriot, Jose Antonio Navarro who, although imprisoned in a Mexican dungeon for three and one half years, uttered these words while under pressure to disavow his allegiance to Texas: "I have sworn to be a good Texan and that I will not forswear. I will die for that which I firmly believe, for I know it is right. One life is a small price to pay for a cause so great. As I fought, so shall I be willing to die. I will never forsake Texas and her cause. I am her son."

Along with Navarro, Jose Francisco Ruiz was a signer of the Texas Declaration of Independence; Juan Martin de Veramendi, father-in-law of James Bowie and governor of the combined state of Coahuila and Texas from 1832-1833, was sympathetic to the Texas colonists; Don Erasmo Seguin about whom these words were spoken by Honorable Guy B. Bryan: "In the infancy of Texas--in the days of her weakness and his strength, he was the faithful friend of the American."

Colonel Juan N. Seguin, like his father, Don Erasmo, an early opponent of Santa Anna, fought in the Battle of Bexar, served as a courier from the Alamo and with Houston in the Battle of San Jacinto; other Tejano patriots were Captain Placcido Benavides, Blas Herrera, Jose Cassiano (an Italian by birth), Lorenzo de Zavala, Ambrosio Rodriguez, Antonio Cruz de Arocha, Alejandro de la Garza, Martin de Leon, the Curbiers. A special honor goes to those who died at the Alamo--Juan Abamillo, Gregorio Esparza, Toribio Losoya, Andres Nava, Damacio Jimenes, Carlos Espalier, Juan A. Badillo, Antonio Fuentes, and Jose Maria Guerrero.

The list is almost endless but time and space do not permit the inclusion of all names. If a reader's kin or some other early Texan is inadvertently omitted, please forgive the author.

COLONISTS DIVIDED BETWEEN CO-EXISTENCE AND INDEPENDENCE

When William Barret Travis rode into Anahuac that May evening in 1831, the colonists were already divided into two camps: those seeking peaceful coexistence led by Stephen F. Austin and those seeking independence led principally by William H. Wharton. But William Barret Travis' personal credo was that "ultimately they bury the meek just as deep as the bold," and he intended to play a bold role. Losing no time, he established a legal presence in Texas by filing an application for a land grant, giving his age as "22," his profession as "law," place of residence - "Alabama," and as stated earlier, his marital status as "single."

Just as soon as he could evaluate the situation, Travis cast his lot with colonists who sought total independence--the so-called War Party. In doing so, however, he did not alienate pacifist Stephen F. Austin because in November of 1825, Austin wrote United States Senator Thomas H. Benton from Missouri, endorsing Travis for an appointment as United States Consul for the port of Galveston. The letter is excerpted below:

The particular object of this letter . . . is to recommend to you the bearer, Mr. W. B. Travis, who probably will apply to you for the appointment of U. S. Consul for the harbor and Bay of Galveston in Texas--

My personal acquaintance with Mr. T. is very short and limited, he has been recommended by persons of respectability and I can with full confidence say that he has acquired the esteem and respect of the better part of the people in the section of the country where he resides which is on the Trinity river near the head of Galveston Bay, and I have my self no hesitation in recommending him as a suitable person for the appointment of Consul.

Meanwhile, Travis had been invited to join another young attorney, Patrick C. Jack, in Anahuac as a partner. It is interesting to note that Jack and his brother, William, had both practiced law in Jefferson County, Alabama before coming to Texas in 1830. The Jack brothers were very capable men and had a patriotic tradition as sons of a father who had commanded a Georgia regiment in the War of 1812. Travis was instantly attracted to the Jack brothers.

"Three-Legged Willie" also became an immediate friend. "Three-Legs," as he was affectionately called by those who knew him, was a fun-loving character with a gregarious temperament-- gifted at telling stories, playing the banjo, and singing in an excellent voice. His office was in San Felipe, the capital of Austin's colony; and he had been there since 1827. Most of that time he had published the *Texas Gazette* and used it to expose the citizens to the poems of Lord Byron as well as inciting them to the idea of independence.

Patrick Jack had introduced Travis to "Three-Legs" and quickly this threesome was known throughout the colony as the "life of any party" and generally described as a trio that loved to drink and gamble but knew when to bridle frivolity. Travis, like Williamson, was addicted to flashy clothes. His favorite attire was a white hat, red pantaloons, and patent leather pumps. To say the least, he was conspicuous in both Anahuac and San Felipe where the dress of the day was predominantly buckskin or drop-front cotton denim.

TRAVIS AND BRADBURN CLASH

Colonel Juan Bradburn continued his tyrannical treatment of the citizens, commandeering slaves to work on his military buildings without compensation to their owners, even encouraging them to revolt by telling them it was the aim of the Mexican government to set them free. He gave sanctuary to three runaway slaves whom he enlisted in his detachment, refusing to surrender them to their rightful owner, William M. Logan.

Just as sure as night follows day, it was inevitable that Bradburn and Travis would clash. This clash was set up by Bradburn's arrest of Travis' friend, Patrick Jack, on a pretext that has never been made clear; but the most likely reason is that Jack had organized a militia company supposedly for protection of the colonists against Indians. Bradburn saw this as a threat to his authority and arrested Jack but detained him only briefly. However, Patrick's freedom was short-lived as within twenty-four hours he was back in jail, this time with his friend, William Barret Travis. Probably the reason for Travis' arrest was the fact he had interceded on behalf of Logan, attempting to recover the slaves Bradburn held. Bradburn continued to drag his feet and finally refused to surrender the slaves to either Travis or Logan.

Upon hearing rumors that the citizens would attempt to free Travis and Jack, he had them moved to an old brick kiln that he had fortified with soldiers and two cannon. He reinforced the walls of the old kiln with unused bricks, stacking them inside the old wall with "commandeered" labor of his prisoners. To prevent their escape, Bradburn had the pair shackled with leg irons to the ground. Friends of Travis and Jack started to gather and threats were made. Bradburn let it be known that he would kill the prisoners if one shot was fired. Travis then shouted, "I would rather die a thousand deaths than permit this oppressor to remain unpunished!"

William H. Jack, Patrick's brother, determined to teach Bradburn a lesson, rallied volunteers from San Felipe and asked his friend, John Austin (no relation to Stephen F. Austin), to gather ninety more at Brazoria. William Jack, with his militia group, left immediately for Anahuac and laid siege, waiting on the arrival of John Austin. On June 4, 1832, the force from Brazoria arrived. Now the total rose to one hundred sixty men, all clamoring for a fight. Bradburn promised he would turn the prisoners over if the colonists would withdraw. They agreed.

Using this interlude, Bradburn strengthened his position but so did the colonists. John Austin and others went to Brazoria for two cannon while the main group camped in Turtle Bayou.

TURTLE BAYOU RESOLUTIONS

"Three-Legged Willie" heard that Santa Anna was engaged in a rebellion to overthrow President Bustamente in Mexico and would probably be successful. Williamson felt it was prudent that their actions at Turtle Bayou not be construed by Santa Anna as an act against his authority. They adopted what became known as the Turtle Bayou Resolutions, in which they declared their actions were in no way to be interpreted as an uprising against Mexico or Santa Anna but only a resistance to Bradburn's tyranny. The Resolutions went on to emphatically state that the colonists resorted to arms only in support of Santa Anna and the Federalists.

BATTLE OF VELASCO

At Brazoria John Austin and his men loaded the cannon on a vessel in the Brazos River with the intention of sailing back to Anahuac. But the military commander at Velasco, Domingo de Ugartechea, would not allow them to leave the area. Ugartechea stated that even though he was not in sympathy with Bradburn, he could never allow insurgents to take up arms against a Mexican garrison. But John Austin persisted, and on June 26, 1832, the Battle of Velasco was fought and Ugartechea surrendered the garrison only after the loss of lives of ten colonists and five Mexican soldiers. This action at Velasco was of no help as the siege at Anahuac had been settled before they arrived.

Colonel Jose de las Piedras (commandant at Nacogdoches) heard of the trouble at Anahuac and rushed to the scene on the coast. He quickly realized that Bradburn's unwarranted actions was the root cause of the problem and skillfully proposed that prisoners receive a legal trial, marshal law be lifted, and the colonists be reimbursed for property Bradburn had confiscated. This was enough to satisfy the colonists and they soon dispersed after seeing the popular Travis and Jack released amid cheers and applause. Bradburn resigned and barely escaped with his life as he ran for the Louisiana border.

Stephen F. Austin was in Mexico when he heard of the Anahuac incident. He was displeased over the taking up of arms by the colonists but was consoled when told of the Turtle Bayou Resolutions, which were a declaration in favor of Santa Anna. It was his opinion that the new emperor of Mexico was a liberal who would favor the colonists and restore the federal Constitution of 1824. General Teran, who so feared the colonists, committed suicide on July 2 rather than leave his fate in the hands of Santa Anna.

THE BATTLE OF NACOGDOCHES AND JAMES BOWIE

Soon after the trouble at Anahuac and Velasco, Texas was cleared of Mexican military presence. Most of the soldiers and their commanders wanted to pledge their loyalty to Santa Anna and to assist him in the revolution still going on in the interior. It was a peaceful exit except in the case of Colonel Piedras, who had aided the colonists at Anahuac. He refused to support the Federalists' or Santa Anna. In a shoot-out that has been called the Battle of Nacogdoches, which cost the lives of thirty-three soldiers and three settlers (including the Hispanic Alcalde of Nacogdoches,) he surrendered his troops who declared their loyalty for Santa Anna. Piedras was escorted to Matamoros in the custody of James Bowie and Stephen F. Austin. Bowie was a man who would play a major role in the battle of independence for Texas.

R. M. "THREE-LEGGED WILLIE" WILLIAMSON
(Courtesy of Eugene C. Barker Texas History Center)

JAMES (JIM) BOWIE
(Courtesy of DRT Research Library at the Alamo)

CHAPTER 5

JAMES BOWIE

James Bowie, more commonly known as Jim, was born in Logan County, Kentucky, in 1796, the eighth of ten children. The family moved to Rapides Parish, Louisiana in 1802.

James Bowie was about six feet tall with a muscular frame. He moved with the ease and stealth of a deer. His eyes were grey, shading to hazel, with hair that was curly and chestnut brown to red. He wore short side whiskers. An original portrait (cir. 1831-34), still in family hands by a great nephew, shows him to be handsome with a strong and determined face. So much has been said and written of this famous man that it is difficult to separate myth from truth in narrating his very interesting life.

If Bowie's manners were more pleasant than those of most men on the frontier, the credit surely goes to the teachings of his mother, Elve Jones Bowie, who had a finishing school education. Well educated for her times, Elve tutored her children at home as there were no schools in the frontier regions where they lived. In addition to the basic courses of study, Jim received instruction from his mother in the social graces. As a result, he was for the rest of his life polite to others and especially to women.

Much of the early information on James Bowie's life comes from his brother, John Bowie, who penned his remembrances for DeBow's *Southern and Western Review* in October 1852. John relates that his brother, James, was only eighteen when he left the family home and struck out on his own. He remained there a number of years and John suspected that many of the old timers (in 1852) remembered the daring deeds and sports the young Jim enjoyed out of a love for excitement. His exploits included roping and catching wild deer in the woods as well as rounding up and riding wild horses. He had even roped and rode alligators in the bayous.

John Bowie remembers his brother, James, as being even-tempered unless he was provoked to the extreme; then his anger could be explosive. But he was never known to take his feelings out on the weak and helpless; even his enemies were treated fairly. Of all the recollections of his associates and the wild tales of his exploits, not one word has reflected any lack of moral character in James Bowie.

Although he was an outdoor man, he also was at ease in social situations. As John puts it, "He loved his friends with all the ardor of youth and hated his enemies and their friends with all the rancor of the Indian." Although he has often been pictured as being an alcoholic, his brother states that Jim (at least in his youth), would only "take a glass to drive dull care away; but seldom allowed it to steal his brains or transform him into a beast."

When Jim was in his late teens, he and his brother, Rezin P. Bowie, went into business for themselves. They installed the first steam-operated sugar cane press in Louisiana and operated a saw mill. The Bowie brothers envied those who were making a lot of money from land speculation. Jim realized that the saw mill would never provide the necessary capital to finance their own land dealings. He sold his bayou property and together with brothers, Rezin and John, went looking for a new business opportunity in raw land. But a chance meeting with Jean LaFitte launched them into the unsavory, but very profitable, business of slave trading.

There has been much criticism of James Bowie's participation in the slave trade and in today's morality this part of his past does warrant condemnation. One can in no way justify this activity but it must be borne in mind that ethics were different then, and in the frontier times in which the Bowies lived, men survived by looking out for themselves, sometimes operating on the fringes of the law. This was true when the Bowie brothers entered into an arrangement with Jean LaFitte. He agreed to sell them sound and healthy blacks at the going rate of $1 per pound. This made the price of a typical slave about $150. In the open market the same slave would fetch from $500 to $1,000.

Bowie was quick to seize upon another and faster way of gain. Under the laws then standing, all Africans brought in were in violation of the statue and were confiscated by the government to be sold at auction. One-half of the price went to the authorities and the balance to the informer. Jim and his comrades began informing upon themselves, and when the slaves were seized and sold, they bought them back, pocketed half the money they paid, and were free to offer their slaves again to whomsoever they chose. The blacks were now lawfully within the United States and represented a commodity as staple and marketable as cotton or sugar. The profits they enjoyed were enormous. Although Jim and his brother John, realized a profit of some $65,000 within two years,(a fortune in those times). they grew tired of the pretense and chicanery of using false names in order to inform upon themselves. They decided to disband the business and spend the profits on land speculation or whatever struck their fancy.

Land prospecting (which he would pursue on and off for the rest of his life) was particularly suited to James Bowie in that he could spend much time in the woods, and above everything else, Jim was an outdoor man.

It was, no doubt, during this period of outdoor life, that the first Bowie knife came into being. Rezin P. Bowie, in a letter to the *Planter's Advocate*, August 24, 1838, stated that "The first Bowie knife was made by myself in the parish of Avoyelles, in this state (Louisiana, Ed.), as a hunting knife, for which purpose, exclusively, it was used for many years." Rezin P. goes on to give a physical description of the knife. He then relates how the knife and Jim Bowie took the first step to legendary fame. It began with an act of self defense in an altercation with a Major Norris Wright, and others, in Alexandria, Louisiana in which Bowie exchanged pistol shots with his adversaries and was wounded. He used his hunting knife to save his life. James Bowie's reputation as a duelist can be trace to this altercation known as the famous "Sandbar Fight". It took place in September 1827 on a sandy jetty on the Mississippi River above Natchez.

It seems a bitter feud existed between the Cunys and the Welles (cousins of the Bowies) and some newcomers to the state: Major Norris Wright and a Dr. Thomas Maddox from Maryland. Also, in the latter's group was a Colonel Robert A. Crain and two Blanchards from Virginia.

Continuing arguments, quarrels, and threats between the two factions finally resulted in an arrangement for a duel to be fought. In the group containing Jim Bowie was the leader of the Welles family, Samuel L. Welles and his brother, General Momfort Welles. Also in the Bowie group were a General Cuney, a Doctor Cuney, and a Mr. George C. McWhorter. The other faction, led by Dr. Maddox, also contained Major Norris Wright of Baltimore, Maryland; Colonel Robert A. Crain of Virginia; Alfred and Edward Blanchard also of Virginia, and finally a Dr. Denny. All of the above-named would act as witnesses, seconds, and surgeons for their particular party.

Arrangements were made for the fight to occur on September 19, 1827, on a little sandbar opposite the town of Natchez. The principals in the duel were Samuel L. Welles on the one hand and Dr. Maddox on the other.

The two main adversaries exchanged a brace of ineffectual pistol shots, and then shook hands, agreeing they had settled their differences in a gentlemanly manner. It was at this moment that General Cuney stepped forward and said to Colonel Crain, "This is a good time to settle our difficulty." Almost at the same instant, Jim Bowie and Major Wright fired; then all others in both parties began firing. Colonel Crain immediately killed General Cuney and shot Jim Bowie through the hip. Bowie drew his knife and rushed toward the Colonel who clubbed him with his empty pistol, landing such a blow to the head that it brought Jim to his knees. Bowie was dazed. Dr. Maddox then tried to choke him; but Jim recovered his strength and hurled Maddox off just as Major Wright approached with cocked pistol and fired point blank at the wounded Bowie but fortunately missed.

Bowie, now armed with a pistol found on the sand, regained his footing and steadied himself against a log, half buried in the sand. Bowie fired at Wright. The shot passed through the latter's body without knocking him down. Major Wright drew a sword-cane and rushed straight at Jim exclaiming, "Damn you, Bowie, you have killed me; but I'll take you with me!"

Jim parried the thrusting sword-cane with his knife. Seizing his assailant, Bowie plunged the knife into Major Wright's body at the navel. Then with both hands on the handle, Jim pulled straight upward, opening Wright's body from his chest to his chin. As Bowie was trying to stem the flow of his own blood, Edward Blanchard approached and shot Jim at close range, the ball passing through his ribs but he still he clung to the half-buried tree trunk. Now a pistol ball fired from the gun of Jefferson Welles shattered Bowie's left arm above the elbow. Jim finally collapsed.

Bowie slowly recovered from his wounds in the "Sandbar Fight." The fact he survived when everyone expected him to die, coupled with the story of how he cleaved apart the body of Major Wright, made him famous in the saloons of New Orleans and gambling boats along the Mississippi. Soon his reputation as a knife-fighter was known all the way to St. Louis and San Antonio.

There were other tales (mostly exaggerated) of Bowie's dueling abilities. Only the "Sandbar Fight" with Major Norris Wright, and the knife fight with "Bloody" John Sturdivant in 1829, can be documented with any degree of certainty. The fight with Sturdivant occurred in 1829 when Bowie was at Natchez-under-the Hill and had a chance meeting with the youthful son of a close personal friend, Dr. William Lattimore. The young man had just sold a large amount of cotton, the proceeds of which he was rapidly losing to a notorious gambler and blowhard by the name of "Bloody" Sturdivant. Sturdivant was cheating the young man in a faro game. Bowie, being quite skilled in gambling himself, observed the cheating. He said to the young man, "Son, you don't know me, but I'm a friend of your father's. Let me play your hand for a while."

The young man gave Bowie his seat and the cheater was quickly exposed. Jim won back all the money young Lattimore had lost and gave it to him with the advice never to gamble again. "Bloody" Sturdivant, ignorant of the identity of the man who won his money, challenged him to a duel. Further, he proposed that they lash their left hands together and fight with knives. Jim accepted. At the first stroke, he disabled the right arm of his antagonist, (his "dealing" arm) although Bowie gallantly let him live.

After the Bowies quit the slave trading business they had time on their hands and money to spend. Their eyes and fancies were attracted to New Orleans; a place where spending came easy on plush hotels, wonderful food, and women of all moral and social levels. This wonderful city, a Paris in miniature, lay glittering before them. They could not resist. Jim Bowie took in all it had to offer and seemed to be as much at home in this atmosphere as he was around a camp fire on the frontier.

Soon, James Bowie tired of the social and business life of New Orleans--and still suffering from the wounds he received in the "Sandbar Fight", grew restless and was ready to move on. New Orleans was becoming over-populated with men of so-called education and distinction, and suddenly he felt uncomfortable in their midst. He related better to the reckless, rough-riding type of man who followed the call of adventure westward. Jim also heard, and answered the call.

Bowie was thirty-two years old when he reached San Antonio in 1828. It was the capital of the province of Texas, which was included in the state of Coahuila. The vice-governor lived in San Antonio. His name was Don Juan Martin Veramendi, an aristocrat and wealthy citizen. Jim knew that all foreigners were required to register with the government if they planned to stay. So he went directly to the governor's office, located in his home on Calle Soledad.

Governor Veramendi had heard of Jim Bowie. He was a legendary hero in Spanish Texas, long before he visited Bexar. The governor was captivated by seeing the man in person. Bowie spoke fair Spanish and informed the governor of events back in the States. This interested Veramendi, and he felt honored by Bowie's presence. Desiring to learn more, Veramendi insisted on introducing him to his family and suggested that Bowie stay for dinner. That night Bowie met Ursula Veramendi the governor's eldest daughter, a beautiful eighteen-year-old.

Jim Bowie was immediately infatuated with San Antonio de Bexar, more often simply called Bexar. The town had been an important center of culture in the days of Spanish rule. But after Mexico's independence, it became just another outpost on the frontier. In the past eight years, over half the population left the city. Yet the place still had a noticeable Spanish charm.

On sunny days, the colorful clothes of the Mexicans contrasted sharply with the drab flat-roofed adobe houses. Mothers bathed their children and washed clothes in the sparkling emerald green waters of the San Antonio River that meandered through the eastern edge of the town. Older citizens gossiped in the two central squares whose names, Main Plaza and Military Plaza, still reflected the flavor of past history. In the evenings, cooking fires glowed in every yard and the pleasing sound of guitar music, intermingled with soft breezes, floated into the streets from doorways and patios. It was quite a change of pace for Bowie; but he loved it. Thanks to Governor Veramendi's friendship, the people accepted him totally.

Because there were hostile Indians all around Bexar, Bowie immediately set about to organize a Ranger Company composed mainly of the local young aristocrats. He was its leader, and they called him "Colonel." Every campaign the Rangers undertook was so successful "Colonel" Jim Bowie became the toast of the town.

Jim was a man after the Governor's own heart--bold, courageous, willing to take a chance, but prudent in business, Veramendi liked to listen to the stories Bowie told of the money and land he had accumulated (though Bowie didn't mention that much of the land he held was by questionable titles). Veramendi invited Bowie to become a partner with him in various enterprises, particularly land speculation. Bowie took quarters on Calle Soledad only a few doors from the Governor's Palace, visiting him frequently. One day the governor suggested that Jim move into the Veramendi home insomuch as they were partners and needed to consult often. Already well acquainted with all the Veramendis, he readily accepted. From that day forward, he never thought of himself as other than a member of the Veramendi family.

Aside from Bowie's sorties with the Rangers, life with the family was easy, carefree and pleasant. They called him "Jaime." While he was the epitome of courtesy and deference to both Don Juan and Dona Maria Josefa Navarro Veramendi, his relationship with the children--including 19-year-old Ursula--was that of an older brother.

Mexican law required that only citizens of Mexico could own Texas land, and Texas land was something Jim wanted very much. Therefore, he decided to become a citizen of Mexico. The first step was to become a Catholic, which he readily did (his baptismal records are on file today in San Fernando Church.) With the governor and his wife as sponsors, his acceptance as a citizen was a foregone conclusion.

The state legislature of Coahuila y Texas at Saltillo passed an act on September 30, offering him citizenship. The oath was administered on October 5, 1830 and Jim Bowie became a naturalized citizen of the state of Coahuila y Texas but with the understanding he would finance a textile mill to be built in Saltillo. Citizenship gave him the right to buy up to eleven leagues (one league = 4,428 acres) of public land. Bowie returned to Texas with fifteen-eleven league grants. (He had induced Mexican citizens to apply, then turn their grant to him.) Many of these worthless grants were found in Bowie's estate inventory after he died.

Bowie had met many women of various shades of virtue in New Orleans and elsewhere, and some had vainly tried to win his heart. But Jim had never felt real love until Ursula's party during the Christmas fiestas in 1830. He suddenly observed how all the young blades of Bexar, mostly members of the Rangers and his good friends, clustered around Ursula, vying for her attention. He must have realized, for the first time that this vivacious, attractive young girl had become a desirable women. At what point Jim realized he loved Ursula, we can only speculate. It must have come as a surprise, even to himself, to realize that he finally wanted to end his bachelorhood.

In all likelihood, Don Juan and Dona Josefa were pleased when Jim Bowie asked for the hand of their daughter. He had impressed them favorably from the start and was now loved as a son. His future father-in-law saw in him a good business partner as well as a proper husband for his adored daughter. They willingly gave their approval.

Bowie signed a dowery agreement which bound him to pay his wife within two years after their marriage $15,000 in cash or equivalent. As a guarantee of his ability to pay, he made a manifest of his principal assets: 60,000 acres in Arkansas valued at $30,000; 15,000 acres in Louisiana at $75,000; notes receivable at Natchez, Mississippi, in the amount of $97,800 and $20,000 in cash in the hands of one Angus McNeill for the purchase of textile machinery--a total of $222,800, a vast fortune at the time. (But Bowie failed to mention that the 60,000 acres in Arkansas had fraudulent title.)

After the long Mexican courtship that custom dictates, James Bowie and Ursula Veramendi were married on April 23, 1831, in the old San Fernando Church (a place where many couples still take their vows today). We can be sure they made a handsome couple--Jim, tall and handsome--Ursula, petite and beautiful in her traditional wedding array. The bells of San Fernando church must have rung joyously and the governor just as surely must have provided an elaborate fiesta for the wedding guests.

Veramendi generously supplied the couple with money, giving them a trip to New Orleans as a wedding present. Legend has it that Jim proudly showed off his bride to his family and friends and she charmed everyone she met.

Rezin Bowie returned to Texas with Jim and Ursula. Rezin wanted to see more of Texas and search for the "lost San Saba silver mine." In the fall of 1831, Jim and, Rezin, with six other men and a boy, set out upon an expedition looking for the mine. Their route would take them through the heart of Comanche country. On the sixth day of travel, the party was surrounded by nearly two hundred mounted warriors--Comanches, who rode like the wind, screaming fierce yells they had never before heard. Resistance seemed hopeless in the face of such great odds, but Bowie was resourceful and took the one desperate chance that might mean victory.

He divided his forces, stationing three in one patch of woods with the animals, and scattering the rest all around. Each was fully armed with rifles, knifes, pistols and plenty of lead and powder. For five days the fight went on. The Indians attacked again and again with arrows and bullets flying thicker than hail. Every charge ended in a rout when they came within rifle range. Bowie's men, crouching behind cover, made every shot count. Indian and horses went down in struggling heaps. They reloaded so quickly and kept up such a sustained fire that the chiefs finally decided their enemy was at least a hundred strong. They counted more than three score of their braves dead and an equal number wounded. The chiefs finally gathered their wounded and rode off. Bowie lost one man whom he reverently buried. Another, badly wounded, was carried back to San Antonio de Bexar. This fight with the Indians became known as the San Saba Fight, for it occurred near the San Saba River. When he returned to Bexar with this story, he was even a greater hero.

He and Ursula lived with her parents in the Veramendi house (later called the Governor's Palace). Bowie was treated even more as a son and furnished with money and supplies without limit. He, apparently, had no regular occupation or income but made frequent trips back East, living like a man who had plenty of money. (He did have money – Veramendi's.)

Bowie was on one of his extended trips East--sometime between the fifth and sixth of September--when a deadly tragedy struck and wiped out the entire Veramendi family, including his beloved Ursula. After hearing that the dreaded cholera had spread to Texas, it seems Don Juan had taken his family to Monclova, Mexico where they had a summer home. But the disease found them and they all perished in three or four days.

Bowie was not aware of their deaths when he executed his will at Natchez, Mississippi, on the following October 21, 1833. He listed as his sole heirs his brother, Rezin P. Bowie, and his sister, Martha Bowie Sterret, and her husband. He explained that his wife had been taken care of by the dowry (which he, apparently, never paid). He further stipulated that $4,000 be paid to a friend who loaned him that amount to buy land and an additional $4,000 to another friend who had secured a loan for him. Apparently, Jim Bowie felt his land investments would pay off, but sadly they never did.

There are those who say the grief he felt over the death of his young wife, Ursula, caused Jim Bowie to become an alcoholic, and that was the reason for his incapacity at the Alamo. Although he drank heavily on occasion, Jim was a sick man when he came into the Alamo. Dr. Amos Pollard, the fort's doctor, called in Dr. John Sutherland for a consultation, but neither physician could come up with a diagnosis except that the sickness "was of peculiar nature, not to be cured by an ordinary course of treatment." In the light of modern research, it seems likely that Bowie had tuberculosis, perhaps compounded by pneumonia.

Some may question Bowie's loyalty to Texas because he was a citizen of Mexico and had taken a Mexican wife. Even Stephen F. Austin labeled Bowie as an adventurer out for personal gain. The Provisional Council of Texas on January 12, 1836, ruled that Bowie was not "an officer of the government or army." His men, however, called him Colonel from his title in the Rangers of Bexar.

But Sam Houston valued him as a leader of "promptitude and manliness" and rated him second to none in "forecast, prudence and valor." In any case, Bowie's fidelity to Texas in the fight against Mexico is clear and unvarnished. He earned his place as "one of the Texas immortals." It is said that after Bowie was killed in the battle of the Alamo and bodies were being burned, an unknown Mexican officer suggested that the body of Bowie not be burned but buried separately from the others, saying, "He was too great a man to sleep in eternity with the common soldiers." But if Bowie could have spoken he would have, undoubtedly, declined this singular distinction, for it is clear James Bowie was an uncommon man for the common man.

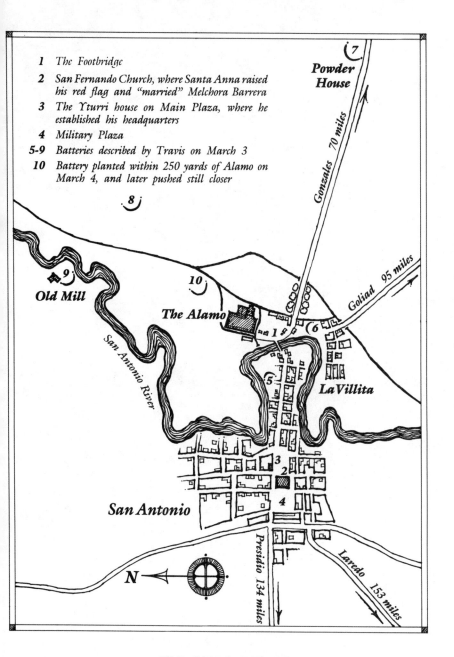

1 The Footbridge
2 San Fernando Church, where Santa Anna raised his red flag and "married" Melchora Barrera
3 The Yturri house on Main Plaza, where he established his headquarters
4 Military Plaza
5-9 Batteries described by Travis on March 3
10 Battery planted within 250 yards of Alamo on March 4, and later pushed still closer

Powder House

Gonzales 70 miles

Goliad 95 miles

Old Mill

The Alamo

San Antonio River

La Villita

San Antonio

N

Presidio 134 miles

Laredo 153 miles

OLD SAN ANTONIO

JAMES BOWIE

CHAPTER 6

WAR OR PEACE

SANTA ANNA TAKES CONTROL IN MEXICO

By the end of 1832 Bustamente and his Centralist followers had been forced to resign. Santa Anna had won the long struggle with Bustamente, but he was not ready to take over government on a day-to-day basis. He still thrilled in leading an army and had many political enemies to eliminate. So he installed as president Gomez Pedraza. By Santa Anna's orders the new president would serve until January 1833 when national elections would again be held. (Santa Anna postponed the elections scheduled in 1832.)

The victorious Santa Anna had fears the Anglo American uprising in Anahuac was the precursor of a general rebellion and sent the Federalist General Jose Antonio Mexia with five hundred troops to Texas. Austin heard of this and joined Mexia at Saltillo and traveled with him into Texas. In each town General Mexia visited, he was met with accolades and pledges of loyalty to the Federalist cause. At San Felipe a fandango (banquet and dance) was held in his honor. The Turtle Bayou Resolutions were read by Austin; toasts were drunk to Santa Anna and to Federalism and to the Constitution of 1824. With this great show of allegiance, Mexia returned to Mexico and assured Santa Anna that the colonists supported him.

COLONISTS ASK REPEAL OF LAW OF APRIL 6, 1830

Santa Anna's overthrow of Bustamente was generally accepted with acclaim in Texas, for he was believed to be a liberal proponent of the Constitution of 1824. The colonists now decided it would be appropriate to protest the hated law of April 6, 1830. The ayuntamiento issued a call for a general convention with delegates from all of the colonies to assemble in San Felipe in October 1832 to draft a resolution. Fifty-eight delegates from sixteen communities gathered and elected Stephen F. Austin as president. The most significant topics in the petition they submitted were as follows: 1) a repeal of the anti-immigration section of the Law of April 6, 1830; 2) separate statehood for Texas, pointing out that it had sufficient population and had traditionally been a separate province under Spain; 3) a school system be established; 4) certain taxes and tariff duties be eliminated; and 5) land titles be issued immediately for all settlers who had not received them.

The convention adjourned in only five days, proud of their work and what they had accomplished in such a short time. The petition was to the political chief in San Antonio, Ramon Musquiz.

Musquiz generally agreed with the colonists' requests, particularly the one for separate statehood. He was distressed, however, over the methods--conventions being entirely unfamiliar to the Mexicans as a way to ask for redress. This spontaneous gathering of citizens was diametrically opposite to the centralized autocracy which Spaniards had followed for hundreds of years. A convention of citizens in his mind was not only illegal but very close to treason. The ayuntamiento he could accept, but a convention--never. He, therefore, refused to forward the petitions and warned them that their convention was a "disturbance of good order."

STEPHEN F. AUSTIN Petitions Santa Anna for Statehood

Meanwhile in Mexico City the postponed national elections were held, and Santa Anna was easily elected. This news heartened the colonists in spite of Musquiz's rejection of their petition. Had they not declared their loyalty to Santa Anna and forced the closure of Centralist garrisons in Texas? They decided to defy Musquiz and called for another convention to meet in San Felipe on April 1, 1833. Two-thirds of the members had not attended the previous one. Among the new members were Sam Houston, who had just arrived from Nacogdoches. He sat in the bar of the Peyton Hotel almost nightly, sipping bourbon. Another was William H. Wharton, son-in-law of an important and successful Brazos River plantation owner, Jarard E. Groce.

The distinguishing feature of this new convention was that it was definitely split into two camps. One would be labeled the Peace Party (moderates) led by Stephen F. Austin seeking peace and continued affiliation with Mexico; the other would come to be called the War Party (radicals), seeking total independence. Wharton was elected president; David Burnett was appointed to draw up the petition for statehood; and Sam Houston was made chairman of a committee to draft a proposed constitution for Texas.

After much debate, the final petitions were almost identical with those of the convention of 1832. However, there was one significant difference. In the petition for separate statehood for Texas, they also submitted a proposed state constitution. This was a bold act, but they were so convinced Santa Anna would approve statehood, they felt it would be expeditious to do so. The convention appointed a committee of three men to deliver this petition to Santa Anna's government in Mexico: Stephen F. Austin; Erasmo Seguin, a prominent rancher southeast of San Antonio and father of Juan Seguin. Seguin had been a member of the congress that drafted the Federal Constitution of 1824; and Dr. James B. Miller, a prominent physician of San Felipe. However, it turned out, only Austin was able to make the trip. He left San Felipe in late April 1833 and arrived in Mexico City in July 1833. He had no inkling of what was in store for him.

THE MEXICAN GOVERNMENT CAROUSEL

With the petition for statehood (and the proposed constitution) in his grip, Austin was now in Mexico City for the second time. To his amazement he found as much or more political confusion as when he had visited ten years earlier. Santa Anna, proven a talented general, would now attempt to demonstrate he was just as skilled as captain of the ship of state. He boldly gambled his political fortune on a secret and complex voyage through the waters of Mexican politics. Santa Anna knew that sudden changes could prove to be unpopular so he decided on a ploy to protect himself. Although he was elected President in the postponed election of 1833, he decided not to be inaugurated. He wanted to orchestrate major changes but was not certain how they would be accepted, therefore, he would use a buffer between himself and the people. Installing as "acting chief executive" his vice president, Gomez Farias, Santa Anna stated that he needed to "recruit his health" and retired to his estate, Manga de Clavo.

Santa Anna, knowing Farias was eager to stage reforms, wanted to be in the balcony watching the show. The proven champion of law and order could always step onto the stage if the audience booed instead of cheered. Santa Anna did not have to wait long for the performance to begin. Farias' first reform was directed against two of the most entrenched hierarchies in Mexico, the church and the army. He declared that henceforth church appointments would be given by the state, and the clergy was forbidden to speak out on politics or enforce tithes.

When Gomez Farias announced his proposed changes, revolution exploded all over Mexico. Six weeks after his inauguration, Farias resigned and Santa Anna returned triumphantly to Mexico City, assumed the presidency he had previously refused, and with bands playing marched triumphantly off to put down the insurrection. There followed a series of apparently staged events, beginning with his so-called "capture" by the insurrectionists who immediately proposed him as their leader to restore the traditional privileges Farias had stripped away. After Santa Anna's "capture," Farias again assumed the presidency, but shortly Santa Anna "escaped from his captors" in June 1833 and reclaimed the presidency. He nullified only some of the smaller reforms instituted by his stooge, Farias, then retired again to his estate in December 1833, but not before again elevating Farias to the position of "acting chief executive," giving him a free reign to initiate other reforms.

It didn't take Farias long to announce a major move--the separation of church and state. There immediately came an explosive uprising. Santa Anna let the smoke blow downwind for a while. Then in April 1834 the astute and cunning Santa Anna, convinced that the vast majority of the Mexican people were fed up with Federalism and Liberalism, again stepped to the forefront and assumed the presidency, proclaiming loudly for conservatism. But he would soon throw off this facade and show his true colors--that of a Centralist, even worse--that of a dictator. Within a twelve-month period, he played musical chairs with his scape-goat vice president five times, letting the hapless Farias suffer the repercussions of reform. He was now moving swiftly toward dictatorship (another volte-face manuever with which he was now a master.) But he must yet decide when the time was ripe.

PRISON FOR AUSTIN

Little wonder Austin was frustrated and bewildered. He had watched in unbelieving amazement as Santa Anna "resigned," "was captured," "escaped," "returned," and "resigned again." The presidency was like a carousel. Sometime in September 1833, during one of the brief periods when Farias was in power, Austin submitted the petition of the 1834 convention; but he was not favorably received. Austin, unusually blunt, told Farias that his colonists would not suffer further delay. Farias took this as a threat and certainly was not prepared to accept Austin's demand for statehood. Both men were angry when they parted. Austin, by now greatly discouraged, made the mistake of writing a critical letter to the ayuntamiento in San Antonio, made up of Hispanics who supported statehood, urging his Hispanic friends there to take the lead in separating Texas from Coahuila. After Austin posted the letter, Santa Anna returned to the presidency for six months from July to December 31, 1833.

Austin visited Santa Anna several times, and found him cordial and friendly; but he denied the petition for statehood. (Santa Anna was legally correct on this, for the Constitution of 1824 required 80,000 population before a territory could become a state.) However, he did agree to repeal the Law of April 6, 1830, and granted every other request of the Consultation, such as (1) repeal of the ban on immigration, 2) better mail service, and 3) modification of the tariff.) So Austin felt that at least his trip was worthwhile and set out overland on December 10 to return to Texas.

He got as far as Saltillo and was stunned when he was arrested there on January 3, 1834. He was immediately returned to Mexico City and thrown in the old Inquisition prison where he languished for six months in solitary confinement. Austin noted in his journal that his cell was only 13 feet x 16 feet and windowless. For the first month, he was not allowed to speak with anyone except his guards and was served his meals through a slot in the door. To add insult to injury, he had to pay for his own food! He was refused bail and was never informed of the charge against him. When the sun was shining, a small skylight gave him enough light to read by, and he was later given writing materials and books by some of his friends in Mexico City.

Later Austin learned his arrest had been ordered by Gomez Farias on the recommendation of General Vincente Filisola, commanding general of the Eastern Interior Provinces. Filisola, an Italian in the service of Mexico, could be compared to Santa Anna and his volte-face maneuvers. He had fought first for the Royalists, then joined Iturbide, later fought with the Federalists, and finally for the Centralists. When he read Austin's letter written to the San Antonio ayuntamiento, Filisola believed it amounted to treason. It had reached his hands in a rather circuitous manner. The San Antonio ayuntamiento had referred the letter to political chief Musquiz, who in turn sent it to the governor, from which it passed it to Filisola, and then on to Gomez and Farias. President Farias, hopelessly caught on the merry-go-round of Santa Anna's schemes, saw the letter as a threat of another revolution and ordered Austin's imprisonment. Now as the carousel of the presidency turned, General Santa Anna again stepped aboard, and in April 1834 ordered Austin removed from solitary confinement and transferred to a city jail with better facilities.

During these long months, it may have seemed to Austin that his plight was being ignored, but this was not the case. In his letters of despair over what he thought was his abandonment, he could not know that due to the lack of communication, friends were working in his behalf. But let's pause for a moment and catch up with developments in Texas after the Bradburn affair in Anahuac--and particularly to Travis.

TRAVIS MOVES TO SAN FELIPE

Travis had been in Texas for almost a year, and though he went there with an open mind, he now had a declared disrespect for Mexican authority. William Barret Travis had left Alabama in the dark of night with a lot of hurt to his heart, his ego, and his fortune. He had a total commitment to restore all of these as soon as possible and to enjoy life at the same time. In May 1832 he packed his few belongings, left Anahuac, and headed for San Felipe de Austin at the urging of his friend, "Three-Legged Willie."

Travis stopped at the Peyton Hotel, which by the standards of the frontier, was first-class. The register reflect its motto, "Headquarters of the most distinctive men in Texas." Some of the more famous names found there were James Bowie, John and William Wharton, Luke Lesassier, Stephen F. Austin, David Burnett, Ben Milam, Gail Borden, Father Muldoon, Erasmo Seguin, Dr. James Miller, and many others. It was definitely the best address in San Felipe and offered Will Travis many amenities not found elsewhere in the colonies.

San Felipe was a lawyer's bonanza. It had a growing population which had land grants with their accompanying problems. It also boasted the general store of Perry and Sommerville, specializing in materials from New York, Philadelphia, and New Orleans. The inventory included "broadcloth, cashmeres, castanets, point and duffel blankets, rich bonnet and felt ribbons, linen and cotton diapers, bleach sheetings and shirtings, and tuckings." Also the firm carried "cutlery and hardware, plow arms, axes, groceries, gunpowder, tea, chocolate, coffee, ginger, raisins, and wines and liquors of all description." They had two prices: "low for cash and higher for cotton, hides, or corn."

Travis must have been a regular customer, as it is recorded that he spent a great deal on his wardrobe as well as on gifts for others. Like "Three-Legged Willie" he favored clothes for his legal practice and social occasions instead of the usual rough boots and other frontier garb worn by most of the local men. His invariably charming manner and good looks accelerated his climb up the social ladder of San Felipe. To women, young and old, he was apparently irresistible--in today's language he would undoubtedly be called a "lady's man." Travis, Patrick Jack and "Three-Legged Willie" turned up at all the balls and fandangos. Some women, in hopes they might be favored with a dance from one or all of this dashing trio, would ride from miles around, carrying their best dress in saddlebags.

Many early Texas stalwarts frequented San Felipe and Travis must have been impressed by these men. Foremost among them was Ben Milam, an exceedingly versatile and interesting soldier of fortune . He had been a seaman, trader, colonizer, and a member of James Long's second filibustering expedition to Texas in 1821. He was taken prisoner with General Long in Mexico, where the latter was assassinated. Milam escaped and returned to San Felipe, where he established a close friendship with Long's attractive widow, Jane Long.

Another of the colorful characters whom Travis met in San Felipe was Captain James "Brit" Bailey from North Carolina. He had come to Texas even before Stephen F. Austin with his wife and six children and settled near the Brazos River on prime land which later became known as Bailey's Prairie in present Brazoria County. He had difficulty in securing a title, but later his claim was validated by becoming one of Austin's "Old 300." Bailey died in 1833 and is probably best remembered for his unusual death-bed request. He told his wife he had never stooped or bowed or was never knocked down by anybody and did not want any man to look upon his grave and be able to say, "There lies old 'Brit' Bailey flat on his back." Therefore, he requested she bury him standing up. After his death, she had a vertical hole dug for his wooden casket and buried him just as he wished.

TRAVIS' DIARY AND REBECCA CUMMINGS

Travis kept a detailed diary beginning August 30, 1833, through June 26, 1834. He made meticulous entries in it regarding loans, bets, and love affairs. Noted were 1,001 legal cases and the names of five hundred persons including twenty or more women.

Mrs. Peyton, who ran the hotel, was a good friend; and he often dined with her, exchanging gossip and news. In fact, he enjoyed feminine companionship when and wherever his legal business permitted. He entered many amorous experiences in his diary, many times giving an exact account. Most of the entries were entered in less than perfect Spanish, e.g. "Chingaba una mujer que es cincuenta y seis in mi pida." -- translated roughly-- "I made love with a woman which is number 56 in my life." Sometimes he would use the girl's initials and other times her first name, e.g. "Chingaba la Susanna que es 59." -- translated-- "I made love with Susanna which is number 59."

In spite of his many casual love affairs, Travis settled down to one girl in the latter part of 1834. She was lovely Rebecca Cummings, who lived at Mill Creek, seven miles above San Felipe. Travis had met Rebecca in September 1833 when business took him to the vicinity of Mill Creek. Not acquainted with that part of the area, he became lost and ended up dining at the Cummings Inn. After meeting Rebecca, he became familiar with the territory in short order. By December he was seeing her often, but judging from his reference to "Miss Cummings" in his diary, the relationship was not serious. However, it must have soon be become serious because shortly he wrote that he planned to pursue her "with schoolboy ardor." By February of the following year he was making regular trips to see her. On March 9, 1833, he noted in his diary "Started to Mill Creek, waters all swimming and prairie so boggy - - could not go - - the first time, I ever turned back in my life--" (a statement that gives credibility to this author's assessment that a ruffian could not run Travis out of Alabama by bobbing his horse's tail!).

He was at the inn just four days later and spent the night there, being invited by her brother, John, to discuss his legal affairs. This time he exchanged gifts with Rebecca, and it is significant that in his diary he no longer refers to her as "Miss Cummings." The entry states, "Gave R. (Rebecca) a breast pin - - took a lock of hair, and C." Accepting a lock of a lady's hair in the early nineteenth century was an indication of a very serious love affair. This was reinforced by his next entry, March 14, "Took ring from R. (Rebecca), swam horse over creek by canoe - - paid J. (John) Cummings $1 for corn and c--." It is presumed that the ring referred to is the famous cat's-eye ring now on display in the Alamo (which he later gave to little Angelina Dickinson at the Alamo.)

Their love affair had advanced to the point where Travis' past had to be discussed. It is believed he told her that he was still married and a father. Apparently, she was willing to wait for him to straighten out his marital affairs. His next entry in the dairy states, "In la sociedad de me inamoratal," - - which translates to "in the society of his beloved." Sunday visits were now routine, but everything did not always go smoothly. His entries sometimes indicated Rebecca's jealousy. This is understandable in light of the fact that while professing his love for her, he was seeing other girls--and still married to Rosanna. Subsequent entries indicate Rebecca vacillated, causing him to write in his diary - - "Went to Cummings - - Recepcion frio, pero conclusion muy caliente - -." - - "A cold reception, but a very warm conclusion." Again he spent the night. In his record for April 2, he states that he had "--spent day at C's (Cummings) - - a noche un conocimento simple . . ." The phrase translates into "Last night, a simple understanding," but it must have meant they had reached a definite engagement to be married when Travis was legally able.

His love affair with Rebecca and diary entries continued. On Friday, June 20, 1834, Travis was back again spending the night at Mill Creek, "Stayed at Cummings all night - - buena (good)". In spite of his serious relationship with Rebecca, Travis apparently never passed up other opportunities. On the very next night, there was an interlude with another girl: Miss J. - - - -. It is also significant that on the following Sunday he did not go to Mill Creek but instead "had an adventure with Miss T."

The cryptic diary of Travis reveals many facets of his personality. He was well read and the books he recorded were by authors such as Herodotus, Addison, Steele, and Scott. Apparently, he was an exceptionally fast reader. According to his diary, he began reading *Westward Ho!* on January 1, 1834, and finished it on January 3.

The diary also indicates Travis was a compulsive gambler. He always entered his poker losses and winnings (the latter were sparse). In one statement to his diary, he lost $200; next time his horse and other personal objects of value. On yet another losing night, he had to leave his flannel shirt, drawers, and handkerchief as security. A later entry relates that he lost "a suit and $14." Apparently, when he did win, he was sporting and generous with his gains. It was typical for him to lend his winnings back to the losers. This is substantiated by one entry as follows--"Won $17.75 at faro - - lent Nowell Scott $1, Howtch, $2 - - Smith $1 - - -." His diary also indicates that he forgave many gambling debts and was generous to those in need and an easy touch for a loan. A recording in his diary on the date of February 12, 1834, is significant. Travis noted that he "wrote bond for J. W. Moore indemnifying him to buy one Boy Joe belonging to Mansfield." Apparently, this is the same Joe who was with Travis at the Alamo and whose account of events there would earn this young black a permanent place in the pages of history.

Both Travis' legal practice and his love affair with Rebecca Cummings seemed to prosper. His major concerns were Austin's fate in Mexico and the problem with his wife, Rosanna. Travis wanted a divorce and also custody of his son, Charles. He pressed Rosanna for an answer but was unprepared for the manner in which it came.

AUSTIN IS RELEASED FROM PRISON

Meanwhile the ayuntamiento at San Felipe held a meeting on April 28, 1834, and voted to send an official petition to the Mexican government for Austin's release. It should be understood that news of Austin's arrest did not reach San Felipe until February 1, 1834, some seven months after Austin's arrival in Mexico City. The San Felipe ayuntamiento resolution to petition the Mexican government was supplemented by other petitions from Matagorda and Liberty. Spencer H. Jack and Peter W. Grayson agreed to take the documents to Mexico and present them for Austin's release. They arrived in Mexico City on October 14, 1834, and employed a skillful Mexican attorney to assist them. Finally on Christmas Day, 1834, Austin was released on bond. He was still restricted to certain generous boundaries.

Austin's final release did not come until six months later in July 1835. A Mexican court finally decided on June 22 that Austin was eligible for freedom under the terms of the general amnesty law covering political prisoners. By July 11, 1835, his passport was issued and he left within a week for Vera Cruz en route to Texas via New Orleans. He had been in prison eighteen months without a trial or even a charge! The erstwhile patient Austin could hardly wait to get back to Texas. For the first time, he realized that regardless of the price, Texas must have its freedom.

In Mexico City, one of the last official acts of President Farias was to send Juan N. Almonte, an educated English-speaking army officer, to make an inspection tour of Texas in the spring of 1834. Almontes' report found the settlements in a state of thriving prosperity with an estimated total population of 21,000. He also reported he did not discover any disloyalty toward Mexico, and in his opinion the government could depend upon the general support of the colonists. Although Almonte was sent out by Farias, his report was made to Santa Anna may have influenced him to free Stephen F. Austin. Perhaps Almonte found the Texans in such a mellow mood because they had heard shortly before his arrival that Santa Anna had lifted the restriction on immigration to Texas. With this news a steady stream of settlers, numbering in the thousands, poured across the Sabine into Texas. They came so fast and numerous many did not receive titles to their lands until long after the Texas Revolution.

SANTA ANNA ABROGATES CONSTITUTION OF 1824

The tranquility in Texas, however, did not prevail in Mexico. In April 1834, Santa Anna took over and ousted Farias for the last time. This was a "new" Santa Anna. In an about-face, he denounced liberalism publicly and dissolved the elected congress, replacing it with "appointees." Further, he abolished all the state legislatures and local ayuntamientos in Mexico. The decrees by Farias concerning the clergy and the army were declared void. In fear of his life, Lorenzo de Zavala, the Mexican liberal leader, fled to Texas. The new and subservient congress legalized all of Santa Anna's acts, including his abolishment of the Constitution of 1824 (officially voided on October 15, 1835.) He replaced it with a document similar to the old Spanish laws called "Siete Leyes," which called for a totally centralized government and made the former states into departments ruled by governors appointed by Santa Anna--an arrangement which made him, in effect, a dictator.

Santa Anna felt no responsibility to the people of Mexico, and a puppet congress passed all his decrees. But some of the states, namely Zacatecas, Coahuila y Texas, and California, defied him. California was too far away to bring to heel; but because of its proximity to Mexico City, Zacatecas would be the first to feel Santa Anna's fury. Liberalism was strong in Zacatecas, and when a decree was issued from the central government, these courageous people revolted. Santa Anna himself commanded the army that defeated the Zacatecan force of 5,000 on May 10, 1835. He had learned well what General Arredondo had taught, not only in tactics but brutality. He was not content with mere submission. Saying he did not want to be burdened with prisoners, Santa Anna extracted a bloody vengeance. After the mass executions, he permitted his troops to rape and pillage the capital.

MORE TURMOIL IN MEXICO

During this time, the state of Coahuila had fallen into disorder under the centralist government. Among other things, the government at Coahuila began to fight over the location of the capital. It was suddenly moved from Saltillo to Monclova. The ayuntamiento of Saltillo, in retaliation for the removal of the capital, set up a rival government and declared their city the capital. Militia forces on both sides prepared to fight, but a clash was averted when Santa Anna, in December 1834, recognized the Monclova government and appointed his brother-in-law, Martin Perfecto de Cos, Commandant of the Eastern Interior Provinces (including Texas), and ordered new elections to be held to select the capital of Coahuila.

Cos resented the Federalist leaning of the Monclova candidates who were swept into office with the election in the spring 1835. He personally wanted the capital returned to Saltillo. Quarrels again broke out between the two cities, and he intervened with force and marched toward Monclova. But before he arrived, the legislature wisely adjourned on May 21, 1835, after authorizing the governor, Augustin Viesca, to use his own discretion in selecting a capital. Viesca did not make an immediate decision which angered Cos. Accompanied by Ben Milam, Viesca fled toward San Antonio but was captured by Cos on June 8. Milam was able to escape and returned to Texas, but the Zacatecas massacre and the Saltillo-Monclova clash were just preludes to the turmoil that would erupt all over Mexico and be felt even in Texas. Santa Anna's declaration that Mexico was a Centralist state in which the President and his National Congress had absolute power had taken the Federalists everywhere by surprise.

ANAHUAC RE-OCCUPIED - TENORIO

At this time Cos, winding up operations in Coahuila, received word from the garrison commander at Anahuac that trouble was brewing. The post at Anahuac was re-occupied by Captain Antonio Tenorio in January 1835; and like his predecessor--Bradburn--quickly made himself unpopular by arresting Andrew Briscoe and DeWitt C. Harris for their refusal to pay custom duties. Cos sent a dispatch rider north with a message to Tenorio that he was sending reinforcements. His message was intercepted at San Felipe, and a citizens committee organized a militia force headed by William Barret Travis to drive Tenorio out of Texas. On June 30, 1835, Travis and thirty men captured Tenorio at Anahuac and forty-four Mexican soldiers without firing a shot and forcing the custom official to sign an agreement to leave Texas immediately.

ACTION AT ANAHUAC SPLITS THE COLONISTS

Travis was not hailed as a hero when he returned to San Felipe after capturing the garrison at Anahuac. In fact, the most immediate effect was to give the vocal Peace Party an issue which cast the War Party in an unfavorable light as war mongers. The Tories (as Travis called the Peace Party members) placed all the blame for the Anahuac affair on Travis and condemned him for his aggressive action. In fear of retaliation nearly every Texas municipality passed resolutions proclaiming their loyalty to the Mexican government. Finally Travis under great pressure and against his better judgment was forced to publish a statement in the newspaper, *Texas Republic*.

> San Felipe, July 18, 1835. W. Barret Travis requests a suspension of public opinion in regard to the capture of the Fort of Anahuac, until he can appear before the public with all of the facts and circumstances attending the capture of the fort.

But not everyone condemned him. "Three-Legged Willie" issued a stirring appeal in his newspaper, *Texas Gazette* which stated:

> All the (Mexican) states have succumbed to the military, and as Texas is the only spot unconquered, Santa Anna is marching his troops here to compel submission - - -. The people will have to determine whether they will yield to the power of the dictator. . . They must submit to the military government, or they must defend their province and their rights with the sword and the bayonet, and they must do this without delay, for the enemy is fast approaching our country.

Some of Travis' friends were derelict in publicly stating their loyalty. Others who had actually participated with him in the Anahuac affair now disavowed their action. Among those was Dr. J. B. Miller, who in a public statement not only denied his part in

WAR OR PEACE

the incident but said he preferred Tenorio. Miller even proposed Ugartechea arrest Samuel M. Williams, "Three-Legged Willie" Williamson, Francis W. Johnson, William Barret Travis, Lorenzo de Zavala, and John H Moore. To further humiliate Travis and his followers, Tenorio was permitted to remain in San Felipe for seven weeks after his promise to leave for Mexico. This was made possible mainly by Dr. Miller's cooperation with Colonel Ugartechea, who demanded the arms taken from Tenorio be returned.

Dr. Miller certainly overplayed his hand and overestimated his influence in suggesting that Travis and the others be arrested. Calmer heads took steps to form a central committee to handle the matter. The committee drafted a letter to General Cos, explaining the situation. The letter was carried directly to him by Edward Gritten and D. C. Barrett. On the way they met another courier sent by Ugartechea with a message addressed to the political chief of San Felipe. The dispatch was an order demanding the arrest of Travis, De Zavala, Johnson, Williamson, Moore, and Williams. Gritten and Barrett persuaded the courier to delay his message to San Felipe until they could deliver theirs to Ugartechea. They continued to San Antonio, but the Colonel stated he would receive no communication until the arrests were made. Further, he stated that if the colonists were really loyal, they would be glad to surrender the men responsible for attacking Anahuac. Gritten and Barrett returned to San Felipe and reported Ugartechea's message to the committee. The majority defied the order. The War Party sensed public opinion was now turning in their favor.

TRAVIS IS VINDICATED AND AUSTIN RETURNS TO TEXAS

On August 8 General Cos issued an arrest for the men. Peace Party representatives, knowing the temper of the citizens, tried to talk with him; but he would have no part of any negotiations until the offenders had been turned in. A feeling of uncertainty swept over Texas, but talk was mostly about war with Mexico. By the middle of August virtually every community had a committee of vigilance. Many of them, like Columbia, with William H. Wharton presiding and William T. Austin acting as secretary, passed a resolution that they would not arrest Travis or the others and, furthermore, passed another resolution requesting all jurisdictions of Texas cooperate in a "general call of consultation" to be held in Washington-on-the-Brazos on October 15, 1835. Velasco immediately named five delegates to the consultation--a speedy response prompted by reliable information from contacts in the interior of Mexico that clearly gave evidence the Mexican government planned to invade Texas with 10,000 soldiers before the end of the year. The informants further stated that "Santa Anna himself had been heard to declare that he would drive every Anglo American beyond the Sabine."

Everything that goes around, comes around; and in this case so would public opinion. Travis was at long last vindicated. He could again walk the streets with his head held high. His euphoria was expressed in a letter written August 24, 1835, to Henry Smith of Columbia (partly excerpted below):

> I am much gratified at the result of your meeting at Columbia. I hope all Texas will follow the example--I admire the spirit of the people of Velasco. Let the town be once garrisoned, and we are slaves.

In his hour of triumph Travis also wrote a friend and former companion in arms, John W. Moore, on August 31, 1835. (Parts of the letter are excerpted below):

> Huzza for Texas! Huzza for liberty and the rights of man!... It is different now, thank God! Principle has triumphed over prejudice, passion, cowardice, and slavery. Texas is herself again...
>
> Principle is gradually working out this glorious end and preparing the way for the march of freedom when the order came for my being arrested and given up to the military to be shot, for engaging in the expedition to Anahuac, etc.
>
> That was too much for the people to bear; it was to great a sacrifice for them to make, and they unanimously exclaimed against this order, and its supporters. The devil has shown his cloven foot, and his lies will be believed no longer...
>
> The word now, a convention of all Texas, to declare our sentiments, and to prepare for defense, if necessary...
>
> ...God grant that all Texas may stand as firm as Harrisburg in the 'hour that will try men's souls.'

...There is no doubt of one thing, they mean to flood the country with troops, and garrison the towns.

San Felipe, Nacogdoches, and all the ports are to be garrisoned in a month or two. They are determined to punish those engaged in the expedition of Anahuac in 1832 and in 1835 and that of Velasco in 1832. If we submit to these things, we are slaves and deserve not the name of freemen. - - -

We are to have a great meeting here on the 12th of September to vote for and against a convention. The citizens of the whole jurisdiction are invited to attend. I hope you will come and bring all the Harrisburg boys you can. Those who cannot come, please get them to sign a paper similar to the one signed at Columbia, expressing their wishes for a convention.

Tender my best respect to all the boys--tell them never fear, fortune favors the brave.

Your friend,
W. Barret Travis

A letter Travis wrote August 31, 1835, to another close friend, Andrew Briscoe, read:

We shall give them hell if they come here. Keep a bright lookout to sea. Allow no pilots in the bay to assist them, and they cannot land before you have time to prepare for them. Secure all the powder and lead.

Remember that war is not to be raised without means. Let us be men and Texas will triumph. I know you can be relied on; therefore, I exert you to be active in preparing the minds of men for the scenes that are to be enacted.

News from New Orleans that we will be liberally aided with men, money, and arms has arrived. Already we have five pieces of cannon, 100 kegs of powder, and lead and shot to correspond, landed in Matagorda and sent from New Orleans.

Another triumphal letter from Travis was written to his friends, Henry Smith and John A. Wharton about August 31, 1835:

Principle has at last triumphed over prejudice, cowardice, and selfishness. The Tories are routed, horse and foot. The unqualified submission men are ashamed to hold up their heads.

On August 24, 1835, Travis wrote to John W. Moore, "The whole upper country are unanimously for convention in which the voice of the people will be freely expressed."

While all of the meetings and activities concerning the general convention were occurring, James Bowie was treating with the Indians, trying to find out whether they would align themselves with Mexico or Texas.

On September 1, 1835, into this whirlpool of meetings, threats of rebellion, consultations, letter writing, and general confusion-- Stephen F. Austin suddenly appeared. He had been absent more than two years. News of his coming swept in front of him like the winds in front of a thunderstorm. Uncertainty would be replaced by leadership as he again took the helm of responsibility and steered a new course for Texas.

TRAVIS SURPRISED - ROSANNA COMES TO TEXAS

For Travis there was another unexpected and significant event in the fall of 1835. One day in the Hotel Peyton, he received a note that Rosanna and his children were waiting at a small inn at San Felipe and wanted to meet with him. To say the least, he was shocked. He had not seen his son, Charles Edward, in over four years and had never seen his daughter, Susan Isabelle.

In the subsequent meeting, Rosanna asked for a reconciliation or a divorce. Seeing that Travis had no affection for her whatsoever, she, therefore, asked him for a statement enabling her to obtain a divorce. He quickly complied. Rosanna agreed to leave Charles with his father. Then she left, taking Susan Isabelle. After returning home, Rosanna enlisted the aid of Judge James Dellett, Travis' old friend and mentor, to assist her in divorce proceedings. On January 9, 1836, the divorce was granted by the General Assembly of Alabama. On February 4 the same year, exactly one month and five days after the divorce, Rosanna married "a rich planter from Louisiana," Samuel G. Cloud--the wedding taking place at Monroeville, Alabama.

The reader should not surmise from the arrangement with Rosanna that Travis did not care for his daughter. In his last will and testament, Travis bequeathed both real and personal property equally to Charles Edward and Susan Isabelle; and he willed his share of his father's estate in Alabama to Susan Isabelle alone. He named guardians for each of the children and specified they receive a proper education.

AUSTIN - A CHANGED MAN

Austin's return to Texas was, indeed, timely. A "Welcome Home Banquet" in his honor was scheduled at Brazoria on September 8. Everyone looked forward with keen anticipation for they all new Austin's key-note speech would outline the course to be followed--if he favored the consultation, then the elections would beyond a doubt go forward--if he did not, the plan would surely fail. In almost an hour-long eloquent speech, he came out strongly for the consultation. Santa Anna, he said, had repeatedly assured him that he wanted to provide the Texans with a "special organization suited to their education, habits, and situation;" and only by such a meeting as a consultation, could it be made known to Santa Anna what sort of organization was needed. He told the gathering that he had warned Santa Anna that the "inevitable consequence of sending an armed force to this country would be war;" yet they still were coming and a Mexican warship had been operating on the coast. The people, Austin said, must decide what to do about these matters, and to do this, it would be necessary to have a convention. Austin thought that war was almost inevitable and, if it were to be avoided, the Texans must be united.

Soon after Austin's welcome home banquet at Brazoria, an important meeting was held September 12 in San Felipe. Austin received a briefing on the political and military situation in Texas and was made a member of the local Committee of Correspondence. The committee called for a Consultation representing all of the colonies of Texas. Two significant resolutions were passed: (1) support for the Mexican Constitution of 1824 and (2) a General Consultation to meet at San Felipe on October 15.

On September 21 Austin issued a general call for Texans to take up arms:

> War is our only recourse. There is no other
> remedy but to defend our right, ourselves, and our
> country by force of arms---.

Then he called for the creation of two forces, one immediately active and the other in reserve. The active force would mobilize by September 28.

Travis, back at Mill Creek and now seriously courting Rebecca Cummings, had heard about the general convention to be held and wrote to Stephen F. Austin on September 22:

> ...All eyes are turned toward you; and the
> independent manly stand you have taken has given
> the Sovereigns confidence in theirselves--Texas
> can be wielded by you, *you alone*, and her destiny is
> completely in your hands--I have every confidence
> that you will guide us safely through all our perils--
> This is not the base of flattery of a servile mind but
> is the reasoning of one ardent in his country's cause
> and who wishes to add his feeble efforts to those who
> have the power & inclination to lead us in safety to
> the desired end.

Travis left Mill Creek after Austin issued his call-to-arms; and on September 28, 1835, he joined the Federal Army of Texas with the rank of lieutenant in Captain Randall Jones' Company.

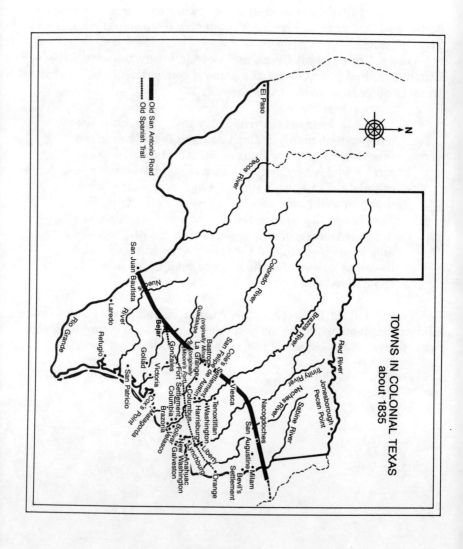

TOWNS IN COLONIAL TEXAS
About 1835

CHAPTER 7

WAR!

GONZALES - THE "LEXINGTON OF TEXAS"

A relatively minor event was about to unfold in Gonzales that would ignite the simmering fire of revolution. Word had reached Mexican Colonel Domingo de Ugartechea that the citizens of Gonzales were repairing a six-pound brass cannon that had been given to them years before as defense against the Indians. Ugartechea sent an order to Alcalde Andrew Ponton to return the cannon, but the citizens of Gonzales heard General Cos had landed four hundred men at Copano Bay south of Goliad and was marching toward San Antonio. They were preparing to do whatever they could to stop him.

Ugartechea sent a detachment of under two hundred men led by Lieutenant Francisco Castaneda to take the cannon by force. The eighteen citizens of Gonzales buried their cannon in a peach orchard and sent for reinforcements. Andrew Ponton stalled Castaneda with various excuses. In the meantime, John Moore and around one hundred sixty others arrived from their farms on the Colorado with Moore in command. By now someone had made a flag with the words, "Come and Take It," painted above a cannon barrel, and the banner was draped over the cannon which had been dug up and mounted on an ox cart. Moore decided to attack at daylight the next day. In the foggy dawn of October 2, 1835, his militia blundered into the Mexican pickets and withdrew. At daybreak there was a parley, but nothing was decided. Moore returned to his lines and opened fire. One Mexican was killed and the rest beat a hasty retreat to San Antonio. This victory at Gonzales launched the war for independence from Mexico and gained permanent recognition for the little town of Gonzales as "The Lexington of Texas." Meanwhile, General Cos slipped into Bexar without opposition.

News about the Battle of Gonzales spread like a grassfire. Some three hundred Texans that had earlier marched toward the coast to intercept General Cos now heard he was already in San Antonio. They decided to march toward Gonzales and en route discovered that Cos had left a small detachment of soldiers at Goliad. On October 9 a company of Texan volunteers, led by George M. Collinsworth, and assisted by Ben Milam, captured the Goliad presidio after a brief skirmish. Three Mexican soldiers were wounded and one killed. The Texans suffered only one man wounded, the first of the revolution, a free black by the name of Samuel McCullough. The capture of Goliad netted the Texans a large quantity of lead and powder and many other military supplies which Cos had left there. More importantly, the control of Goliad by Texans prevented Cos from receiving reinforcements by sea.

COS OCCUPIES BEXAR AND AUSTIN ELECTED TO LEAD TEXAS ARMY

General Cos arrived in San Antonio with only four hundred men. With Ugartechea's troops already there, the total Mexican force in Bexar was now approximately one thousand men. Cos immediately set about fortifying San Antonio, determined to defend himself against an attack.

Now there was a mad rush of volunteers toward Gonzales. Austin arrived on the afternoon of October 11, and when votes were cast for commander-in-chief, he was elected unanimously. By this time, Cos was firmly entrenched in San Antonio, establishing his headquarters at the Alamo. Austin did his best to shape raw recruits into the semblance of an army, but he was not a military man. However, his very presence did elevate morale.

Back in San Felipe an illness kept Travis from going to Gonzales. By the time he recovered, he was thinking more about the general Consultation which would shortly convene, and he knew how important these deliberations would be. But his thoughts were changed on October 11. A message from Austin arrived in San Felipe requesting all who could possibly fight to come to Gonzales immediately and that the Consultation be adjourned until the first of November. At Austin's direction, R. R. Royall, acting chairman of the Council, issued the following bulletin:

FELLOW CITIZENS:
Col. Austin has Just Written for more help, help, help. He took the line of march for San Antonio on the 13th and Wrot for help, help, help, he fears being forced into a fight before the Nacogdoches troops arrive Fellow Citizens you have false reports among you I pledge my Head for the truth of what I write when I say to you that your Countrymen are in danger and have written here for help and that in a

few days. Your Immediate assistance may save our troops and our country. I would Gladly be in the field but cannot be permitted to leave San Felipe. Turnout Turn Out, and that Hastily. Repair to the Camp.

SAM HOUSTON ARRIVES IN TEXAS

Travis and most of the others at the Consultation immediately left for Gonzales, bringing Austin's force up to four hundred fifty men. On October 19, 1835, Austin convened a council of war and decided to proceed to Salado Creek, five miles east of San Antonio to await more reinforcements.

On October 25 a discussion arose among the delegates of the Consultation who had joined Austin. Just when they were trying to decide whether they should return to the Convention or remain with the army, a new voice was heard for the first time. Sam Houston had just arrived in camp from Nacogdoches and immediately made his presence felt. He flatly stated that the army should either disband or suspend operations until an efficient force could be trained and a government organized. He further counseled that a commander in chief must be chosen; he added it was vital to treaty with the Indians (the largest force in Texas) before entering into an all-out war with Mexico. Finally, Houston recommended the army fall back to the east bank of the Guadalupe and go into winter quarters.

William H. Jack gave an angry rebuttal; he emphatically recommended they stay and fight. Austin, after listening patiently, ordered all Consultation delegates, with the exception of certain key officers, to return immediately to the convention at San Felipe. One delegate, William Barret Travis, chose not to return.

Austin now ordered his army to march on San Antonio. It must have been a scraggly lot to view, but their appearance did not dim their high spirits. One of the volunteers, Noah Smithwick, described the procession:

> Words are not adequate to convey an impression of the appearance of the first Texas army as it formed in marching order... it certainly bore little resemblance to the army of my childhood dreams. Buckskin breeches were the nearest approach to uniform, and there was wide diversity ever there, some being new and soft and yellow, while others,

from long familiarity with rain and grease and dirt, had become hard and black and shiny....Boots being an unknown quantity, some wore shoes and some moccasins. Here a broad-brimmed sombrero overshadowed the military cap at its side; there a tall "beegum" rode familiarly beside a coonskin cap, with the tail hanging down behind, as all well-regulated tails should do. Here a big American horse loomed above the nimble Spanish pony...there a half-broke mustang pranced beside a sober, methodical mule...In lieu of a canteen each man carried a Spanish gourd....A fantastic military array to a casual observer, but the one great purpose animating every heart clothed us in a uniform more perfect in our eyes than was ever donned by regulars on dress parade.

So, with the Old Cannon flag flying at the head, and the "artillery" following at the heels of two yokes of long-horned Texas steers occupying the post of honor in the center, we filed out of Gonzales and took up the line of March for San Antonio.

This army may not have been a precision unit but it was grimly efficient. Many were grandsons of the American Revolution. Each carried a long rifle that was deadly at two hundred yards. Ugartechea had faced similar weapons at Velasco and surely had told General Cos their "escopetas" (muskets) were no match for these frontier marksmen with their rifles.

THE BATTLE OF CONCEPCION AND THE SIEGE OF BEXAR

Austin and his rag-tag Volunteer Army of Texas reached the missions just south of the city, and a camp was set up near Mission San Francisco de la Espada. James Bowie and James W. Fannin, with about ninety men were dispatched to reconnoiter the Mexican position and find a campsite closer to the city.

On October 28 Bowie and Fannin were attacked by a force of about four hundred cavalry troop near Mission Concepcion. In the ensuing battle, some sixty Mexicans were killed or wounded and the others withdrew to the safety of San Antonio. Left behind were field artillery pieces and several wagons.

After this battle, Austin and his army set up headquarters at the Old Mill just north of the Main Plaza of San Antonio. He then laid siege to the city, hoping to force Cos to surrender by cutting off his food supplies.

Austin was impressed with the activity of the Mexican cavalry and realized how valuable a cavalry unit could be. On October 27 he ordered Travis to "raise a volunteer company of cavalry of not less than fifty or more than eighty--each man to be armed with a double-barreled gun or a Yager and a brace of pistols." Thus, Travis became s captain in the cavalry of the Texas army.

THE "GRASS FIGHT"

Austin's army remained camped at the Old Mill; and November passed without any real fighting, although on the 10th of November, Captain Travis captured three hundred Mexican horses. On November 26, about three in the afternoon, Erastus ("Deaf") Smith (the most famous scout of the revolution) galloped into camp and reported the approach of a Mexican pack train guarded by a few soldiers. It was decided that the pack animals were carrying silver to pay the Mexican troops. An attack force was organized and the Texans led by Jim Bowie rode out to capture the silver. This activity in the Texan camp was observed by General Cos, and he immediately sent reinforcements with a piece of field artillery. In the following skirmish, the Texans suffered no losses but about fifty of the Mexicans were killed. The remainder retreated to San Antonio.

The Texans seized the pack mules and eagerly broke open the bags. But alas, they found no silver, only grass for the starving horses of Cos' cavalry in San Antonio. Apparently, the siege was having its effect. This little skirmish has forever been dubbed "The Grass Fight."

THE "BATTLE" AT SAN FELIPE

Meanwhile back at San Felipe, a truncated Consultation met on October 11 and organized a temporary government called the Permanent Council, which undertook the handling of affairs, outside the military, until the required number of delegates arrived for the full Consultation. With the help of a Texas merchant, Thomas F. McKinney, the Council was able to borrow $100,000 from New Orleans which was quickly used to buy supplies for the army.

After three weeks, the Council turned the government over to the Consultation when enough members had gathered by November 3 to

WAR!

After three weeks, the Council turned the government over to the Consultation when enough members had gathered by November 3 to form a quorum. The Consultation elected as president, Branch T. Archer. Two and a half days were spent debating the causes that had forced Texas to take up arms and the objectives for which they were fighting. The following day a declaration in support of the Constitution of 1824 was adopted; then the delegates turned their attention to the establishment of a Provisional Government.

Henry Smith (a strong proponent of independence) was elected governor and James W. Robinson, lieutenant governor. Before they adjourned on November 14, the Consultation passed a flurry of resolutions. They ordered all army operations halted, appointed Sam Houston commander of all troops except those at San Antonio, authorized the Provisional Government to borrow money, commissioned Stephen F. Austin, Branch T. Archer, and William H. Wharton as Commissioners to the United States to appeal for aid, and immediately sent a dispatch to Bexar to notify Austin of his appointment.

On November 25 Austin turned command of the army over to Colonel Edward Burleson, an experienced Indian fighter, and left for San Felipe.

"WHO WILL GO WITH OLD BEN MILAM" - THE BATTLE OF BEXAR

"The Grass Fight" proved Cos was in dire need of fodder for his livestock and should have shown Burleson and his staff the effectiveness of the siege; but for some strange reason, Colonel Burleson chose to ignore these signs and decided to lift the siege. This was partly due to the fact that many of the soldiers were getting restless and tired. They were mostly farmers and needed to return home and prepare their land for spring planting. On December 3, 1835, the baggage wagons were packed, and Burleson was about to retire the army to Gonzales when three Texans made their way into camp. One was Samuel A. Maverick. They had been prisoners in San Antonio but managed to escape and brought a first-hand report on the shortage of hay and supplies in the city and the low state of the soldiers' morale. Still Burleson hesitated. Milam charged from his tent shouting, "Who will go with old Ben Milam into San Antonio?" Instantly there were cheers of approval. After the group had formed some semblance of order, he counted three hundred one, including a number of Tejanos under Juan Seguin. Milam had captured the heart and spirit of the army, and he was to play a hero's part in the drama of Texas history.

Meanwhile in San Antonio, Cos planned for his defense by dividing his command into two divisions: one would hold the Alamo on the east side of the San Antonio River, and the other division was strongly entrenched in the stone buildings on the west side of the river along the two main plazas. Both divisions were supported by artillery.

At 3:00 a.m. on the morning of December 5, the assault began with Milam, Francis W. Johnson, and Edward Burleson each in charge of a column. They immediately broke through the Mexican picket line and charged into San Antonio. Here the Mexican defense stiffened, and the fighting became house to house. This type of fighting was an advantage for the Texans, as their long rifles could pick off the Mexicans if they showed themselves at two hundred yards. Slowly, street by street, the Mexicans steadily fell back. The deadly shooting of the Texans took a terrific toll. Word reached Cos and he began to realize his situation was desperate. The Mexican troops fought valiantly and after three days still held tenaciously to much of the city. As a diversionary movement, Colonel James C. Neill with a company, attacked from a different direction.

On the third day the bad luck that seemed to follow Ben Milam through life struck again. He was shot through the head while leading a bloody advance. Milam was buried in the courtyard of the Don Juan Veramendi house, almost on the same spot where he met death. Ben Milam became the first in a long pantheon of Texas heroes.

Now Johnson was chosen commander. He appointed Major Robert C. Morris of the New Orleans Greys as second in command. The assault continued. The sharp crack of the Texan rifles and the duller boom of the escopetas was continuous. The Mexican cannons thundered again and again; but still the Texans came, using logs as battering rams to knock down doors and barricades. On December 9 the Texan forces finally reached the San Antonio River, and the remnants of the Mexican forces fell back to the Alamo. On December 10, 1835, General Cos raised the white flag of surrender.

Colonel Burleson, the senior officer, now took command. Cos signed a covenant in which he pledged he would never again take up arms against the colonists and would support the Constitution of 1824. Burleson permitted them to retain sufficient muskets and

General Cos, leading his army of some 1,000 men, marched south in defeat and disgrace and crossed the Rio Grande on Christmas Day 1835. In less than two months, Cos would break his pledge never to bear arms against Texas and would once more cross the Rio Grande, headed for San Antonio.

"BATTLE OF SAN FELIPE" CONTINUES

Back in San Felipe the victory was received with euphoria. Some even labeled it a triumph for Texas and the end of the war, but elation soon gave way to confusion and dissension. On December 10, the same day that Cos capitulated, the Council passed a resolution calling for a new convention to meet at Washington-on-the-Brazos in March to draft a constitution for a new government; but Governor Smith felt that this Council should stay in session and draw up the constitution now. He vetoed the resolution, but it was passed over his veto on December 13. Tempers flared anew on both sides.

"THE MATAMOROS INVASION"

In San Antonio Dr. James Grant, who had fought in the Battle of Bexar, proposed the army march south and seize Matamoros. He felt they could carry the war to Mexico and bring it to a quick end. (It must be stated that Grant had a personal interest behind this scheme. When Santa Anna nullified the Constitution of 1824, Dr. Grant, who lived in Mexico, lost vast silver holdings in northern Coahuila. In fact, Dr. Grant had never been a resident of Texas and did not own one inch of Texas soil.) His plan to carry the war below the Rio Grande was prompted by a selfish desire to regain his silver mines and land. By promising the Texans plunder and riches they would gain in capturing Matamoros, he won their support.

Dr. Grant took his invasion idea direct to the government at San Felipe. The Consultation delegates were already divided over the war effort, and his radical idea served to split it further. Houston, backed by Smith, warned against marching the whole army southward and pointed out the logistic problems of supplying an invasion of Mexico. However, a majority of the Consultation favored the idea for reasons ranging from false confidence over the recent Bexar victory to wanting to see Anglo-Saxon liberties spread into Mexico. Probably the most honest reason was their desire to put down Governor Smith and his "high and mighty" General

Houston. (Here-in-after Council and Consultation are used interchangeably.)

On January 3, 1836, the Council authorized Dr. James Grant and Colonel Francis W. Johnson, (still in Bexar), to make an invasion of Mexico at Matamoros. When Colonel Johnson received word of this, he declined the command after being advised the invasion was opposed by Governor Smith and General Houston. The Council then appointed James W. Fannin to replace Johnson. Dr. Grant protested, declaring that Colonel Burleson intended for him to command inasmuch as the invasion was his idea. So the Council appointed Dr. Grant as commander of volunteers and Fannin, commander of the regulars. This meant a split command with no one really in charge. Just a few days later, Colonel Johnson changed his mind and accepted the position of commander they had offered him earlier. Unbelievingly, the Council committed the ultimate military folly and also made Colonel Johnson commander but allowing the other appointments to stand. The Matamoros invasion would have three co-commanders but no executive commander. General Houston, was not even advised of the appointments. When the news reached Governor Smith, he immediately vetoed the Council's actions, and they quickly overruled his veto. To say the least, he was unhappy.

Governor Smith received a message from Lieutenant Colonel James C. Neill, now in command of the Alamo. He advised Smith that Dr. Grant and Johnson had stripped the Alamo of most of its blankets, warm clothing, medical supplies, guns, ammunition, and some of the smaller cannon for their planned expedition. With this news the governor verbally exploded, publicly denouncing these acts as treasonous, slandering the Council in explicit and personal terms. He culminated his attack by demanding an apology from the Council for its outrageous support of the hair-brained idea of an invasion of Mexico and told them plainly they would either agree to cooperate or he would dissolve them.

The Council was equally adamant and in turn vilified the governor. Immediately there was a vote of impeachment. They replaced Henry Smith with Lieutenant Governor James W. Robinson. But there was just one small problem; Smith refused to vacate his office. Seizing the official seal and the state archives, he declared he would shoot "any S. O. B." who tried to take them from him. He continued to act as governor, making Robinson's efforts to operate totally futile. The biggest war in Texas at the moment

WAR!

was in San Felipe. On January 17 the Council was unable to raise a quorum. In effect, government in Texas was non-existent.

This comedy in San Felipe was watched with amusement by most of the colonists who were now getting their fields ready for spring planting. The thought of war was not on their minds. To the casual observer of the day, it may have been amusing; but in retrospect the results of this ignominious comedy of errors proved to be tragic and doomed hundreds of men to die needlessly.

Governor Smith still held the loyalty of General Sam Houston, Lieutenant Colonel James Neill at the Alamo, and his recruiting officer at San Felipe, Lieutenant Colonel William Barret Travis; but the majority of the army, both regulars and volunteers, were consumed with the idea of not only ending the war quickly but gaining personal riches by seizing the silver mines in northern Mexico and looting Matamoros. Undoubtedly the images of beautiful senoritas also entered their minds.

A FRUSTRATED HOUSTON GOES ON FURLOUGH AND SENDS BOWIE TO BEXAR

Smith now ordered Houston to proceed to Goliad to talk some sense into the army that seemed to be acting on its own. Houston caught the forces of Grant and Johnson, now numbering about five hundred volunteers, at Refugio. Fannin had recruited volunteers from Velasco and went to Copano Bay near Goliad with some four hundred fifty men including the "Georgia Battalion." This meant a total force of 1,000 misguided stalwarts under Fannin, Johnson, and Grant, with each commander conducting separate and unrelated operations except for the objective of invading Mexico. Houston was told by each "commander" that he had no authority over them, as their orders came directly from the Council. Thus, the Council had utterly destroyed Houston's command over the only army in Texas. Houston did what he could and advised the rank and file of the folly of the expedition and asked them to give it up. He probably convinced some three hundred who returned to their farms and homes.

Now Houston received a dispatch from Colonel Neill at the Alamo asking for reinforcements. Houston had originally planned to garrison both Goliad and the Alamo, but since Grant and Johnson had removed most of the army from Bexar to the Goliad area, he now had serious doubts about defending Bexar. He asked Colonel James Bowie, with about thirty men including James Butler Bonham, who had recently arrived in Texas, to inspect the situation at the Alamo and make his own decision whether it should be held or abandoned. (Evidence indicates Houston had anticipated a decision by Bowie to demolish the Alamo and withdraw from Bexar.)

Houston, disgusted and in despair, wrote a letter to Governor Smith on January 30, washing his hands of the Matamoros affair, implying it was more of an act of piracy than a military operation and impugned the leaders' motives. He further stated it was beyond any logical military mind to comprehend the developments now seizing Texas. He concluded by saying he was furloughing himself until March 1 and would go north to treaty with the Indians. This was something Houston was qualified to do. Houston, at age 13, had been adopted as a "blood" son of Chief Oo-loo-te-ka of the Cherokee nation.

SYNOPSIS OF THE 1835 CONSULTATION AND THE 1836 CONVENTION

The Consultation of 1835 met a few times at San Felipe in October. With only a few delegates present on October 11 they formed a temporary government called the Permanent Council to handle military affairs until a quorum from all municipalities arrived for the Consultation. The Permanent Council only lasted until November 3, 1835 when most of the other delegates arrived.

Now with a quorum the Consultation quickly organized and elected Branch T. Archer, President, and soon adopted a resolution to support the Mexican Constitution of 1924. Then they proceeded to elect Henry Smith Governor, and James W. Robinson Lieutenant Governor, and appointed Sam Houston Commander of all troops except those at San Antonio and commissioned Austin, Archer, and William H. Wharton to go to Washington D.C. and appeal for aid. (Consultation and Council are used interchangeably.)

Smith and the Council were at odds from day one. Smith dissolved the Council and they impeached him and appointed Robinson as Governor. Smith refused to give up the State Seal and Archives and declared "I'll shoot any S. O. B. who tries to take them." The main disagreement was over a ridiculous plan, the brain child of Dr. James Grant and endorsed by Colonel Francis Johnson to invade Mexico at Matamoros. Houston labeled it a hairbrained idea from the beginning even though his friend, Governor Smith, originally endorsed it but quickly changed his mind. By January 31, 1836, a quorum was no longer present. Before they disbanded they agreed to a Convention (Consultation)

WAR!

on March 1, 1836. In the interim Texas did not have an effective government.

The next Convention (Consultation) assembled at Washington-On-The-Brazos on March 1, 1836 and elected Richard Ellis of Jonesborough President and unanimously passed a resolution that Texas declare its independence. The resolution was supported by Lorenzo de Zavala and two other Mexican delegates. George Childress headed the committee to draft the declaration of independence and on the following day, March 2, it was unanimously adopted. But it was the forceful Sam Houston, delegate from Refugio, that kept them from adjourning and rushing to the Alamo. Most historians would agree he was the most influential man in Texas. On March 4, Sam Houston, was reaffirmed as Commander in Chief of all Texas forces and he left immediately to take over a nonexistant army. The convention also elected David G. Burnett, President of the new Republic; Lorenzo de Zavala, Vice President; Samuel P. Carson, Secretary of State; Thomas Jefferson Rusk, Secretary of War; Bailey Hardeman, Secretary of Treasury; Robert Potter, Secretary of Navy; and David Thomas, Attorney General.

note: Both the Texas Declaration of Independence and the Texas Constitution are patterned after and closely reflect the work of Thomas Jefferson and others who drafted similar documents for the colonies some sixty years earlier.

SAM HOUSTON
© Lajos Markos, 1984

117

WAR!

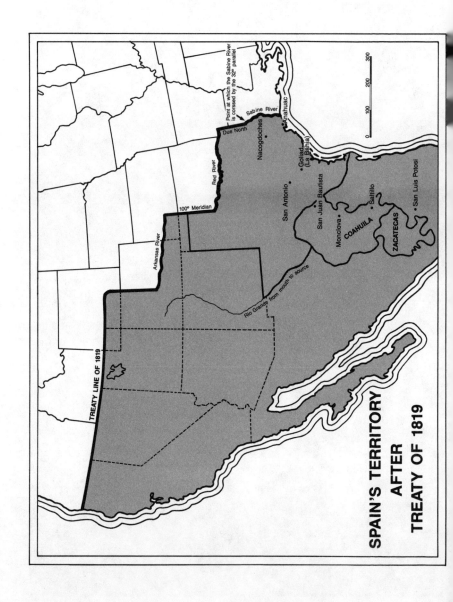

SPANISH TERRITORY AFTER 1819

CHAPTER 8

THE ALAMO

BOWIE ARRIVES

Jim Bowie and his thirty volunteers, with James Butler Bonham and Louis "Moses" Rose reached San Antonio on January 19, 1836. In his saddle bags, Bowie carried Houston's quasi-order to demolish the Alamo. He was warmly greeted by Colonel James Neill, but Neill quickly painted a dismal picture--only eighty-four healthy men, no winter clothing or blankets, no money, no medical supplies, and very little powder and lead. They had twenty-four cannon but little ammunition. Grant and Johnson had stripped the Alamo.

In spite of the gloomy report, Bowie began to look the situation over with the view in mind that it might be defended. His thirty volunteers brought the garrison up to one hundred ten men, including about nineteen New Orleans Greys. But probably the most distressing problem was the lack of sufficient cannon balls for the priceless 18-pounder (which had been dragged all the way from San Felipe by Damacio Jimenes using a double team of oxen.) Bowie had good reasons to do what Houston thought he would--blow up the Alamo. On the other hand, if he destroyed the Alamo, he would be faced with the problem of what to do with all the cannon. He had no wagons, oxen, or horses to transport them; and they were far too valuable to the revolution to destroy.

He also had personal reasons for not wanting the Alamo razed. From the walls he could view thousands of acres owned by the Veramendi family. (Jim still cursed the trip he took, causing Ursula to go to Monclova, and death. He reasoned if he had been home, she would not have gone.) He drank to dim the memory of Ursula's tragic death and perhaps the memory of Bexar, for it was here he found the only happiness he had ever known. The Alamo was a reminder of those happy days; maybe the old mission cast a spell on him. But his drinking aggravated and accelerated a lung disease he wouldn't admit he had--tuberculosis.

Another factor in Bowie's ultimate decision to defend the Alamo was his independence. Jim Bowie was never one to obey orders unquestioningly from anyone, not even General Houston. His independent nature, together with sentimental values, was enough reason for Jim Bowie to decide that he was not about to hand the old fort over without a fight. Sentiment aside, Jim Bowie was enough of a soldier to appreciate the strategic location of San Antonio and the Alamo. He genuinely believed it was worth defending and expressed this opinion to Colonel Neill, who readily agreed. Neill had already written Houston on January 14, 1836, of his resolve to stay and fight. Bowie and Neill put the idea to the men and they also voted to stay and fight. That settled it. They would defend the old fort.

The decision having been made, there was much work to do-- and quickly. Bowie's Mexican friends in San Antonio had informed him they had heard Santa Anna was marching with many men and cavalry and intended to retake San Antonio at all costs.

The reports about Santa Anna depressed Colonel Neill but stimulated Bowie. He even drank less as he went to work full-time on the fortifications. Again, his Mexican friends in San Antonio rallied to his support. Provisions poured in--forty-two head of cattle, one hundred bushels of corn, gun powder and shot--and more importantly--cannon balls for the 18-pounder.

With skillful hands and the eye of Green B. Jameson, the garrison engineer, the Alamo began to change into a real fort. Jameson closed the breach on the southwest side, running from the front of the mission almost to the main gate. He did this with a palisade of sharpened stakes and posts, reinforced with a mound of dirt on the backside that would permit men to take positions to fire. He used more dirt and timber to construct the parapets and gun mounts all along the walls. Inside the Alamo, he built a dirt ramp and parapet on the east wall and mounted three cannon at the top. For the big 18-pounder, he built a special parapet in the southwest corner where it had a commanding view overlooking the entire town. Almeron Dickinson, the creative blacksmith from Gonzales, also had a real knack for handling artillery. Hiram Williamson from Philadelphia was better than average as drill master, and John Baugh of Virginia acted as adjutant and kept records. In the midst of all this activity, Bowie was almost his old self. By the end of January, with the concerted effort of everyone, the Alamo began to look like a fort even though it was never intended to be one.

Even with all of the absorbing work, the men were still interested in the politics of San Felipe. They kept abreast of the tug-of-war between the Council and Governor Henry Smith as best they could; and though they were suffering due to the conflict, the men were solidly behind Smith. On January 25 they held a mass meeting in support of the governor with Jim Bonham acting as chairman. And it was Bonham's carefree and cocky attitude that had done much to elevate their morale through all the hard work. All the meeting amounted to was a patriotic rally, ending in a unanimous resolution to hold the Alamo at all costs. Bonham and Bowie were the first to sign, followed by all the others. Then the group voted to ask the government for five hundred dollars (they might as well have asked for five thousand dollars, because none would be forthcoming).

At least the rally served to renew the spirits of the men, and they returned to work with vigor. Any traces of insubordination and quarreling vanished, and they were rededicated to the task. Bowie knew the money requested would not be sent soon, if at all. So he contacted a Mexican friend and negotiated a loan of five hundred dollars. This was an almost impossible achievement given the circumstances. but the loyal Mexicans of Bexar did more. With their help, he managed to get horses and sent out scouting parties as far as the Frio River. However, the physical strain of all the work began to take its toll. Bowie's illness reappeared with vengeance. Fierce coughing racked his once-strong body. Bowie had no patience with weakness--above all his own. He sought relief, albeit temporary, in whiskey. As Bowie began , Jim Bonham tried to do his work and Bowie's. Little is generally known about Jim Bonham. He is one of the unsung heros of the Alamo, holding the singular distinction of being the only courier to leaveand return twice to the Alamo. Albert Martin was the only other messenger that returned. Other known couriers are as follows: Dr. John Sutherland, John W. Smith, James Highsmith, Johnson (first name unknown), Juan Seguin, Antonio Cruz y Arocha, James Allen, James Walker Baylor, Alejandro de la Garza, Andrew Jackson Sowell, Byrd Lockhart, William Oury, and Lancelot Smithers. Another possible courier was William B. Patton.

JAMES BUTLER BONHAM
(Artist's Conception)

JAMES BONHAM   122

CHAPTER 9

JAMES BONHAM

(Author's Note: Some of the following story cannot be verified)

James (Jim) Butler Bonham was born February 20, 1807, at Redbank, Edgeville County, South Carolina. He came from a large family of eight children, five sons and three daughters. James was the fourth son born to Sophia and James Bonham. It was his father's second marriage, as his first wife, Hannah, had died at a relatively young age. One might say James was born into a clan, for the Bonhams and their kin, the Butlers and Brooks of South Carolina, were a tightly-knit family. They were all champions of states' rights and each had a strong sense of "noblesse oblige." Various men of the clan, younger and older than James, distinguished themselves in battle and politics.

When Jim was eight years old, his father died, leaving his mother a comfortable estate. She had already inherited a sizable estate from her father, and one could say Jim Bonham enjoyed many amenities that were denied his younger friend, William Barret (Buck) Travis, who was two years his junior. Jim's mother combined her inheritances into one large plantation. To say the least, Jim Bonham did not lack for comfort while Mark Travis (Buck's father) worked hard to eke out a living for his family.

When Jim was now in his teens, his mother sent him to an academy with a touch reputation for academic skills and discipline. But whatever rule Jim thought he could bend, he did. He finished the academy and entered South Carolina College in 1824.

While in college, Jim met a living hero whom he learned to admire, Marquis de Lafayette, the French soldier and statesman who had fought with the colonists during their struggle for independence. Lafayette was also a prominent leader in Revolutionary times in France. His heroic actions won the respect of patriots on both sides of the Atlantic. Lafayette visited South Carolina College in 1826. After listening to him speak, Jim decided Lafayette was a man he would like to mold his life after, the kind of man willing to risk everything he had and fight for what he believed in.

All students at the college had to belong to one of the two debating clubs, the Clariosophic and Euphradian. These two clubs served as a platform to debate topics of political, social, paternal, and intellectual ideas. The experience he gained in open debate among fellow intellectuals not only presented him a challenge he loved but developed in him an eloquence of speech. He would use this eloquence later as a lawyer, expressing himself dramatically and convincingly.

The debating club also allowed him to form bonds with many who felt the same way he did about rigid rules imposed by the school authorities which he felt were unfair. He organized a group called "The Black Shirts," and invited all who were dissatisfied with one thing or another to join. They demanded more students' rights and asked to have a part in deciding college rules and practices. They demanded better food at the dining hall and more lenient hours for bed check in the dormitories. They wanted their voices heard by the college's board of overseers.

The school administration looked with great disdain on "The Black Shirts" and demanded they leave school. All were summarily expelled; three freshmen, six sophomores, fourteen juniors, and twenty-three seniors. Among the seniors was Jim Bonham. However, it should be noted he was in a rather distinguished group. Jim's roommate was James P. Carroll, later to become a distinguished jurist and a writer of law. Another was William H. Gist, who was to become governor of South Carolina and a distinguished jurist himself. Another was Francis W. Pickens, who would follow Gist as governor.

By age twenty-three Jim was an extraordinarily handsome man and brave to the point of rashness. His six-foot, two-inch frame was powerful and straight as that of an Indian. His quick smile, black hair and eyes were the finishing touches to a ruggedly handsome face that won the hearts of most young women he met.

After being expelled from South Carolina College (now the University of South Carolina), he studied law and was admitted to the Bar in 1830 and decided to settle in Pendleton. He quickly became one of the most sought-after bachelors in the community. He was still interested in political change, and he settled in Pendleton mainly because John C. Calhoun, then Vice-President of the United States, also had a law office there and a family residence just a few miles away. Calhoun was a champion of states' rights and so was young Bonham. Most of the states were upset over the new federal tariff laws. South Carolina was particularly angered when President Andrew Jackson stationed troops at the Port of Charleston to enforce these laws. The governor indicated he would meet force with force. Jim Bonham volunteered his services and was appointed a captain in an artillery battery. Soon they were ordered to Charleston to oppose the federal troops and to assert states' rights. Jim looked forward to a conflict. He cut a dashing figure in his uniform with a bright red sash and silver epaulets. However, he was denied the taste of battle as a compromised tariff bill was passed in 1833 that satisfied the states. Disappointed, Jim Bonham returned to Pendleton.

The next two years he continued to practice law, but his impetuousness continued to get him into trouble. One day an opposing attorney made disparaging remarks about a woman whom young Bonham was defending. Bonham insisted the opposing attorney apologize. He refused and Bonham dragged him from the courtroom and gave him a good old-fashioned thrashing. Upon reentering the courtroom, the judge was adamant and immediately asked that Bonham come before the bench. "You, sir, will make a public apology for your actions immediately," ordered the judge to the haughty Bonham.

"I will not apologize, your Honor; and furthermore, I'm going to tweak your nose!" So saying, he proceeded to lean across the bench and caught the surprised judge by the nose and gave it a good pinching.

The startled judge stammered and sputtered, his nose as red as a cherry and his eyes watering. Bonham stepped back to survey the results, dusted his lapels, and straightened his coat and tie. He had a rebellious gleam of satisfaction in his eye.

When the judge finally regained his wits and realized what had happened, he stammered, "You . . . young whipper-snapper! I sentence you to ninety days in jail for contempt of court." The judge had to shout over the laughter of people in the courtroom who thought the incident rather amusing. Because Bonham had defended the honor of his female client, his stay in jail was certainly made easier by the many women who came to his aid. They showered him with all kinds of foods, decorated his cell daily with flower arrangements, and furnished clean linens for his bed each day. Additionally, his clothing and shirts were taken away and not only washed but perfumed before being returned.

It can truthfully be said all the girls loved Jim Bonham except the one whom he loved, a beautiful belle of the town by the name of Caroline Taliaferro. Bonham's heart would race each time he saw her; and when she danced the Virginia Reel, mostly with someone else, he couldn't take his eyes from her. He would wait in eager anticipation all evening for one short waltz so he could touch her tiny waist and hold her elegantly-gloved hand. She looked even more beautiful as the candlelight of the ballroom danced on her blonde curls and rosy cheeks as they moved to the rhythm of the music.

Bonham was crushed when he read in the paper one day that she was engaged to marry a Dr. Miller. He decided immediately to leave Pendleton, but in defiance he did attend Caroline's wedding, escorting a very beautiful girl. He even went to the reception and took the lovely bride's hand to wish her well; but as he gazed into her eyes and realized he still loved her very much, he knew that he had made the right decision to leave. He could not stand to stay in Pendleton and see her occasionally, knowing she was married to another.

In 1834 Jim Bonham moved his law practice to Montgomery, Alabama. But his unsatisfied quest for adventure and a cause to fight for, seethed within his mind. He expressed his disappointment with Montgomery in a letter dated October 1834 to his mother wherein he stated he "was as sickly as the country around." Bonham was ready for a change when (in a story later told to members of Bonham's family) a letter reached him from his boyhood friend, Buck Travis.

Travis must have described the opportunities in Texas and ended by saying, "Stirring times are afoot here, Jim; do come to Texas and take a hand in these exciting affairs."

Jim Bonham must have read and reread the letter; each time with growing excitement. He knew he had to go. He immediately closed his office in Montgomery and returned home to say a last farewell to his beloved family.

Sometime in early October 1835, he set out for Texas, stopping at Mobile, Alabama, en route. On October 17 in Mobile, he participated in several Texas rallies, speaking to the crowds that jammed the Shakespeare Theater. Jim Bonham must have been at his zenith in eloquence as he appealed to their sense of liberty and freedom to join him and others in Texas. Assisted by E. C. Horton and S. P. St. John, Bonham recruited within two weeks enough men to form the "Mobile Greys." Undoubtedly, he looked forward to this new adventure with great anticipation.

The date of his exact arrival in Texas is not known, but in a letter to Governor Henry Smith dated November 30, 1835, James Walker Fannin wrote:

> Allow me to also to name to you in an especial manner, my friend, Major J. B. Bonham, just arrived from the U. states (sic) & who enters warmly into the good cause - The Artillery is also his favorite corps.

Bonham wrote a letter of introduction to Sam Houston dated December 1, 1835, from San Felipe in which he stated:

> Permit me through you to volunteer my services in the present struggle of Texas as without conditions I shall receive nothing, either in the form of service pay or lands, or rations.

It is interesting that if, indeed, Bonham and Travis were boyhood friends, there is not some record of contact when he first reached Texas. But it is possible that Travis was still with Austin's army at Bexar on December 1, for there is an entry wherein he reported eight men of his company present and two absent without leave on November 26, 1835. Even if he left for San Felipe on that date, the trip could take four or five days, depending upon weather and other factors. It is worthy to note that on his trip from San Felipe to the Alamo in January, Travis took eleven days. It is also interesting to note that when the Consultation promoted Travis to major in the regular army on December 1, 1835, he did not learn of the appointment until December 17 when he was visiting Rebecca Cummings at Mill Creek. It is just possible that the two friends' paths did not cross in San Felipe due to Travis' absence.

Houston was impressed enough to make special mention of Bonham in a letter to Acting Governor, J. W. Robinson, on January 11, 1836. It reads as follows:

> Colonel Bonham ought to be made a major by all means. His influence in the army is great and more so than some who would be generals.

A study of the men in the Bonham family shows a strong sense of "noblesse oblige" for liberty, freedom, states' rights, and family honor. An example of just how seriously the Bonham-Butler-Brooks clan took their sense of duty is exemplified by their service in the war between the United States and Mexico in 1846. Knowing they had lost their kin, James Bonham, at the Alamo, two members now joined the new fight. Preston Brooks served as a company commander in the famous Palmetto Regiment of South Carolina Volunteers. Another member of the clan, Pierce Butler, was the commander of that regiment and was killed leading it in the bloody battle of Churubusco.

Interestingly, the younger brother of James Bonham, Milledge Luke Bonham, also followed the family tradition. Unlike James, he graduated from South Carolina College (as did most of the men in the family) and like his older brother, became a lawyer. He also joined the military service, but instead of going to Texas served in the Seminole Uprising of 1836. But ten years later in 1846, Milledge also served in the war with Mexico. He commanded the 12th United States Infantry during Scott's Mexico City Campaign. (Later he would serve as a brigadier general in the Confederate Army.)

In view of the above, it is not hard to understand why James Butler Bonham chose to step across the line and die in the Alamo.

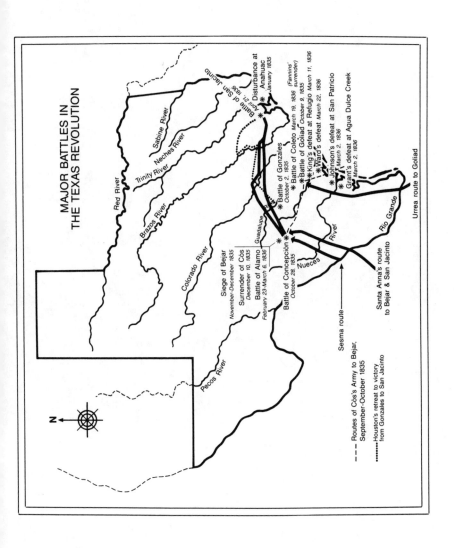

MAJOR BATTLES IN THE TEXAS REVOLUTION

MAJOR BATTLES IN
THE TEXAS REVOLUTION

Red River

Sabine River

Neches River

Trinity River

Brazos River

Colorado River

Pecos River

Guadalupe

Nueces

River

Rio Grande

Disturbance at
Anahuac
January 1835

Battle of San Jacinto
April 21, 1836

Battle of Coleto *March 19, 1836*
(Fannin's
surrender)

Battle of Gonzales
October 2, 1835

Battle of Goliad *October 9, 1835*

King's defeat at Refugio *March 11, 1836*

Ward's defeat *March 22, 1836*

Johnson's defeat at San Patricio
March 2, 1836

Grant's defeat at Agua Dulce Creek
March 2, 1836

Siege of Bejar
November–December 1835

Surrender of Cos
December 10, 1835

Battle of Alamo
February 23–March 6, 1836

Battle of Concepción
October 28, 1835

Urrea route to Goliad

Sesma route

Santa Anna's route
to Bejar & San Jacinto

N

– – – Routes of Cos's Army to Bejar,
September–October 1835

.... Houston's retreat to victory
from Gonzales to San Jacinto

129   *JAMES BONHAM*

CHAPTER 10

DIRE DECISIONS

"---DIE IN THESE DITCHES"

As early as February 2, 1836, Bowie heard from his scouts that General Sesma with two thousand troops was, indeed, in Laredo but had not yet crossed the Rio Grande. He also knew that General Cos with one thousand men was lingering at Presidio de Rio Grande. Rumors were rife that Santa Anna was forming an army. But would Santa Anna invade before spring? It wouldn't be sensible to do so. He thought he had time to reinforce the Alamo and a personal letter to Governor Smith would bring results. On February 2, he hastily scribbled on brown paper the following:

> The Alamo
> February 2, 1836
>
> Dear Sir:
>   In pursuance of your orders, I proceeded from San Felipe to La Bahia and whilst there employed my whole time in trying to effect the objects of my mission. You are aware that Gen. Houston came to La Bahia soon after I did; that is the reason why I did not make a report to you from that post. The Comdr. in Chf, has before this communicated to you all matters in relation to our military affairs at La Bahia; this makes it wholly unnecessary for me to say any thing on the subject. Whilst at La Bahia Genl Houston received dispatches from Col Comdt Neill informing him that good reasons were entertained that an attack would soon be made by a numerous Mexican army on our important post of Bexar. It was forthwith determined that I should go instantly to Bexar; accordingly I left Genl Houston and with a few very efficient volunteers came on to this place about 2 weeks since. I was received by Col. Neill with great cordiality, and the men under my command entered at once into active service. All I can say of the soldiers stationed here is

complimentary to both their courage and their patience.

But it is the truth and Your Excellency must Know it, that great and just dissatisfaction if felt for the want of a little money to pay the small but necessary expenses of our men. I cannot eulogize the conduct & character of Col. Neill too highly: no other man in the army could have kept men at this post, under the neglect they have experienced. Both he & myself, have done all that we could; we have industriously tryed [sic] all expedients to raise funds, but hitherto it has been to no purpose. We are still labouring night and day, laying up provisions for a siege, encouraging our men, and calling on the Government for relief.

Relief at this post, in men, money, & provisions is of vital importance & is wanted instantly. Sir, this is the object of my letter. The salvation of Texas depends in great measure in keeping Bexar out of the hands of the enemy. It serves as the frontier picquet guard and if it were in the possession of Santa Ann there is no strong hold from which to repel him in his march towards the Sabine. There is no doubt but very large forces are busy gathering in several of the towns beyond the Rio Grande, and late information through Genr. Cassiana & others, worthy of credit, is positive in the fact that 16 hundred or two thousand troops with good officers, well armed, and a plenty of provisions, were on the point of marching, (the provisions being cooked &c). A detachment of active young men from the volunteers under my command have been sent out to the Rio Frio; they returned yesterday without information and we remain yet in doubt whether they intend an attack on this place or go to reinforce Matamoros. It does however seem certain that an attack is shortly to be made on this place & I think & it is the general opinion that the enemy will come by land. The Citizens of Bexar have behaved well. *Col. Neill & Myself have come to the solemn resolution that we will rather die in these ditches than give it up to the enemy.* These citizens deserve our protection and the public safety demands our lives rather than to evacuate this port to the enemy.-- Again we call aloud for *relief*; the weakness of our post will at any rate bring the enemy on. Some volunteers are expected; Capt. Patton with 5 or 6 have come in. But a large reinforcement with provisions is what we need.

James Bowie (Rubric)

I have information just now from a friend whom I believe that the force at Rio Grande (Presidio) is two Thousand complete; he Stated further that five thousand more is a little back and marching on, perhaps the 2 thousand will wait for a junction with the 5 thousand. The information is corroborated with all that we have heard. The informant says that thy intend to make a decent [sic] on this place in particular, and there is no doubt of it.

Our force is very small, the returns this day to the Comdt. is only one hundred and twenty officers & men. It would be a waste of men to put our brave little band against thousands.

Shortly after Bowie dispatched his letter, Colonel Neill received an answer from the governor to his earlier letter. The message said the governor would do all in his power to send help. This news bolstered the men's morale, and they worked even harder. After posting his letter to Neill, Governor Smith ordered Lieutenant Colonel Travis to recruit one hundred men and proceed with all haste to reinforce Neill at Bexar.

In the meantime, Colonel Fannin dallied at Copano Bay, wishing for ships to transport his troops to Matamoros; but no ships were available. He was true to form, always waiting, never acting. The other two "commanders," Grant and Johnson, with their force cut by Houston's persuasion, also dallied at Refugio and San Patricio, trying to catch enough mustang horses to form a cavalry.

SANTA ANNA PREPARES TO INVADE TEXAS

General Santa Anna had been informed as early as December 18, 1835, of the humiliating defeat of his brother-in-law, General Martin Perfecto de Cos, and his retreat from Bexar. Santa Anna flew into an enormous rage, vowing to vindicate the honor of

Mexico. He had always been energetic, but now he moved with unusual briskness. Proceeding at a fast clip to San Luis Potosi, he began assembling an army that would eventually number around five thousand men. On January 7, 1836, he moved the army to Saltillo, where he set up training operations. Santa Anna, always a detail man, now issued staccato orders. He was never happiest than when planning a campaign. Over a month ago, on December 2, 1835, General Joaquin Ramirez Sesma with fifteen hundred men had been ordered to reinforce Cos at Bexar. He marched north but now waited at the Rio Grande. The main army, forming at Saltillo, would be made up of two divisions. The first division under the command of General Sesma had attached the battalions from Matamoros and Jimenes as well as elements from San Luis Potosi and a regiment from Dolores and eight pieces of artillery. The second division under the command of General Vincente Filisola was made up of three brigades. The 1st Brigade would be under the command of General Antonio Gaona, composed of the Aldama, Toluca, and Queretero battalions, plus six pieces of artillery. The second brigade, under the command of General Eugerio Tolsa, would consist of a battalion from Guerrero and a contingent from Mexico City as well as one from Guadalajara and Tres Villes. There were also six pieces of artillery attached and later the Morales battalion would join them. The 3rd would be a cavalry brigade under the command of General Juan Jose Andre and consisted of a permanent regiment from Tampico, an active unit from Guanajuato, plus an auxiliary unit from El Bajio. The Sapper battalion, Santa Anna's pride and joy, was attached to his headquarters.

General Vincente Filisola was also appointed by Santa Anna as second in command of the army. Brigadier Generals Juan Arago and Adrian Woll were appointed major general and quartermaster respectively. The commanding general of artillery was Colonel Pedro Ampudia.

Santa Anna covered every detail in his general order for the army down to the changes of clothing each soldier would take, the number of pairs of shoes and sandals, canteens, and plates; also he specified the cavalry corp would be provided with the best horses possible and each officer would be supplied with a spare horse and all officers' horses would be given priority in pasturing.

The army would train at Saltillo. Santa Anna would personally supervise this phase and, "whip them into shape." Always thinking ahead, Santa Annaknew he would need protection on his flank as he marched into Texas. This assignment went to the experienced and principled General Don Jose Urrea, with three hundred infantry, three hundred lancers, and one field artillery piece, a 4-pounder. General Urrea would proceed at once to Matamorosand take command of the battalion already en route there from Campeche. Then he would proceed across the Rio Grande, paralleling the coast about 30-40 miles inland. Santa Anna had been well informed by Mexican rancheros in south Texas regarding Dr. Grant and Colonel Johnson. Urrea would search out and destroy them and then proceed to Goliad and end forever Fannin's dream of invading Matamoros. By messenger, Urrea coordinated all of his movements with His Excellency, leading the main army on a direct route to San Antonio. After the recapture of Bexar, Santa Anna with Urrea and all the other generals would proceed eastward to drive every Norte Americano beyond the Sabine. (It should be mentioned that two of his generals were foreign mercenaries; his second in command, General Vincente Filisola of Italy and General Adrian Woll of France.)

Actually Santa Anna had not planned to invade Texas until spring, but he felt the disgraceful surrender of Cos at Bexar demanded satisfaction. He had made a bold decision. He would not wait for the end of winter and spring grasses. Santa Anna was a professional soldier, and somehow he would make do on what the land provided. His policy which had already been approved by his puppet congress was simple: (1) every colonist found in arms or who had taken part in the rebellion would be executed; (2) those who had not participated would be transplanted to the interior of Mexico; (3) all properties of the colonists would be seized to pay for the cost of the operation, and (4) never again would a North American be permitted to enter Texas. These details were on his mind as he personally attended to the most trivial matters of the coming invasion. Santa Anna left San Luis Potosi on January 2 and arrived in Saltillo on January 7, 1836. The army would prepare to march as soon as possible. Saltillo would be the "jumping-off place" for the attack on San Antonio, approximately 365 miles north. Santa Annaprobably had some thoughts about his first mission to Bexar in 1813 with General Arredondo.

SANTA ANNA'S INVASION ROUTE

On January 25 came the final Grand Parade. The die was now cast. The glittering Generalissimo watched from his horse as troops and officers went past, some in good order, some not. But generally it was an impressive sight--the senior officers in their dark blue and scarlet uniforms, the dragoons with polished brass breastplates, followed by endless rows of soldiers in white cotton fatigues, wearing on their heads a tall black shako, complete with a colorful pom-pom and tiny visor. Santa Anna was pleased overall with his army which he patterned after his idol, Napoleon.

As the "Napoleon of the West" watched his troops parade, he must have thought, "How can an unorganized group of mountaineers stand up to the superiority of the trained Mexican soldiers? My officers have over twenty years of fighting experience and cannot be intimidated by colonists ignorant of the art of war, undisciplined, and known to be insubordinate!" But he overlooked one fact that should have been revealed by Cos after Bexar and Ugartechea after Velasco. The rifles of the frontiersmen and mountaineers in Texas were accurate at two hundred yards while the "escopetas" (muskets)--authentic English surplus from the days of Waterloo--could barely reach, and would not kill even at seventy yards. Nevertheless, the Generalissimo's spirits were high as he gave the order on January 25, 1836, to "move out."

IN SAN FELIPE TRAVIS LEAVES FOR ALAMO

Meanwhile back in San Felipe Travis had tried valiantly to recruit a hundred men; but in the time allowed fell tragically short, coming up with only thirty-nine. On January 21 Travis invested more than $50 of his own money in supplies such as flour, tinware, twine, leggings, and spurs. His list also showed he purchased a flag. The author's version of the flag is shown on page 139. (Authors note: No one knows what flag Travis purchased, but I cannot accept the idea it was the "1824" flag. A study of the words and deeds of Travis leads me to the firm conclusion he would never have purchased or flown a Mexican flag of any design. He had a total commitment to independence--not co-existence under Mexico.) This conclusion is reinforced by his letter written from the Alamo and dated March 3, 1836, to the President of the Convention, meeting at Washington-on-the-Brazos, excerpted below:

> The citizens of this municipality are all
> enemies except those who have joined us heretofore;

we have but three Mexicans now in the fort: those
who have not joined us in this extremity, should be
declared public enemies, and their property should
aid in paying the expenses of the war.

The bearer of this will give your honorable body
a statement more in detail, should he escape through
the enemies lines.

God and Texas--Victory or Death!!

W. Barret Travis
Lieut. Col. Comm.

His list also included a powder flask, a bridle, blankets, a tent,
frying pan, and rope. The next day, January 22, he received $100
from Governor Smith for supplies, which were sorely needed, as he
had already invested an additional $50 of his own money for corn,
coffee, sugar, and more blankets and advanced $17 to his men.

On January 23, 1836, as Santa Anna was about to review his
army at Saltillo, Travis left San Felipe for Bexar with thirty-nine
men. He was disappointed that with the rank of lieutenant colonel,
he had ended up with less than a company officer's command. The
only pleasant thought he carried as he rode toward the Colorado was
the fact he had taken time out to visit his son, Charles, at Montville
a week earlier. It would be the last time he would ever see him.

Travis was even more discouraged on January 27 when he
reached Burnham's Crossing on the Colorado and awoke the next
morning to discover nine of his men had deserted. Worse, they had
taken the precious equipment and provisions he had purchased.
Two of them were horse thieves, one stealing a fine sorrel and the
other a dun, each horse with saddle, bridle, blanket, gun and shot
pouch--total value $150--all of which Travis had personally
subsidized. Travis immediately reported the desertions to
Governor Smith and again described the difficulty he had in trying
to recruit soldiers. Before the report was finished, he was so
depressed he submitted his resignation to Governor Smith. He
dispatched the letter by express and bivouacked on the Colorado for
a reply, but the reply never came. After waiting a reasonable
length of time, Travis gloomily resumed the march to San Antonio.
Smith had received the letter but chose to ignore it. He needed men,
and he particularly needed Travis at the Alamo.

AUTHOR'S VERSION OF TRAVIS' FLAG

FLAG OF NEW ORLEANS GREYS
(Sent back to Mexico by Santa Anna
as the flag of the Alamo)

TRAVIS ARRIVES AT THE ALAMO

On February 3, 1836, Travis and his motley little group arrived at the Alamo. He was disillusioned more to find Bowie and Neill only had one hundred sixteen able-bodied men. His group brought the strength up to one hundred forty-six. Bonham, glad to see his boyhood friend, expressed his view that they would need a thousand; Travis agreed.

Travis pushed his thoughts into the background and pitched in wherever he could. Even with all the work, he couldn't forget the political situation back in San Felipe. He took a part in influencing the election of Samuel Maverick and Jesse Badgett to represent the garrison at the convention meeting in Washington-on-the-Brazos on March 1. For the next week, there was so much to do Travis hardly slept. On February 8 finally came excitement enough to make them forget Santa Anna. At mid morning the thirteen "Tennessee Mounted Volunteers" headed by Captain William B. Harrison, rode in from the east, laughing and cheering; but the "star" of the group was the ex-Congressman, bear hunter, story teller, and "gentleman from the cane," David Crockett. In his foxskin cap (its tail jauntily dangling) with Old Betsy cradled in his arms, he appeared bigger than life itself. He was just the tonic needed at the right time. Soldiers and citizens alike, instantly jammed the Main Plaza to welcome him.

DAVID CROCKETT - THE POLITICIAN

With wild applause and invigorating cheers resounding in his ears, Crockett must have felt like a conquering hero as he mounted a packing case that someone hastily provided for a stage amid calls of "Speech! Speech!" As soon as he could get their attention, he began:

> I've fought bears and I've been a member of Congress...and fightin' bears is a lot less trouble. Course, you can kill a bear. In the last election I was defeated by a peg-legged cuss from the camp of Andrew Jackson. I told my constituents, "Since you have chosen to elect a man with a timber toe to succeed me, you may all go to hell, and I will go to Texas."

Then Crockett concluded with inspirational words that he rarely projected in Congress:

> Fellow Citizens, I am among you. I have come to your country, though not I hope, through any selfish motive whatsoever. I have come to aid you all I can in your noble cause. I shall identify myself with your interest, and all the honor that I desire is that of defending, as a high private, in common with my fellow citizens, the liberties of our common country.

Stirring words! David Crockett came to Texas to rouse people and hopefully find here a new political future. Crockett, always the politician, had arrived at Nacogdoches from Tennessee about January 12, 1836, and learned to his dismay delegates from Nacogdoches already had been elected to the convention meeting on March 2. The thought may have entered his mind that Bexar and the Alamo may not yet have elected delegates and might just elect him. If this was his reason for going to San Antonio, he arrived one week too late. (Sam Maverick and Jesse Badgett were elected on February 1.) For whatever reason, he was at Bexar and would soon be in the Alamo; and like the others, trapped by a steadfast devotion to duty and liberty, and (in Crockett's case) reputation. He really had no other choice but to stay and die.

Soon after the speech, Crockett and his "Tennessee Mounted Volunteers" proceeded to the Alamo. Crockett asked, "Who's in charge?"

Colonel Neill introduced himself and advised that he was commander.

"Colonel, I'm David Crockett from Tennessee. We hear old Santa Anna is giving you some trouble; and like I told the folk back at the Plaza, we've come to help."

"Welcome, David Crockett, and welcome to your men," replied Colonel Neill with a smile. After introductions all around, Crockett and the Tennessee Volunteers got some much-need rest. The next morning they pitched in like all others, working to fortify the Alamo.

THE FANDANGO

But men who work hard need to play a little. On February 10 Colonel Neill declared a fandango (singing, dancing, drinking and barbecue) would be held in San Antonio to celebrate the arrival of David Crockett and the Tennessee Mounted Volunteers.

There were shouts and yells as the men scrambled into San Antonio to invite the citizens, particularly the senoritas. Everyone was looking forward to the evening and men who hadn't bathed in weeks hit the cold river with eagerness, lye soap in hand.

Soon fires were going and the smell of barbecued meat filled the air. Fiddles and guitars were tuned, and a festive mood took over the Main Plaza in Bexar; war and battle seemed oceans away.

There were plenty of shouts and applause for Crockett. He made more speeches and told yarns that sounded better after a few drinks. The men of the Alamo had worked hard and now they intended to drink and play hard. The fandango soon began in earnest. But it was suddenly interrupted by a rider galloping into the town around 1:00 a.m. shouting, "Santa Anna is crossing the Rio Grande!" The courier was one of several scouts sent out by Bowie and Juan Seguin, (son of Erasmo Seguin, an influential Texas citizen and staunch friend of the Texans.)

This news momentarily stopped the fandango and sent Travis, Bowie, and Crockett into a council of war. The most important decision coming out of the meeting was that the message was unimportant and the party should continue. It did--all nightlong. It is significant that the meeting did not include Colonel Neill. This must have offended him deeply. He had been pushed aside by others who considered themselves more able, and it hurt.

DAVID CROCKETT
(Courtesy of DRT Research Library at the Alamo)

143   *DIRE DECISIONS*

ANTONIO LOPEZ DE SANTA ANNA
(Courtesy of Eugene C. Barker Texas History Center)

COLONEL NEILL LEAVES ALAMO

The next day Colonel Neill called all the men together and made the following announcement: "Gentleman, due to illness in my family, I find it necessary to return home. Therefore, I am transferring command of this fort to Lieutenant Colonel Travis." (A logical choice for Travis was the next senior regular army officer.) There was unbelieving silence in the ranks. Travis had only been in the Alamo one week--besides, he was too young! Jim Bowie, fired by his usual morning drink, was the first to speak. "Now hear me, Colonel Neill, I'm not taking any orders from a 26-year-old kid."

There were also angry shouts from Bowie's men. Colonel Neill realized he had created a problem. Travis also sensed the problem. He and Bowie had gotten along fine until now. But would Bowie at forty-one, the best-known fighter in Texas, take orders from a 26-year-old? Not likely. The rumbling of the Volunteers continued, and Bowie did nothing to quell them. Travis saved Neill further embarrassment by ordering an election. "Let the men vote." Bowie was elected in a landslide.

Colonel Neill had no choice. "Very well, gentlemen, all regular army troops will be under Lieutenant Colonel Travis, and all volunteers will be under the command of Jim Bowie, except for the Tennessee Volunteers. They will be under Colonel Crockett."

There was small talk in the ranks as the men mulled over this new situation. Before they could say anything else, Colonel Neill continued, "I now bid you farewell and good luck." With those words, he rode out the gates of the Alamo. (He later fought with distinction at the Battle of San Jacinto.)

As the days passed Bowie became intolerable. The more he drank, the worse he coughed; and the more he coughed, the more he drank. He constantly did everything he could to embarrass Travis. At one point he shouted, "I am in sole command of this fort. Everyone fall in for close-order drill." Most were afraid of Jim Bowie sober, but when he was drunk they were terrified. To placate him they obeyed. He administered the drill in a slovenly manner. Travis was furious. He dispatched the following letter to Governor Smith:

> February 13, 1838
> Dear Sir,
>   Lieutenant Colonel Neill being suddenly called home because of illness in his family appointed me as senior officer to command this garrison in his absence. Jim Bowie protested and as a consequence, Colonel Neill split the command with regular under me and volunteers under Bowie. Ever since he has been roaring drunk and has assumed all command on occasion. If I did not feel my honor and that of my country compromised, I would leave here instantly for some other place with the troops I command, as I am unwilling to be responsible for the drunken irregularities of any man. I beg of you to immediately order some regulars into this place, as it is more important to keep this post than I first imagined. The Alamo is the key to Texas from the interior. Without a footing here, Santa Anna can do nothing against the colonies. I did not solicit command of this post, and if I am to defend it, please send troops.
>
> William B. Travis, of the Alamo
> in the absence of Colonel Neill

JOINT COMMAND

Bowie sobered up on the morning of the 14th and actually apologized to Travis. As sick and drunk as he had been, he believed the Alamo was the key to Texas and to defend it was a far bigger thing than who would command it. They agreed to keep separate commands but to confer on all major decisions.

With the conflict between their commanders at least temporarily resolved, morale improved and a new atmosphere of excitement and dedication took hold of the defenders. Captain Almeron Dickinson and his men had successfully mounted nineteen serviceable cannon and hoped to mount two others. Dr. Amos Pollard made a hospital of sorts on the second floor of the main barracks. He found most of the surgical instruments he needed except syringes, but he would make do. The blacksmith and ordinance chief of the Alamo, Sam Blair, chopped up horseshoes and nails to substitute for grape shot. Travis was everywhere, and he pitched in even on menial jobs. The volunteers observed no one worked longer or harder, and the regular army troops discovered that Jim Bowie, in spite of his habit of hard drinking, was a fair and dedicated man. The garrison now acquired a unity that was not present before.

There had been no recent information on Santa Anna's whereabouts, and it was incorrectly assumed that he was waiting for spring grass to feed his horses before marching north. But they should have known, for on February 16 another dusty courier on a lathered horse reined up at the house of Ambrosio Rodriguez. His name was Rivas Rodriguez, a cousin. He had ridden all the way from Laredo to warn them Santa Anna was preparing to cross the Rio Grande and march on Bexar. Ambrosio sent for Colonel Travis, who listened patiently as Rivas repeated his story. Finally Travis thanked Rivas but decided that he had erred as to Santa Anna's plans. (In Travis' mind there was no way Santa Anna could move his army eight hundred miles in the dead of winter.) He would come--about that Travis had no doubt--but not now.

On February 18 Ambrosio passed to Travis another report that Santa Anna was marching north; still Travis refused to believe. Another courier arrived on February 20--this time one of Juan Seguin's own scouts--the experienced Blas Herrera, a member of Seguin's company of local Mexicans (Tejanos) who supported independence for Texas. Herrera said he had seen Santa Anna's army crossing the Rio Grande with his "own eyes."

That night Travis called a council of war in his room and asked Herrera to repeat his story. Travis, Bowie, Crockett and others argued for hours whether to believe him. Some accepted it but others, including Crockett, were doubtful. Again, Travis chose to ignore the warning. (He was not alone; many experienced observers agreed, John W. Smith and David Cummins among them.) Travis expected Santa Anna about March 15. But Herrera

DIRE DECISIONS

was right. They were stupid not to believe him. Santa Anna was coming and fast.

Actually Santa Anna crossed the Rio Grande on February 16, the Nueces on the 17th, and was joined there by Sesma's brigade. Now only one hundred seventeen miles to go! Texan scouts had burned the Nueces bridge but Santa Anna's engineers quickly built another temporary bridge.

His army trudged onward in spite of cold rains and hostile Indians. (Governor Musquiz's son, a soldier in Santa Anna's army was one killed by an arrow.) On February 19 Santa Anna crossed the Rio Frio and on the 20th crossed the Hondo. Only fifty-four more miles! On February 21 Santa Anna advanced to the head of the column when it reached the Medina. Here Sesma's crack dragoons had been waiting. Santa Anna ordered a halt so all columns could catch up. Now his goal was only twenty-five miles away! Informants from San Antonio told him of a great fandango to be held that very evening in Bexar on Soledad Street. Most of the Alamo defenders would attend. Ah ha! He would surprise them. All the Texans would be trapped! Quickly Santa Anna issued orders to Sesma's cavalry. The dragoons would attack at midnight; let the Texans get drunk first. It would make the slaughter easier.

It began to rain heavily just as the dragoons started saddling up. By the time they were ready, the normally emerald green Medina turned into a dark brown raging torrent. Santa Anna knew they couldn't cross, but he didn't fret too much. The Texans would die soon enough.

In San Antonio light rain put a damper on the festival and most turned in early. February 22 was like any other day at the Alamo-- drill and drill, work and more work, repair the breach in the north wall, etc.

Now the principals in this great drama about to unfold were in position. Santa Anna had sworn to teach these rebel Texans and Americans a lesson, to vindicate the honor of Mexico, and to avenge the defeat of his brother-in-law, General Cos. Leading the vanguard of his great army, he was at the Medina River only eight miles from the city! The day was February 23, 1836. The Alamo was about to become the hub of a battle to rival that of Thermopylae for historical significance, and its defenders would pay the supreme price for freedom. But like a phoenix, the old fort would rise from its own smoke and ashes to become a revered monument to valor.

Countless words have been written about the Alamo, but none have captured its true meaning better than those of Miss Clara Driscoll:

> Watch it in the silence of eventide, when the glow of a departing day throws its radiant color like a brilliant mantle about the old ruin. How clearly its battle scars stand out, vivid and lurid in the stones, red as the blood of the men who fought and died there - - -

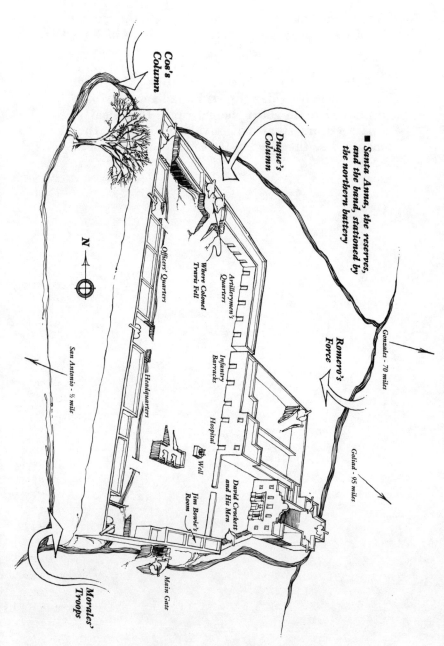

Cos's Column

Duque's Column

N

■ Santa Anna, the reserves, and the band, stationed by the northern battery

Romero's Force

Gonzales - 70 miles

Goliad - 95 miles

Officers' Quarters

Where Colonel Travis Fell

Artillerymen's Quarters

Infantry Barracks

San Antonio - ½ mile

Headquarters

Hospital

Well

David Crockett and His Men

Jim Bowie's Room

Main Gate

Morales' Troops

ATTACK ON THE ALAMO

"THE HOUR THAT TRIED MEN'S SOULS"

CHAPTER 11

"THE HOUR THAT TRIED MEN'S SOULS"

DAY 1 - FEBRUARY 23 - TUESDAY

SANTA ANNA RETURNS!

At an unusually early hour, candles and oil lights flickered before dawn in most houses of Bexar. About 3:00 a.m. on the morning of February 23, 1836, a wet and muddy courier knocked on the Rodriguez door. Ambrosio was gone. The courier warned Mrs. Rodriguez to get out of town and not wait for Ambrosio's return; Bexar would be attacked that very day. The news spread from house to house; soon there were flickering lights, quiet conversations, running feet, and the hushed noise of belongings being loaded into carts and wagons.

The first rays of sunlight revealed streets full of creaking carts and wagons rumbling along as the drivers urged their teams to move faster.

Travis awakened early and looked out his window. What was this? A stream of carts were lumbering out of town towards the east and southeast. People were still dashing in and out of houses and talking excitedly. Travis asked for information and was told it was time to do farm work. Farming in February? And at 6:30 a.m.! Frustrated, he ordered the exodus stopped, but they hurried even more. What was going on?

It was around eleven o'clock before a friendly citizen of Bexar told him about the courier who had visited Mrs. Rodriguez. Santa Anna's cavalry was camped about eight miles out on Leon Creek!

Now Travis grabbed Dr. John Sutherland and a garrison private. All ran to the San Fernando Church between Main and Military Plazas. The bell tower of the church was the highest point in town. Dr. Sutherland, with his last ounce of breath, scrambled up its winding stairs trying to keep up with Travis and the young private. Each selected a window and stared at the horizon, Travis looking south southwest with his spyglass.

The winter mesquite, bare of leaves, and the scraggly chaparral were motionless in a calm wind and bright sun. The only things visible were the outbound carts to the east and southeast.

"THE HOUR THAT TRIED MEN'S SOULS"

Seeing nothing to be alarmed about, Travis told the sentry to keep a sharp eye to the southwest and ring the bell if he saw cavalry.

Travis returned to his quarters, and Dr. Sutherland stopped at the general merchandise store of Nat Lewis on Main Plaza. Lewis had heard enough to make him wary. He was taking inventory and slowly packing, figuring he would leave, but not that day. The doctor helped count spools of thread, bolts of cloth, and talked with Lewis about the situation in Texas. At 1:00 p.m. the two men were still counting when they suddenly heard the tower bell ringing. Sutherland, leaving Lewis with his merchandise, dashed for the church. Travis and others beat him there and again they saw nothing. Travis patted the private on the shoulder, but the sentry cursed and swore he'd seen lances flashing in the sun. He was unconvincing, and the crowd soon dispersed.

Travis was also skeptical but wanted to know for sure. Dr. Sutherland volunteered to ride out to the Leon Creek and have a look if someone who knew the terrain would go with him. John W. Smith (who had distinguished himself in the Battle of Bexar in December) quickly agreed to go. Travis tossed Smith his spyglass. As they rode off, Smith turned and looked up at the sentry, "Son, if you see us coming back riding hell bent for leather, ring that bell cause we've got trouble."

Sutherland and Smith proceeded about four to five miles southwest of town and topped out on a small hill. They could see dust in the distance, and Smith brought the spyglass to his eye. He exclaimed, "My God, doctor, have a look!" The doctor quickly brought the spyglass into focus, then wheeled his mount, exclaiming, "Let's get the hell out of here fast!" They spurred their horses to a full run, but Sutherland's mount slipped and fell upon him, damaging the doctor's right leg. With Smith's aid he remounted, and they continued their break-neck race to town. The sentry saw them coming and pulled with vengeance on the bell rope.

Bexar exploded with activity at the sound of the bell as the sentry repeatedly pulled the rope so hard the bell almost flipped over. Travis barked orders, "Captain Baugh, get everybody back to the Alamo and take all the provisions you can find!" Young James Allen, a sixteen-year-old, came running up (Allen had been with Milam's men who captured Bexar from Cos in December). Travis, spotting him, requested, "Allen, spread the word to everyone, and tell Captain Carey to get his cannon in battery and ready to fire." Then Travis, looking half bewildered at all the activity, muttered to himself, "It's just not possible that Santa Anna has entered Texas!"

The exodus of San Antonio begun that morning by some of its citizens was now almost a stampede. All of the defenders of the Alamo who had been living in town headed for the garrison. Citizens who had wavered on leaving earlier now grabbed all the belongings they could and swarmed past Travis on foot, horseback, mules, burros--in carts, wagons, or any conveyance they could find.

Juan Seguin, with ten others in his company, rode up and asked Travis what he could do. "Round up all the loose cattle in town you can find, and head them for the Alamo. We'll need more beef than we've got in the corrals now."

Jim Bowie was helping his sisters-in-law, young Juana Navarro Alsbury, (twenty-four years old) with her baby and her younger sister, Gertrudis Navarro, (about nineteen) carry their belongings from the Veramendi house and load them into a buggy. Jim had not been feeling well for some time and was coughing up blood. Leaving the house, he picked up a small portrait of his late wife, Ursula, and touched her face lovingly, then tucked it inside his coat.

Out on the street the black servant of Captain Francis DeSauque (who had left on February 21 for Goliad to get provisions) reported to Colonel Travis, saluted, and proudly stated, "Private John, reportin' for duty, sir."

Travis smiled pleasantly and returned the salute as he said, "Fall in with my men, John. I've just made you a real private in the Texas Army." Captain Almeron Dickinson, with his horse in a dead run, pulled up in front of his quarters at the Musquiz home. His wife was outside. "Give me the baby, Susanna! Jump on behind and ask me no questions." She handed little Angelina to her father, and then Almeron gave Susanna a hand as she swung behind him onto the horse. The three of them forded the San Antonio River to the west bank, not waiting to cross the crowded footbridge further down. Captain Dickinson headed for the Alamo, passing on the way other Mexican women struggling with their belongings. Two of whom were Trinidad Saucedo a pretty teenage girl, and an old woman, Petra Gonzales.

As the men of the Alamo garrison and other civilians swarmed across the footbridge and headed to the old mission, some of the native Mexicans who had stayed in their homes stared at the scene in disbelief. Undoubtedly some wanted Santa Anna to win; others

"THE HOUR THAT
TRIED MEN'S SOULS"

wanted him to lose, while others felt caught in a situation not of their making.

Seguin and his men rounded up thirty head of cattle, and the air was filled with their bellowing and the crack of whips as the cursing men herded the animals into the corral on the east side of the Alamo. Some of Bowie's men were searching the jacales (huts) just outside the Alamo, lugging in pecans, grain, ears of corn, and whatever else that was edible. Inside the fort, mothers were trying to comfort crying children and find a safe place in the rooms of the old church. It was well they didn't know that the Alamo's supply of gunpowder lay in the adjacent rooms.

Nat Lewis had been too busy packing his belongings to pay attention to all of the activity around him. Now with all of his inventory he could carry on a pack mule, he stopped momentarily inside the Alamo compound. Without dismounting from his horse, he took one look at all the preparations for war and said to himself, "To hell with this; it's time to go. I'm not a fighter; I'm a merchant." Urging his horse and pack mule forward, he headed for open country; on the way he saw two soldiers leaving--a Captain Dimitt and a Lieutenant Nobles.

Travis was now in his headquarters room in the west wall. "Damn," he said to himself, "where are the reinforcements?" He had sent Bonham to Goliad on February 16 asking for Fannin's help. Surely Fannin would send help--or would he? His thoughts were interrupted by David Crockett and Dr. Sutherland. Sutherland's knee had been severely wrenched when his horse fell, and it was now stiff and almost useless. Crockett supported him as they came into the room. Travis mumbled something about help and Dr. Sutherland said, "If someone will get me on a horse, I'll ride to Gonzales and rally support."

"Bless you, doctor," replied Travis, "but you'd better not ride alone."

Turning to Joe, his slave, Travis said, "Find John Smith."

By this time Crockett was fidgeting for an assignment and blurted out to Travis, "Colonel, here am I. Assign me to a position, and I and my twelve boys will try and defend it."

"Take the palisades, Crockett; it's our weakest point, and I know of no one I would rather have at that location."

"Then consider it mine." As Crockett left he said to the other Tennessee Volunteers, "Come on, boys, we've got the palisades."

"David," Travis called out as Crockett was leaving.

"Yes."

"THE HOUR THAT
TRIED MEN'S SOULS"   154

"You're the only Congressman I ever liked."

"Damn shame you weren't there when I needed your vote," said the smiling Crockett.

SANTA ANNA ENTERS BEXAR

It was now about 1:00 p.m. the same day. Santa Anna fidgeted while he waited for the rest of his army to catch up so they could make a grand entry into San Antonio. He had ordered all officers and men into dress uniforms. Finally at about 2:30 p.m. the long columns started moving, using both the Old San Antonio and Laredo Roads. There would be no element of surprise to their entry into the city, though Santa Anna tried twice. The flooded Medina thwarted the first attempt, and last night Sesma's dragoons started to San Antonio but halted at the Alazan Creek, only a mile and a half from town. Thinking they had been discovered by Texan scouts, the soldiers returned to the main column without attacking.

Now everybody in Bexar knew Santa Anna was coming. They had been seen by the sentry, John W. Smith Dr. Sutherland and others. In the afternoon sun, the Mexican army was highly visible as it advanced on the city. Juan Seguin's company had hoisted their red, white, and green banner with two stars in the center representing Coahuila and Texas; but they lowered it and retired to the Alamo as Santa Anna's advance guard approached within musket shot of the Main Plaza. Shortly behind the advance guard, His Excellency rode in front of the main army, proud and erect, savoring every minute of his return to San Antonio. These "perfidious foreigners" would be routed. In his mind he was reliving 1813 all over again, but now he was the commander of a grand army! And a magnificent sight it was--the dragoons with their polished breast plates glistening in the sun, the guidon ensigns (flags mounted to a staff) of each battalion! But the proudest were the bearers of the national emblem of Mexico, the red, white, and green banner with an eagle clutching a serpent in its beak and cactus in its claws; a menacing omen of the vengeance that would be extracted from the Texans.

As Santa Anna, astride his prancing dapple horse, neared Main Plaza, the band struck up one of its lively parade marches. Even the horses seemed to match the cadence. The citizens who had remained in town watched in wonder and amazement as the seemingly endless column rode by. Suddenly His Excellency reined up his prancing charger, doffed his plumed hat and bowed in the direction of the fountain. All eyes turned to a pretty young

"THE HOUR THAT
TRIED MEN'S SOULS"

senorita sitting there. Santa Anna rode on but looked back more than once toward the fountain.

As soon as General Santa Anna occupied the city, he had his aides hang a blood red flag, the symbol of "no quarter," from the San Fernando Church tower, visible to the Alamo only eight hundred yards away. When Travis saw the banner, he ordered a shot fired in defiance from the 18-pounder and his own emblem be raised (see page 139) over the hospital. The 1824 flag (the Mexican tri-color with 1824 in the center instead of an eagle) already flew from the Alamo.

Travis gazed transfixed at the Mexican cavalcade pouring into the plaza. He must get help from Colonel Fannin! The four hundred men in Goliad were of little use to Texas there. Fannin had returned to Goliad from Copano Bay and was now ensconced in Ft. Defiance, still undecided about his ill-conceived plan for an invasion of Mexico at the Port of Matamoros. Travis calculated riding time (it takes a good horse and rider, in excellent shape, to cover thirty-five miles in one day). Surely Bonham should be back with help at any moment unless something (perhaps Indians) had deterred him.

"Santa Anna must not have stopped at the Rio Grande long enough to water his horse," Travis thought to himself. Here he was in San Antonio in all his splendor. (Actually, since Santa Anna crossed the Rio Grande on February 16, he had covered one hundred sixty-five miles in seven days--with an army in the dead of winter. An extraordinary feat!)

Travis realized a new plea for help must be made and by men who knew the seriousness of the situation. Dr. Sutherland still insisted he could ride, and now John W. Smith was eagerly waiting.

"Men, Indians or a Mexican patrol may have gotten Bonham. I've got to get another message to Fannin. He has the only army in Texas."

Turning to Smith, Travis said, "John, you and Doc ride immediately to Goliad. Tell Fannin we must have his help and soon. There's a thousand Mexicans here now, and there'll be thousands more in a few days. Tell him not to waste a minute. Now hurry, boys, while you can still get out." The gates opened and they dashed away to the east. Travis climbed on a gun barbette to watch them leave. He wondered if his friend, Bonham, had been killed. He silently prayed not. How much he needed him! Then he mused that perhaps Fannin was on the way, and he was worrying for nothing.

Travis' thoughts retraced the events of that morning. He was glad Samuel W. Maverick had dropped by the Alamo and left for Washington-on-the-Brazos as a delegate to the Convention before the Mexicans arrived. (Jesse Badgett had left days before.) Travis had asked Maverick to spread the word at Gonzales and San Felipe that he needed men and supplies. From his saddle, Maverick promised he would do what he could. That statement satisfied Travis that morning, but now things were different. "What he could" might take days or even weeks. There wasn't much time; the need was now!

Travis turned his thoughts to Jim Bowie. What a time for Jim to be sick! Bowie's chronic, wracking cough had not improved even with Dr. Amos Pollard's treatments. In fact, it had grown much worse, and he appeared feverish. Travis wished the feud between them would end. There was no room in the Alamo now for dissension.

BONHAM RETURNS

Jim Bonham, approaching San Antonio, had heard the shot from the 18-pounder and wondered what it meant. He was soon to find out. He had just topped Powder House Hill and gotten a view of the town which congealed his blood. The plaza was full of parading, marching Mexican cavalry and soldiers with yet more coming in, the columns stretching out to the southwest as far as he could see! Bonham thought, "Fannin, if you could only see this and still refuse to come, you are a coward!" Bonham's eyes focused on the blood-red flag that fluttered from the San Fernando Church. He knew its meaning, but this did not deter him. He spurred his tired mount into a run down the hill and headed straight for the Alamo gates. The sentry saw him coming, swung open the gates, and Bonham thundered in unchallenged. The Mexican soldiers probably thought, "Just one more fool to kill."

Travis' hopes were dashed when Bonham gave his report. Fannin wasn't coming. "He said he might need all his men for the invasion of Mexico if he decides to go. Says he's waiting on ships. He can't make up his mind what he wants to do."

"Damn Fannin," Travis answered. "The invasion is outside these walls! He can forget Matamoros! We need those four hundred men! It's the only army in Texas. Fannin must come! He cannot ignore our plight. Get some rest, Jim; I must send

"THE HOUR THAT
TRIED MEN'S SOULS"

another messenger." He summoned a young man by the name of Johnson (first name unknown) and Ben Highsmith, issuing instructions, "Ride to Goliad and tell Fannin I cannot accept his reason for refusing to come; Texas needs every man from Goliad here in the Alamo and quickly. Tell him if there's going to be a republic, it will be born here in these old walls." Shortly, two more messengers rode out the Alamo gates bound for Goliad. (In all, Travis sent out around eighteen messengers.)

Bowie, for some unknown reason, thought the Mexican officers had asked for a parlay just before Travis fired the 18-pounder. Perhaps Bowie knew the odds before him and questioned the wisdom of confrontation if there was a chance for negotiation. Seizing the only paper in sight, he quickly wrote a note, apologetically explaining the garrison had fired before hearing that the Mexicans wanted a parlay. He sent the message by his aide, Green B. Jameson. (The message Jameson carried did not indicate capitulation.) Bowie originally had signed it, "God and the Mexican Federation." But this he boldly marked out and substituted, "God and Texas," proving once and for all that he was as committed to independence as anyone.

Santa Anna refused to see Jameson. He took one look at the note and scornfully tossed it to his aide, Colonel Jose Batres. Batres wrote in reply, "His Excellency cannot offer terms to rebellious foreigners for whom there is no recourse left. If they wish to save their lives, then they must place themselves immediately at the disposal of the supreme government---." Jameson headed back with written emphasis of what the red banner already had told them, "Unconditional surrender."

Travis was furious when he saw Jameson leave the fort under a flag of truce. No sooner than Jameson returned, he sent his own messenger, Albert Martin, though no one knows for sure why. Probably it was in anger as he and Bowie had agreed not to take any major steps without consulting each other. So perhaps it was the reaction of a sensitive man, wanting the Mexicans to know that Travis, the co-commander, could send his own messenger to parlay.

Albert Martin met the English-speaking Colonel Almonte (Santa Anna's chief of staff) on the footbridge over the San Antonio River. There was no written note. Martin told Colonel Almonte he was speaking for Travis and that if he wanted to meet with the co-commander, Travis would greet him with "much pleasure." Colonel Almonte explained, "it did not become the Mexican government to make any propositions through me" and that he was only there to listen. Almonte must have laid out the terms of surrender. They talked for over an hour with Martin finally saying that he would return with Colonel Travis if the terms were agreeable, otherwise, the Texans would resume fire.

Colonel Almonte didn't have to wait long for his answer. Within minutes after Martin walked inside the Alamo gate, the big 18-pounder roared again. Later Travis reported in a letter to Houston, "I answered them with a cannon shot."

As twilight approached over San Antonio on the first day of the siege, the usual sounds of Bexar had changed. Music and laughter were replaced with the clacking of steel against steel as men stacked rifles; the rattling of chains as cannons were unhitched from horses; the sounds of cursing and sweating soldiers as they shoveled earth, placing into battery their five-inch howitzers.

Santa Anna had ensconced himself in the Yturri house on the northwest corner of Main Plaza and Colonel Almonte was in the Nixon house. The Yturri home was a flat-roofed one-story building but had been built very strongly. It may not have been too comfortable, but at least Santa Anna felt secure. Soon he and Almonte were in conference. Santa Anna thought it would be a good idea for Francisco Ruiz to remain as Alcalde. When they interviewed him, he seemed very cooperative and capable of administering the duties of that office.

The darkened streets were mostly crowded with soldiers. But a few of the town's people slipped along quietly in the shadows. The houses were either silent or noisily occupied by soldiers. At the Gregorio Esparza house, there was hushed excitement. Family members were gathering their belongings. It was dark now and Gregorio would put his plan into action. He was one of Seguin's best men and an expert in handling artillery. Collecting his wife, Ana, and four children, including eight-year-old Enrique, Gregorio led them into the dark night, forded the San Antonio River, and quickly headed for the Alamo. One by one, they were lifted into the church through an open window. Enrique later recalled memorable and historically valuable events of the Battle of the Alamo. Gregorio knew full well that his brother, Francisco, could possibly be with the army outside; for he was a presidial soldier and had fought with Cos in the first Battle of Bexar.

Travis was in his quarters, reflecting on what had been a disappointing day--the failed attempt to parlay, Bonham's return with disappointing news, and the lingering problem with Bowie.

"THE HOUR THAT TRIED MEN'S SOULS"

Travis didn't realize it when he went to sleep that night, but by the next day, fate would solve the latter problem.

DAY 2 - FEBRUARY 24 - WEDNESDAY

TRAVIS GETS SOLE COMMAND

Jim Bowie was gravely ill and knew it. Every breath he took was difficult and felt like a thousand knives in his chest. Travis stopped by to check on his condition.

"I'm getting weaker, Travis." He continued in a voice hardly audible, "Would you summon my men?" When they all gathered, Bowie announced he was relinquishing his joint command. They must follow Travis and obey his orders. Travis was a good soldier, he told them, and just as willing as he to "die in these ditches." Travis now realized the Alamo was under his sole command; he felt equal to the task. The volunteers quickly dispersed, as the bombardment of the Alamo began in full fury. It did not abate even during the night.

TRAVIS' FAMOUS VICTORY OR DEATH LETTER

At the end of the second day of the siege, Travis had gone to his room at dusk. Lighting a candle, he fell into his chair and again picked up the pen that had written so many pleading messages. The one he was about to write this evening of February 24, 1836, would become the epitome of all calls to arms. Even today it quickens the heartbeat and surges the blood of any man who calls himself a patriot and cherishes freedom.

> Commandancy of the Alamo-
> Bexar, Fby 24th, 1836-
>
> To the people of Texas & all Americans in the world.
>
> Fellow citizens & compatriots-
> I am besieged, by a thousand or more of the Mexicans under Santa Anna--I have sustained a continual Bombardment & cannonade for 24 hours and have not lost a man--The enemy has demanded a surrender at discretion, otherwise, the garrison are to be put to the sword, if the fort is taken--I have

answered the demand with a cannon shot, & our flag still waves proudly from the walls-*I shall never surrender or retreat.* Then, I call on you in the name of Liberty, of patriotism & everything dear to the American character to come to our aid with all dispatch--The enemy is receiving reinforcements daily & will no doubt increase to three or four thousand in four or five days. If this call is neglected, I am determined to sustain myself as long as possible & die like a soldier who never forgets what is due to his own honor & that of his country-

VICTORY OR DEATH

William Barret Travis
Lt. Col., Comdt.
(Rubric)

P. S. The Lord is on our side--when the enemy appeared in sight we had not three bushels of corn--We have since found in deserted houses 80 or 90 bushels & got into the walls 20 or 30 head of Beeves--
Travis

Send this to San Felipe by Express night & day--.

Travis knew this was a special message. It must be carried by a courier whom he trusted and who was familiar with the local terrain. Summoning Albert Martin, a 30-year-old captain from Gonzales, Travis gave him the document with these words: "Our very existence and the future of Texas may well rest in your hands. This message must be read by General Houston, Governor Smith, and all the delegates at the Convention. Ride with all haste, my friend. There's not one moment to lose!" Martin folded the note and stuck it inside his buckskin shirt. Riding out of the Alamo, he slipped through the Mexican lines and galloped down the road to

"THE HOUR THAT TRIED MEN'S SOULS"

Gonzales seventy miles away, carrying a message he did not realize would become immortal.

By the time Albert Martin delivered Travis' letter to Gonzales on February 25, he had written on the outside: "Hurry on all the men you can get in haste." Waiting to relay the message ninety miles to the east at San Felipe de Austin was Lancelot Smithers who had arrived in Gonzales from the Alamo with another plea only the day before. Riding through a "blue norther," young Smithers reached San Felipe February 27. Adding his own postscript to the letter, he had written: "I hope that Every one will Randeves at Gonzales as soon as poseble as the Brave Soldiers are suffering. do not neglect the powder. is very scarce and should not be delad one moment."

DAY 3 - FEBRUARY 25 - THURSDAY

In the early morning light of February 25--the third day of the siege--the men in the Alamo saw that another Mexican earthwork had gone up during the night just across the river.

By 10 a.m. all Mexican batteries opened fire, creating a smoke screen which enabled their soldiers to cross the river and dart among the jacales (huts) along the east bank. This area, known as La Villita, might be a site where the enemy could move cannon close to the Alamo.

Colonel Travis, knowing something must be done about this dangerous situation, ordered his own cannon to return the fire, mainly as a diversion, while Robert Brown, Charles Despallier, and James Rose made a daring dash out the front gate and through the smoke with flaming torches which they applied to the nearest huts. The burning of most of these jacales gave the Texans a clear view of the area and a new field of fire. Losing their cover, the Mexicans fell back to the river.

But with the arrival of nightfall, additional Mexican troops had arrived, and two new batteries went up - one just three hundred yards south of the Alamo; the other near the powderhouse about a thousand yards to the southeast. The ring was tightening around the Texas garrison.

Travis countered with rifle fire and sent a group outside for a brief skirmish with some of General Ramirez y Sesma's men. Another group was sent out to raid La Villita to bring in timber from the remaining jacales for firewood.

Alarmed that none of his couriers had returned, Travis feared they might all be dead. He must try again to get a message outside-- this time to the Commander-in-Chief, General Sam Houston. Reaching for his pen, he wrote the following message:

> Today at ten o'clock, a.m. some two or three hundred Mexicans crossed the river below, and came up under cover of the houses, until they arrived within point blank shot, when we opened a heavy discharge of grape and canister on them, together with a well directed fire from small arms, which forced them to halt and take shelter in the houses about ninety to one hundred yards from our batteries. The action continued to rage for about two hours, when the enemy retreated in confusion, dragging off some of their dead and wounded. During the action the enemy kept up a continual bombardment and discharge of balls, grape and canister. We know, from actual observation, that many of the enemy were killed and wounded--while we on our part, have not lost a man. Two or three of our men have been slightly scratched by pieces of rock, but not disabled. I take great pleasure in stating, that both officers and men conducted themselves with firmness and bravery--Lieut. Simmons of the Cavalry, acting as Infantry, and Captains Carey, and Dickinson and Blair of the Artillery, rendered essential services, and Chas. Despallier and Robert Brown, gallantly sallied out and set fire to houses which afforded the enemy shelter, in the face of the enemy's fire. Indeed the whole of the men, who were brought in to action, conducted themselves with such undaunted heroism, that it would be injustice to discriminate. The Hon. David Crockett was seen at all points animating the men to do their duty. Our numbers are few, and the enemy still continues to approximate his works to ours. I have every reason to apprehend an attack from his whole force very soon; but I shall hold out to the last extremity, hoping to secure reinforcements in a day or two. Do hasten on aid to me as rapidly as possible. As from the

superior number of the enemy, it will be impossible for us to keep them out much longer. If they overpower us, we fall a sacrifice at the shrine of our country, and we hope posterity and our country will do our memory justice. Give me help, oh my country! Victory or death!

Travis
(Rubric)

Looking over his roster for yet another courier, Travis noted the name of Juan Seguin. Captain Seguin was a fiercely loyal Texan and an avowed enemy of Santa Anna. He had come into the Alamo with a small contingent of Mexican volunteers who felt as he did. If anyone could get through the Mexican lines, it would be Seguin. On the other hand, Travis desperately needed him in the Alamo. Calling in his staff, Travis put the matter of selecting a courier to a vote. Seguin was everyone's choice to carry the message to Houston.

Outlining the seriousness of the situation, Travis told Seguin the Alamo was now almost completely surrounded, and his chances of getting through were slim; but Seguin's knowledge of Spanish and the countryside made his chances better than that of anyone else. Readily agreeing to the mission, Seguin volunteered not only himself but also his aide, Antonio Cruz y Arocha. After leaving Travis' command headquarters, Seguin dashed across the plaza to the hospital where he asked Jim Bowie if he could borrow his horse. Bowie, burning with fever, answered in the affirmative. Seguin thanked him and ran to the stables with Arocha. They quickly saddled their mounts and quietly left the Alamo.

Shortly after leaving the Alamo gates, Seguin and Arocha were stopped by Texan pickets, not knowing they were on a mission assigned by Travis. Insults were hurled at Seguin and his aide, as the Texan sentries thought the two Tejanos were deserting. They took these slurs silently and rode leisurely eastward. Shortly they were revealed to a dismounted Mexican cavalry unit as the moon suddenly broke through the clouds. The captain ordered them to approach. Seguin answered casually in Spanish saying they were friendly vaqueros, and they continued slowly forward. Suddenly both men raked their mounts with spurs, leaned forward as flat as possible, and dashed past the dazed Mexicans. Fortunately, clouds again covered the moon and they fled in a wild flurry of bullets and escaped into a wooded area. They soon turned toward Goliad with a cold north wind at their backs.

DAY 4 - FEBRUARY 26 - FRIDAY

Up early on a cold Friday morning, Travis could see that Sesma's cavalry had now blocked the road to Gonzales. Some members of the Alamo garrison went out the northern postern (gate) to engage the Mexicans in an exchange of fire. Captain Green B. Jameson and his men spent the day digging trenches, dodging cannon balls, throwing up earth works, and improving parapets with the lumber obtained the night before by Brown, Despallier, and Rose. The Mexican gunners continued to fire steadily but did little damage. Crockett and his men were busy taking long-range shots at careless Mexicans and rarely missed.

FANNIN'S ABORTED ATTEMPT TO COME

While Santa Anna's army of close to 2,000 men was investing the Alamo, an incident was unfolding at Goliad that, properly executed, could have affected the outcome of the battle of the Alamo. Colonel Fannin had finally decided to go to the aid of Colonel Travis. In the afternoon of February 26, he left Ft. Defiance with three hundred twenty men and four cannon. About two hundred yards from town, while still in sight of the fort, one wagon broke down. The entire column stopped for repairs. About an hour later the caravan again crept toward the river. Before they could cross, two more wagons came apart. Again repairs were made. Once more they started forward, and once more they halted because it was decided the single yokes of oxen pulling the guns weren't strong enough to drag them across the river--more aimless hours of waiting around while the oxen were double-teamed. The crossing was slow and tedious. It was late afternoon when all the artillery was on the far bank. Now the men were weary, wet, and discouraged even more by a cold north wind that started blowing. Fannin decided to let them rest. After giving the command to "fall out," he discovered the ammunition wagon was still on the Goliad side of the river. What a comedy of errors!

Evening was fast approaching and Fannin made another bad decision. His troops couldn't march in the dark, so he reasoned they might as well camp for the night on the riverbank, starting fresh the next day. He ordered his troops to stack their arms and turn the oxen loose to graze--untethered.

A cold dawn on the 27th revealed the significance of his bad decision. The untethered oxen had wandered off and were nowhere to be seen. Fannin sent out scouts to find them. More precious hours were lost!

By midmorning Fannin received a request from some of his officers to hold a council of war. It was convened in some thick brush to partially block the biting wind. Some of the more hesitant officers raised the question--"Was this expedition really a wise idea?"

A few zealots were shocked. Fannin sided with those who had serious doubts about the wisdom of leaving Ft. Defiance. After all, he had attended West Point and knew something about logistics. He noted they were short of supplies (something he should have known before ever leaving the fort). He further stated there was only a little dried beef, a half barrel of rice, and no cattle to slaughter except those needed to draw the cannon. He concluded by saying the nearest supplies lay at Seguin's ranch some seventy miles away.

One of the officers asked if he was suggesting they ignore the Alamo's call for help. Fannin replied he sympathized and wanted to help; however, as a trained soldier he had been taught to look at military odds. Realistically, what could three hundred twenty volunteers with four cannon and little ammunition hope to accomplish against thousands of well-equipped and superbly trained Mexican troops? Furthermore, if they did go to San Antonio, Goliad would be left virtually undefended, exposing the Texans' entire left flank.

Fannin's professional use of words like "tactics," "left flank," and "logistics" ruled the day. Even the zealots were quieted. The guns and wagons were withdrawn across the river and the "relief expedition" trudged back up the hill to the old stone compound ridiculously named "Ft. Defiance." Thus ended the only chance Travis ever had of getting significant aid.

DAY 5 - FEBRUARY 27 - SATURDAY

The idea they were isolated and nobody cared began to invade the Texans' minds on this bitter cold Saturday, February 27. They pictured Fannin en route, hooves thundering to their aid. But the only thunder they heard was the Mexican cannons. Their weary minds also conjured up Houston riding west at the head of a huge army of volunteers. They did not know Houston was a commander-in-chief without an army and was somewhere in Indian country. Nerves were beginning to fray and even the normally jovial Crockett told Mrs. Dickinson, "I hate being hemmed in! I'd rather go outside and shoot it out with the Mexicans." Doubt was in everyone's mind. If only one of the many couriers sent out got through, he should be back by now saying help was on the way. Even Travis, staring at the fading white-wash on the walls of his room, wondered if his hopes for help weren't just that--fading. Why didn't Fannin come? Why didn't Houston come? Why didn't Governor Smith order them to come? Why--why--why?

His thoughts broken by rifle shots, Travis ran outside. The Mexicans were trying to block the acequia that supplied part of their water. Captain Jameson put some men to work on a half-finished well in the south end of the compound. The sharp-shooting Tennesseans dropped six of the enemy in rapid order and the rest fled. The defenders filled skin bags and tubs from the ditch, and some went back to complete the well.

Now Travis called Bonham to his room. Pouring two drinks he said, "Jim, I guess up to now we've both been rebels without a cause, but now we have one that's not only good enough to live for but to die for if we have to."

"I agree," said Bonham.

"My friend, will you go once more to ask Fannin's help? He's our only chance."

"You know I'll go, but that man can't make up his mind about anything."

"You must convince him, Jim. It's our last hope."

"I'll try my damndest, Will." Bonham answered as he turned to leave. Travis called him back.

"If you come back through the Mexican lines in daylight, you'll be riding hard. Tie this to your hatband so we'll know it's you." He handed Bonham a white handkerchief. Travis watched his friend ride out of the north postern into the night and wondered if he would ever see him again.

DAY 6 - FEBRUARY 28 - SUNDAY

By Sunday the norther had abated to be replaced by drizzle. A Mexican platoon was observed making another attempt to cut off water. Again, the deadly shooting of Crockett and his boys lessened their ranks, and the effort failed again. The defenders also

"THE HOUR THAT
167   *TRIED MEN'S SOULS"*

observed a new Mexican battery being placed by the old mill eight hundred yards to the north. Cannonading continued without let up. General Santa Anna's tactic of harassment was having its intended effect on the Texans.

David Crockett and a Scot by the name of John McGregor decided to try and cheer them up. Crockett with his fiddle and McGregor with his bagpipes staged a musical duel. The winner was McGregor, based upon the amount of noise that he created. But in spite of this cheerful interlude, the Alamo was now almost completely boxed and the defenders knew it. There were gun batteries to the northwest, southwest, south, west, and north, all on the Alamo side of the river. Only the east did not have a Mexican battery.

URREA CATCHES GRANT AND JOHNSON

Meanwhile, the other two principals in the ill-fated Matamoros expedition, Colonel Frank Johnson and Dr. James Grant, had left Goliad with about one hundred men to round up mustangs, much needed by Fannin. They in turn split up, each taking about fifty men. On February 28 Colonel Frank Johnson was at San Patricio. He was surprised by General Jose Urrea sweeping up the Texas coast to protect Santa Anna's flank. Johnson and a few others miraculously escaped, but the rest were massacred. Urrea then sought out and destroyed Dr. Grant's command at Agua Dulce Creek on March 2. There were no survivors. Johnson brought the news of both disasters to Goliad. Fannin was now convinced his action in aborting the Alamo relief effort was justifiable, but he failed to consider that Ft. Defiance was the next target of the hard-marching General Urrea.

Back at the Alamo, the men continued to hope for help. They figured Jim Bonham could reach Goliad by the 28th; and if Fannin and his men started shortly thereafter, they could arrive as soon as March 2 and certainly by March 3. Hope springs eternal for the doomed. Each day they spent endless hours peering over the parapets, gazing down the Goliad road and visualizing a phantom army led by Fannin.

DAY 7 - FEBRUARY 29 - MONDAY

The sun came up bright and warm. The cold north wind no longer whistled through the low barracks where Jim Bowie tossed and coughed on his cot. He asked to be moved outside to get some sun. However, a high gray overcast soon obscured the sun, but a mild southwesterly breeze warmed the old fort. The men needed this interlude. Their nerves were on edge from six nights of endless cannon fire, punctuated by shouts and wild bugle calls in the night, serving to keep the men edgy, constantly expecting a charge. Bitterness and discouragement were apparent, yet they hung on doggedly, proud of the reason they were there, bound together by a common peril and a common purpose. They shared a deep-down conviction that now was the time, and this was the place to make their stand for freedom. Each felt this damp, moss-covered old fort was really the womb from which the Republic of Texas would emerge, healthy and crying for nourishment. They sincerely felt sooner or later their compatriots in Gonzales, Goliad, San Felipe, Washington-on-the Brazos, and Velasco would come to their aid. Alas, except for Gonzales, it wasn't to be.

Today marked their first full week in the Alamo, and there was still no sign of help; but neither had there been an all-out Mexican assault. However, each morning as they looked across the parapets, they could see the Mexican earthworks and cannon had moved closer during the night. Even as they watched, a Mexican infantry battalion crossed the San Antonio River to the south, circled to their left, and passed the Gonzales Road to take up a position in the open brush just to the east. Then for no apparent reason, the same battalion marched back again over the same route. Darkness fell before the Texans could determine where the battalion finally ended up. Due to all of this maneuvering, they felt Santa Anna was making some kind of plans for attack; and so he was. He had heard Fannin was marching from Goliad, so he called on General Sesma to take the Allende battalion and the Delores cavalry and head for Goliad. However, long before Sesma reached Goliad, he learned through Mexican informants that Fannin had returned to Ft. Defiance, so he wheeled his troops and headed back to San Antonio.

DAY 8 - MARCH 1 - TUESDAY

In the little town of Gonzales, seventy miles east of San Antonio, recruitment of volunteers had commenced soon after the arrival of Dr. Sutherland and John W. Smith on February 24 with the news that the Alamo was under siege. Gonzales had earned a reputation for fighting, established in October 1835, when the "Come and Take It" taunt greeted the Mexican company under Lt.

"THE HOUR THAT TRIED MEN'S SOULS"

Francisco Castaneda. It is interesting to note two men now in the Alamo--Almeron Dickinson and Jacob Darst--participated in that fight and a third, Albert Martin, now on his way back to the Alamo also took part.

Reflecting this same "Come and Take It" attitude, thirty-two men from Gonzales were now going to the aid of the Alamo, under the command of Captain George C. Kimball. Although they knew their small number would be insufficient to stem the Mexican tide, they went anyway. A call had been received for help they could not ignore. The group set out from the town square at 2:00 p.m., February 27. John W. Smith was returning to the Alamo to guide them through the Mexican lines and then past the Texan outposts into the Alamo. Albert Martin, who had arrived in Gonzales February 25 with Travis' letter, "To the People of Texas and All Americans in the World," was among the thirty-two men. So was Galba Fuqua, another sixteen-year-old. Reaching the Alamo on March 1 about 3:00 a.m., in a pouring rain, the group slipped safely through the sleeping soldiers. The Alamo was immensely cheered by the new arrivals. They concluded if those thirty-two men could get through, so could Fannin.

DAY 9 - MARCH 2 - WEDNESDAY

UNKNOWN IN THE ALAMO--TEXAS DECLARES INDEPENDENCE

The ninth day of the siege dawned clear and cold with the thermometer at thirty-four degrees. The weary men in the Alamo were only aware of the heavy Mexican cannonading and did not know Texas independence had been declared that day--March 2, 1836--at Washington-on-the-Brazos.

Aware the Alamo couriers had been coming and going, Santa Anna directed a search be made for their routes. In the afternoon, a covered road was discovered within a pistol shot of the fortress. The Jimenes Battalion was ordered to guard it.

It has to be said Santa Anna was a bold and courageous leader, because he exposed himself to fire more than once as he inspected his lines and troops. However, he was sent scurrying once when his headquarters building came under fire from the 18-pounder. Whether opium-fortified or inherently brave, he was as fearless as he was ruthless. It is recorded he made personal inspections of the battlefield and entrenchments on both February 29 and March 1. Both times he was observed and shot at by the defenders, but he was

"THE HOUR THAT
TRIED MEN'S SOULS" 170

out of accurate rifle range; and by this time, the defenders were so short on powder that their cannons were not fired. They were saving the precious powder for the final assault.

The mood in the Alamo went from elation over the arrival the of the thirty-two men from Gonzales, to foreboding as the defenders watched the enemy move ever closer. They were now completely encircled, making it very doubtful any more messengers could get through the Mexican lines.

But they had not reckoned with the daring of Captain James Butler Bonham, who was riding hard across the prairie toward the Alamo. As he came through Gonzales from Goliad, he learned that thirty-two men had already left for the Alamo. Ignoring a grim warning from courier, Ben Highsmith who had barely escaped earlier, Bonham declared: "I will report the result of my mission to Travis or die in the attempt." (Bonham's ride: He covered 235 miles on horseback in five days--San Antonio to Goliad = 95 miles; Goliad to Gonzales = 65 miles; Gonzales to San Antonio = 75 miles. An average of 47 miles a day!)

DAY 10 - MARCH 3 - THURSDAY

Santa Anna's army was bolstered by the arrival of troops from General Antonio Gaona's brigade--the Tolucas "activos," the Aldama Battalion, and the crack unit of Zapadores. Now with 2,500 men, new batteries were placed closely around the Alamo. Another red flag was hoisted, this time on Powder House Hill.

At the very moment Colonel Juan Almonte was writing his sister that victory was near, he observed a lone horseman dashing on a frothing horse direct for the Alamo entrance by the corral. It was Bonham returning from his second trip to Goliad and Gonzales. He had Fannin's note of refusal in his pocket.

Only modern-day tracer bullets would have shown an observer how fortunate Bonham was to escape being hit as he bolted pell-mell toward the Alamo with the white handkerchief flying from his hatband. Cheers rose as he thundered inside, reporting back as promised.

Travis now gave up on any help from Fannin. If help was to come, it would have to be from other sources. He decided to make one last appeal direct to the President of the Convention at Washington-on-the-Brazos. To the intrepid scout, John W. Smith, he entrusted this desperate message which read in part:

"THE HOUR THAT
TRIED MEN'S SOULS"

...I look to the colonies alone for aid; unless it arrives soon I shall have to fight the enemy on his own terms. I will, however, do the best I can ... and although we may be sacrificed ... the victory will cost the enemy so dear, that it will be worse for him than defeat. I hope your   honorable body will hasten reinforcements....Our supply of ammunition is limited....God and Texas. Victory or Death.

William Barret Travis

After writing this official message, Travis then took time to write some personal letters. The first was so personal that only the outside instructions were ever known: "Do me the favor to send the enclosed to its proper destination instantly." Legend states that his message was to Rebecca Cummins in San Felipe.

The next letter was to his friend, Jesse Grimes, in which he explained his reasons for staying with the Alamo. Travis' last letter was to David Ayres, who boarded his young son, Charles. He wrote:

Take care of my little boy. If the country should be saved, I may make him a splendid fortune; but if the country should be lost and I should perish, he will have nothing but the proud recollection that he is the son of a man who died for his country.

As Smith saddled up, other defenders handed him letters to their families and friends. Now it was time to leave, but Travis had one last instruction: he would fire the 18-pounder three times a day--morning, noon and night--as long as the Alamo stood. As long as these shots were heard, they would know he was still fighting.

It was almost midnight when John W. Smith mounted his horse for his final ride from the Alamo. The northern postern was opened and a few Texans slipped outside and worked their way north a short distance where they began firing as a diversionary tactic. Meanwhile, Smith dashed through the gate, reined his horse eastward, and vanished in the pale moonlight.

DAY 11 - MARCH 4 - FRIDAY

Mexican batteries continued to fire into the Alamo, making effective hits on the north and west walls. Their infantry was entrenched now on all sides. That night General Santa Anna called a staff meeting at which he declared his intention of making a full-scale assault on the Alamo. General Sesma and Colonel Almonte joined the Generalissimo in favor; but his brother-in-law, General Cos, General Manuel Fernandez Castrillon, and Colonel Jose Maria Romero opposed, arguing they should wait until the two 12-pounders arrived on March 7. They warned him that unless the walls were breached, assaulting the walls with ladders would be disastrous. Santa Anna overruled all objections saying, "I did not invite you here to ask your opinion but rather tell you mine. Less than two hundred perfidious foreigners are defying the 'Napoleon of the West.' Hear me, gentlemen, they must be quashed and now!"

Through his native spy network, Santa Anna knew the colonists had held a meeting March 2 to declare their independence and now planned to appeal for help from the United States. Before they could pull themselves together and get such help, he had to hit them. He had already lost ten days sieging this measly fort, and he felt every day Sam Houston grew stronger. In fact, the Alamo was a cocklebur in his blanket of well-laid plans to drive the Texas rebels beyond the Sabine and end the revolution.

Ben, his American Negro cook, later reported a conversation he overheard between Santa Anna and Colonel Almonte in which the latter told Santa Anna, "General, the cost will be high."

"The cost doesn't matter; it must be done! The assault, gentlemen, will begin Sunday at dawn. This is my order of battle. Make copies for all commanders involved. Tell them to study it carefully and prepare their troops accordingly."

DAY 12 - MARCH 5 - SATURDAY

General Santa Anna's battle plan was ready by 2:00 p.m., March 5, and copies prepared by Secretary Ramon Caro for all commanders involved in the assault.

GENERAL SANTA ANNA'S ORDER OF BATTLE
The following is a translation of General Santa Anna's order of March 5, 1836, by Juan Valentine Amador.

"THE HOUR THAT
173   *TRIED MEN'S SOULS"*

General Order of March 5th, 1836, 2:00 p.m. To the Generals, Chiefs of Sections and Corps Commanders:

Being necessary to act decisively upon the enemy defending The Alamo, the Most Excellent General-In-Chief has ordered that tomorrow at four o'clock the attacking columns, placed at short distance from the first trenches, undertake the assault to begin with a signal given by the General by means of the sounding of a bugle from the North battery.

General D. Martin Perfecto de Cos will command the First Column. If he cannot, I will. The Permanent Battalion, Aldama, with the exception of the Grenadier Company and the three first Active Companies of San Luis, will form the First Column. The Second Column will be commanded by Colonel D. Francisco Duque. If he cannot, by General D. Manuel Fernandez Castrillon. The Active Battalion, Toluca, and the three Active Rifle Companies, San Luis, with the exception of the Grenadier Company, will form this Second Column.

Colonel D. Jose Maria Romero will command the Third. If he cannot, Colonel D. Mariano de Salas. The Rifle Companies from the Permanent Battalion, Matamoros and Jimenez, will form this column.

The Fourth will be commanded by D. Juan Morales. If he cannot, by Colonel D. Jose Minon. It will be formed by the Scouting Companies from the Permanent Battalions, Matamoros and Jimenez, and the Active Battalion, San Luis.

The points from which these columns will mount their attacks will be designated by the General-In-Chief at the opportune time, and then the Column Commanders will receive their orders.

The reserves will be formed by the Sapper Battalion and the five Grenadier Companies from the Permanent Battalions, Matamoros, Jimenez and Aldama, plus the Active Battalions, Toluca and

San Luis. The reserve force will be commanded by the General-In-Chief at the moment of attack; but the gathering of this force will be carried out by Colonel D. Augustin Amat, under whose orders the reserves will remain from this afternoon until they are placed in positions to be designated.

The First Column will carry ten scaling ladders, two crowbars and two axes; the same number by the second; six ladders by the third, and two by the fourth.

The men carrying the ladders will sling their rifles on their backs until the ladders are properly placed.

The Companies of Grenadiers and Scouts will carry ammunition at six rounds per man and at four the riflemen, and two flints in reserve. These men will not wear cloaks, carry blankets, or anything else which will inhibit them to maneuver quickly. During the day all shako chin-straps will be correctly worn--these the Commanders will watch closely. The troops will wear shoes or sandals. The attacking troops will turn in after the night's prayers as they will form their columns at midnight.

The untrained recruits will remain in the camps. All armaments will be in good shape--especially the bayonets.

As soon as the moon rises, the riflemen of the Active Battalion, San Luis, will move back to their quarters to get their equipment ready; this will be done by leaving their stations in line.

The Cavalry, under the command of General D. Joaquin Ramirez y Sesma, will occupy the Alameda and will saddle up at three o'clock in the morning. Their duty will be to guard the camp and keep anyone from deserting.

Take this into consideration: Against the daring foreigners opposing us, the Honor of our Nation and Army is at stake. His Supreme Excellency, the General-In-Chief, expects each man to fulfill his duties and to exert himself to give his country a day of glory and satisfaction. He well

"THE HOUR THAT TRIED MEN'S SOULS"

knows how to reward those brave men who form the
Army of Operations.

General Santa Anna

"STEP ACROSS THE LINE"

During the day the Mexican batteries to the north moved even
closer. Miraculously after twelve days of bombardment, not a
single defender had been killed. Strangely, the Mexican
cannonade began to taper off at noon, and by mid afternoon there
was total quiet. Colonel Travis assembled his men, single file, in
the plaza. He positioned himself at front and center. For a moment
he stood silently, looking up and down the line. For the past two
hours he had steeled himself for the following address (excerpt
from the speech reconstructed by William P. Zuber):

Gentlemen:

My pleas for help have fallen on deaf ears. Our
choices are clear. We can surrender and betray the
dream of independence. We can try to escape and
suffer the shame of one who runs from his enemy.
Or we can remain and face a destiny that is certain
doom.

But we shall die for the cause of liberty and
freedom; and although we may be sacrificed, the
victory will cost the enemy so dearly, that it will be
worse for him than defeat.

For me, I shall stay in this fort and fight as
long as there is breath in my body. And this I will do
even if you leave me alone.

But if I am destined to die, let my scabbard be
empty and my sword red with the blood of men who
would deny freedom.

With these words Travis took his sword in hand and walked the
full length of the file of men in front of him, scribing a fine line in
the packed dirt of the Alamo.

"Those who choose to stay and die with me, step
over this line."

"THE HOUR THAT
TRIED MEN'S SOULS" 176

(Author's note: It has been presented by some authors that five to seven of these valiant men survived the coming battle and surrendered only to be promptly executed. I can find no irrefutable evidence that this is true. It is possible some of the badly wounded from the Battle of Bexar, in the hospital at the Alamo, were taken alive and immediately executed. But little does it matter how each man died; they all, in effect, died when they stepped across the line.)

Immediately there was movement. First came Tapley Holland, leaping over. Then came Jim Bonham, followed by David Crockett and his volunteers, Micajah Autry, Gregorio Esparza, Almeron Dickinson, and all the others--only Bowie and Louis "Moses" Rose remained. Bowie raised his pain-racked body on one elbow saying, "Carry me across, boys!" Now "Moses" stood alone. He was twice the age of many who had crossed the line (therefore, the nickname, "Moses"). He had served with Napoleon and survived the retreat from Russia. He had come to America to live--not die. The silence was broken by Bowie, his old friend. "Aren't you willing to die with us, Moses?"

"No, Jim," he replied, "I'm not prepared to die, and I shall not do so if I can avoid it." His eyes measured the height of the nearest wall. He sprang forward and climbed to the top. Turning, he looked down briefly at his doomed friends and leaped to the ground.

Travis thanked all the defenders and dismissed them. Then he stood alone, looking at the line he had drawn in the dirt. The thought occurred to him that it was just a shallow line which would soon be obliterated by the shuffling feet of the defenders. He did not realize when drawing that thin line, it would deepen with time and tales until it was etched into the bedrock of human emotions. Some historians have tried to purge it from their pages, but they will never expunge it from the imagination of students, teachers, orators, adventurers, writers, and patriots. Long live the line!

Travis now retired to his low-ceilinged room and lit a candle. He watched the flickering light reflect from his cat's-eye ring. His thoughts went back to Alabama, Rosanna, and his own little daughter. After a few moments, he removed the ring and reaching for a nearby piece of string, made a small necklace. He arose and went directly to the quarters of Mrs. Dickinson. Little Angelina, who was just learning to walk, toddled to him, grasping one of his boots with both hands. Travis bent over, swooped her up, and kissed her. Reaching into his pocket he pulled out the ring necklace and

"THE HOUR THAT TRIED MEN'S SOULS"

slipped it over Angelina's head saying to Susanna, "I'd like her to have this. I don't think I'll be needing it."

Travis went back to his room and hurriedly drafted another appeal to Fannin. Travis didn't believe it would do any good, but he felt he had to try. He called for young James Allen.

Soon young Allen stood before him. Travis handed him the message saying, "James, get this through to Colonel Fannin; it's our last hope." Travis walked with young Allen as he led his horse toward the postern. Travis spoke. "James, from Goliad go to all the colonies. Tell the people Texas can be a republic, but it will require greater courage to declare for independence than to stand defiantly in these old walls and die."

"And remember, James, whatever happens, wherever you go, carry this message forth--*freedom rests finally upon those willing to die for it.*"

Travis ordered the north postern opened a final time. The daring young man dashed through the gate, riding bareback without even a bridle. Racing safely through the Mexican lines, Allen vanished into the darkening night--the last messenger to leave the Alamo.

A priest of San Fernando moved along the line of kneeling Mexican soldiers, blessing each one. Finally he came to Francisco Esparza, brother of Gregorio. Making the sign of the cross before addressing the padre, Francisco implored, "Father, my brother, Gregorio, fights in the Alamo. Will you pray that I do not kill my brother?" The priest laid his hand on Francisco's head and prayed.

Back at command headquarters, Travis wrapped himself in his blanket and turned in, a shotgun and sword by his side. His faithful servant, Joe, was asleep across the room.

The night was very dark as the moon had not risen. The Mexican cannons fired only sporadically all afternoon and as night approached, they ceased altogether. Just after dark, three exhausted defenders went out of the fort as pickets to keep watch against a surprise attack. The unusual quiet of the night tranquilized the sentries, and soon they were asleep. They were rudely awakened at three in the morning by their relief; but they, too, fell asleep, their weary minds and bodies succumbing to the silence of the first night without bombardment since the siege began. They would never open their eyes again, for about 4:00 a.m. stealthy Mexican scouts, crawling silently, put their tired bodies to eternal rest with single, deep thrusts of their daggers. The sleeping defenders inside the Alamo would now have no pre-warning of the coming attack.

DAY 13 - MARCH 6, 1836, 5:00 A. M. - SUNDAY

THE FALL OF THE ALAMO

A red glow was beginning to appear in the eastern sky, a harbinger of the blood that would soon stain the ground around the Alamo, collect in pools on her earthen floor, spatter her walls and gun barbettes, discolor the uniforms and clothing of both attacker and attacked, and soak the bed and bedding of the sick and wounded.

Some 1,800 Mexican soldiers were tensely coiled with an excitement that was almost irrepressible, knowing at any minute the staccato notes of a bugle would propel them en masse toward the old fort they had waited for thirteen days to take.

The signal to the first bugler would come from Santa Anna himself. He now raised his white-gloved right hand and would drop it as a signal to the bugler. He looked toward Almonte and nodded.

Suddenly from the ranks, a shout, "Viva Santa Anna!" Others took up the cry, and it rolled like an avalanche through the ranks. His Excellency knew the time had come. The cheers had already cost the edge of surprise. He dropped his hand. The shrill notes of the blood-curdling strains of "Deguello," the traditional Spanish march of "no quarter"--of throat-cutting and merciless death, penetrated the chillness of the early morning air. Other buglers took up the sound, and it rolled around the periphery of the Alamo like an echo. Eighteen hundred yelling men surged forward. Ten cannons shook the ground in synchronized thunder, their eerie flashes reflecting off the white-fatigue uniforms of the Mexican hordes now surging toward the silent, silhouetted walls of the Alamo. Each cannonball trailed sparks in the heavens as it gracefully arched its course of death and destruction.

The massed bands of all the battalions now simultaneously blared the Deguello, and this brought a faint smile to the lips of the Generalissimo as he watched his troops rolling forward like water.

On the north Alamo wall a sleepy Captain John Baugh stared into the erupting bedlam surrounding him. He was accustomed to alarms in the night--but nothing ever like this. There was no signal from the pickets posted outside the walls, and the din in front of him could mean only one thing--they were already dead. He

"THE HOUR THAT
TRIED MEN'S SOULS"

raced for the barracks crying for all to hear, "Colonel Travis! Everybody! The Mexicans are attacking!"

Travis, sleeping fully clothed, bolted from his blanket and called to Joe. Then he grabbed his double-barreled shotgun, belted on his sword, and dashed across the plaza yelling, "Come on, boys; the Mexicans are upon us, and we'll give them hell!" He passed a group of Juan Seguin's loyal Texans including Juan Abamillo, Carlos Espalier, and Antonio Fuentes. (Nine Tejanos would die that morning.) Travis, still running, shouted in Spanish, "No rendirse, muchachos; no rendirse!" He leaped to the barbette of the north battery and looked out over the wall. He could only see mass movement, but the yells, bugles, and exploding shells told the story only too clearly.

Already the Mexicans had set two of their scaling ladders against the wall which now were loaded with clamoring soldiers. Travis kicked one ladder backward, then fired his shotgun point blank down the other. Suddenly he was spun around by a musket ball in the forehead, fired from the semi-darkness. He slid to the floor of the gun barbette and down a bank of earth that had been piled against the inside wall. Travis ended up in a sitting position, looking back up the slope and braced against a post. He was mortally wounded but still firmly clutched his sword. The Mexicans had set another ladder. Led by a Mexican officer of high rank, he leaped over the wall into the gun barbette and stared at the fallen Travis. Raising his sword, the officer raced down the slope to deliver a fatal blow. Travis waited until the last second and thrust his own sword through the officer's body which fell upon him. An unbelieving Captain John Baugh rushed up to his dying commander, rolled the dead officer's body aside, and lifted Travis' head just in time to hear his last words, "Never surrender!" One of the first to die in defense of the Alamo, William Barret Travis would have been twenty-seven on August 1 of that immortal year.

The Alamo was now alive with rifle and cannon fire. Eight-year-old Enrique Esparza covered his ears as the 12-pounders thundered into action. In the barbettes, Captain Dickinson's artillerymen blasted grape and canister into the on-rushing horde. Damacio Jimenes and other Hispanic Texans--Andres Nava, Juan A. Badillo Toribio Losoya, and Jose Maria Guerrero--were spread throughout the compound. (Losoya had grown up inside these walls--and here he would die.) Some of these men helped man the 18-pound cannon, others the 12-pounders in back of the chapel, or the smaller cannon elsewhere.

All Texans were now at their posts, and each had four or five guns loaded and ready. The women and children huddled in the chapel. Private John took his position on the wall.

In the seclusion of the dark sacristy of the Alamo church, Susanna Dickinson heard the rising crescendo of the battle. She held Angelina tighter as the tumult outside her door intensified. Suddenly the door was flung open and 16-year-old Galba Fuqua of Gonzales burst into the room. He was pale and haggard as blood trickled through his fingers held over his mouth. A bullet had shattered both jaws. His eyes were screaming but no words were uttered. He gurgled something to Mrs. Dickinson, but she could not understand. Desperately, she pressed his jaws together; and he tried again to speak; nothing but blood came from his mouth. Gesturing, he indicated for her to wrap his jaws with a bandage. She quickly tore the hem from Angelina's dress and fitted it around the boy's jaws and head. This youth of uncommon valor turned and rushed back into the fight where he gave his life before he had a chance to live it.

To Santa Anna, standing behind the protection of the earthwork to the north, the whole fort now seemed lit by blazing gunpowder. He saw his columns pushing into this barrage of fire--brave soldiers charging into the face of almost certain death for the honor of Mexico. To the east and north his troops had been stopped, pinned down by the long-range accuracy of the Kentucky rifles and salvos from the 18-pounder. On the southwest, two blasts of grape shot from Captain Dickinson's guns ripped into Morales' troops. Over forty men went down. On the northeast another blast took out half a company. The battalion commander, Colonel Francisco Duque, fell with a broken leg. Surging troops, pushing forward, trampled his body like hay under the hooves of stampeding cattle.

A few Mexican soldiers reached the walls but were cut down by shotgun blasts. Not one ladder stayed up. The attackers wavered, then fell back. Their shouting and cursing officers urged them forward a second time--and again they were met head on with the Texans deadly fire. They stumbled, halted, and again retreated.

A third time they came. Now they were yelling and shouting, "Viva Santa Anna!" and "Viva la Republica!" Colonel Romero's column on the east was hard hit and again stopped, but he would not let them retreat. He shifted his men to the right and mixed them with the Duque battalion (now led by General Castrillon) on the north. At the same time General Cos' column had been stopped on the northwest corner, but now he veered to the left, also ending up

181

"THE HOUR THAT
TRIED MEN'S SOULS"

with the Duque battalion. This had the effect of a single, unplanned, throng of men--all surging toward the north wall. The charge ended up in a confused mass under the wall, safe from cannon fire but easy targets for the Texas rifles and shotguns right above them. Bullets rained down like hail. They continued to squeeze together and in the dust and semi-darkness fired blindly, more often hitting friend than foe. Unable to clearly see the soldiers in front, troops in the back killed many of their comrades. Most of those carrying the scaling ladders were either killed or trampled.

Santa Anna, looking on from his vantage point, was seeing his Napoleonic warfare tactics fail before his eyes. He had personally planned all the details, assigning the twenty-eight scaling ladders and working out the four-column charge--a model military operation taken right out of Napoleon's manual--and now utter chaos.

He barked orders to Colonel Augustin Amat, "Commit the reserves!" These were the experienced grenadiers and the tough Zapadores--pride of the Mexican army. Eager to see action, they charged across the rough ground around the Alamo wall, firing and shouting. Again Santa Anna called for the massed bands to strike up the Deguello. This time His Excellency would see his troops go over the northern wall, aided unintentionally by Captain Green B. Jameson. During the siege Jameson had tried to strengthen a breach in this wall by building a timbered structure to reinforce the crumbling stone on the outside. Inadvertently, he had constructed a large rough ladder, thinking it would be impossible to climb. But the Mexicans proved him wrong. Up this hodge-podge lattice of logs and lumber, they climbed, grasping at the chink holes and log ends, falling back only to be pushed forward as easy targets for the Texans above. But still they came and eventually the Texans, even with four or five guns each, couldn't stem the tide surging over the wall. The first group of Mexican soldiers that rolled onto the north gun barbette was led by Lieutenant Colonel Juan Amador, who only realized a brief moment of glory before taking a bullet through the head.

General Cos, exasperated with the mass of men at the north wall, ordered an oblique movement and attacked the west wall. His men were now bunched at the north end, flanking the gun battery overhead. The wall still had to be scaled, and there were no wooden structures here to climb. Worse, the troops carrying the ladders were either dead or missing. However, the Texans again had unintentionally aided Santa Anna. At several points along this wall, they had made embrasures to fire through. Unfortunately, for the defenders, these embrasures were large enough for the small Mexican soldiers to squirm through. They scrambled through the openings like sheep--faster than the Texans could dispatch them. To make matters worse for the defenders, the northern postern had been forced open, and the surge of Mexicans was like water through a breached dam.

Almeron Dickinson, seeing what was happening, and rushed into the sacristy where his trembling wife, Susanna, sat holding Angelina. "Great God they are inside our walls! Sue, if you're spared, save our child, and tell her how much I love her." He embraced them before rushing back to his guns on top of the church. When he arrived, his men had already turned the cannons and depressed them to fire point blank at the enemy inside the fort. Other gun squads did the same, and grape shot ripped the Mexican ranks from two directions.

This "shooting of birds in a rain barrel" was brief as a fourth Mexican column charged the south side, wisely passing up the palisade defended staunchly by Crockett's Tennesseans. Now all walls leaked Mexicans like flour through a sifter, and soon Morales' men had their chance. Taking refuge in jacales near the southwest corner, they quickly regrouped and charged across a short, open distance to the fort where they ascended the barbette up to the 18-pounder. They were upon the stunned Texans before they could react and after a few bayonet thrusts by Morales' men, the big cannon went over to the Mexican army.

Gregorio Esparza died at one of the two 12-pound cannon mounted atop the Alamo. Later, his son, Enrique(who survived), said his father was killed in the church near the south window. (Other survivors included Juana Navarro Alsbury, Gertrudis Navarro, Trinidad Saucedo, Petra Gonzales, Susanna and Little Angelina Dickinson, Gregoria's wife Ana, the other three Esparza children, Joe - Travis' slave, and Sam - Bowie's slave.

Now the Mexicans were scrambling over the west wall of the plaza, and Morales' troops charged the main gate from the inside, opening it to those attacking from the front. A virtual avalanche of flashing bayonets surged in. The surviving defenders desperately fought in all directions, shooting at every target of opportunity. There was now no semblance of resistance on the north wall; Romero's and Castrillon's columns flowed into the Plaza, joining with Morales' men coming in through the main gate. The Texans

"THE HOUR THAT TRIED MEN'S SOULS"

continued to fight, giving ground foot by foot. Most were out of ammunition but fought with gun butts, knives, tomahawks, fists, and feet. The attackers were equally tenacious--shooting, clubbing, and bayoneting anyone not in a Mexican uniform.

Crockett and his Tennessee boys, cornered near the palisade, fought with a savage fury. But raw courage is never a shield; and one by one these paladins perished. Apparently, David Crockett died as he lived--defending with his life the principles he believed to be right.

Long after the battle, one of the Mexicans, a sergeant Felix Nunez of the Aldama battalion said, "One I remember, a tall man with buckskin coat and a fur cap with a foxtail attached, fought like a cornered cougar. He must have been charmed, as many of our soldiers fired with deliberate aim and missed, yet he killed at least eight of us and wounded many more. He was finally felled by a saber blow to the head by one of our officers and slumped to his knees. Immediately, he was pierced by not less than ten bayonets." (For different authors' versions of Crockett's death, see Appendix.)

Some of the Texans had retreated to the barracks where the doorways had been blocked by hides stitched together and filled with earth and high enough for protection to fire a rifle. The defenders who had retreated there took up positions behind these new parapets and fired point blank at the on-rushing hordes. The Mexicans wavered and scattered, looking for cover; but there was none in the open plaza. They fell in heaps and their co-mingled blood ran red and steaming in the cold early morning light. General Castrillon, now atop the north wall, could see his troops were again being cut to pieces. He knew something had to be done and quickly. On order his men swung around the two cannon in the north barbette.

On the southwest wall, Colonel Morales had also turned the big 18-pounder, and it completely devastated the long barracks and all therein.

Bowie, sick and secluded in his darkened room like a wounded bear, lay in wait. He listened to the thunder and din of battle outside his door. He knew it would soon open. He had made peace with God and prayed he would see his beloved Ursula again. With a brace of pistols Crockett had given him cocked and ready, he silently hoped whoever opened the door had made the same preparation to meet his Maker. He would use his last energies to see that they did. Suddenly there were shouts and footsteps; and as the door was flung open, Bowie's two pistols fired as one. The three foremost men, one carrying a torch for light, crumpled in the threshold, the flickering torch giving the room an eerie light. But the multitude behind surged in; and the once-great body of Jim Bowie was pierced with at least eight bayonets. They lifted his body aloft like fodder, his blood ran streaming down their upstretched arms. (For different authors' versions of Bowie's death, see Appendix.)

Now the battle began to wane and Lieutenant Jose Maria Torres of the Zapadores battalion suddenly noticed on the Alamo roof a strange flag gently fluttering in the first rays of sunshine. He couldn't read the English words emblazoned thereon and didn't know what they said; but it certainly wasn't Spanish. He was determined to replace it with his own country's flag and raced to the Alamo roof only to find the corpses of several of his comrades who had tried before him to bring the Texans' flag down--each had been shot by the mortally wounded Jim Bonham, who was determined to keep it flying. Torres quickly stepped over and around the bodies, slashed the rope securing the flag mast, letting the flag and mast fall to the roof. He quickly cut off the enemy flag and attached the national emblem of Mexico. He was about to tie off the raised mast when he buckled with a bullet in his chest fired by the dying Bonham. Torres' body, his fists clenching the mast, slowly slid to the Alamo roof--pulling down his own flag to cover his lifeless form like a sheet. Quickly, a sergeant grabbed the mast from the fallen officer's hands and again raised the Mexican flag.

Now there was quiet. No more shooting, shouting, cursing, or screaming--just an eerie silence as soft sun rays started to illuminate the ghastly scene of death and destruction that covered the ground both inside and outside the Alamo. The hush was broken only now and then by moans of the wounded Mexicans and dying Texans.

The eyes of the surviving attackers looked upward to their flag, waving in a gentle breeze and emblazoned by the morning sun. Wild cheering now broke the silence. What a price had been paid for the glory of that moment!

But, apparently, Santa Anna thought it minimal. Riding through the carnage, he was accompanied by the Alcalde Francisco Antonio Ruiz and the slave, Joe, to identify for His Excellency the bodies of Travis, Bowie, and Crockett. The corpse of Travis was pointed out, the young commander's hand still clutching his sword. Santa Anna looked downward. Slowly he removed the sword from Travis' hand with the toe of his boot.

Captain Fernando Urizza approached, saluted, and said, "Congratulations on a great victory, your Excellency." Santa Anna, shrugged and without returning the salute replied, "It was just a small affair."

His remark was heard by Colonel Almonte, who whispered to Colonel Morales, "One more such small affair, and we are ruined." There were over six hundred Mexican dead and wounded, one-third of all the attackers, and some of them the cream of the Mexican army. It would take weeks for the survivors to recuperate, and many of their severely wounded never would.

Captain Urizza then asked Santa Anna, "Your Excellency, what shall we do with the bodies?"

He curtly replied, "Burn them all! Order your men to start gathering timber. The cavalry will drag the bodies, but the infantry will secure the ropes and stack them. Be certain not one of our valiant soldiers is on the pyre even if every face has to be wiped clean!"

Francisco Esparza heard the order. He desperately searched for and found his brother's body. Then with his widowed sister-in-law, Ana, he pleaded with Santa Anna to give Gregorio a Christian burial. In a rare moment of benevolence, Santa Anna agreed, and Gregorio Esparza thus became the only defender so honored. He was buried in the Campo Santo (cemetery) just west of the San Fernando Church.

Despite the statement from His Excellency, it was no "small affair." It forever changed the course of history. Those thirteen days bought precious time for General Sam Houston to rally his army. Seven weeks later, Santa Anna was crushed in humiliating defeat at San Jacinto by Houston's smaller force...a force driven by the burning passion and resounding cry of "Remember the Alamo." That immortal clarion call would echo through the canyons of time and inspire future generations of Texans and other Americans as they defended freedom on battlefields all over the world.

(Courtesy of DRT Research Library at the Alamo)

THE ALAMO--*may we never forget and forever may it stand as a shrine to the Price of Freedom!*

"THE HOUR THAT TRIED MEN'S SOULS"

HEROES OF THE ALAMO

NAME	BIRTHPLACE
Juan Abamillo	Texas
James R. Allen	unkknown
Mills DeForest Andross	Vermont
Micajah Autry	North Carolina
Juan A. Badillo	Texas
Peter James Bailey	Kentucky
Isaac G. Baker	Arkansas
William Charles M. Baker	Missouri
John J. Ballentine	unknown
Robert W. Ballentine	Scotland
John J. Baugh	Virginia
Joseph Bayliss	Tennessee
John Blair	Tennessee
Samuel C. Blair	Tennessee
William Blazeby	England
James Butler Bonham	South Carolina
Daniel Bourne	England
James Bowie	Tennessee
Jesse B. Bowman	unknown
George Brown	England
James Brown	Pennsylvania
Robert Brown	unknown
James Buchanan	Alabama
Samuel E. Burns	Ireland
George D. Butler	Missouri
Robert Campbell	Tennessee
John Cane	Pennsylvania
William R. Carey	Virginia
Charles Henry Clark	Missouri
M. B. Clark	unknown
Daniel William Cloud	Kentucky
Robert E. Cochran	New Jersey
George Washington Cottle	Tennessee
Henry Courtman	Germany
Lemuel Crawford	South Carolina
David Crockett	Tennessee
Robert Crossman	Massachusetts
David P. Cummings	Pennsylvania

NAME	BIRTHPLACE
Robert Cunningham	New York
Jacob C. Darst	Kentucky
John Davis	Kentucky
Freeman H. K. Day	unknown
Jerry C. Day	Missouri
Squire Daymon	Tennessee
William Dearduff	Tennessee
Stephen Dennison	England
Charles Despallier	Louisiana
Almeron Dickinson	Tennessee
John H. Dillard	Tennessee
James R. Dimpkins	England
Lewis Duel	New York
Andrew Duvalt	Ireland
Carlos Espalier	Texas
Gregorio Esparza	Texas
Robert Evans	Ireland
Samuel B. Evans	New York
James L. Ewing	Tennessee
William Fishbaugh	Alabama
John Flanders	Massachusetts
Dolphin Ward Floyd	North Carolina
John Hubbard Forsyth	New York
Antonio Fuentes	Texas
Galba Fuqua	Alabama
William H. Furtleroy	Kentucky
William Garnett	Tennessee
James W. Garrand	Louisiana
James Girard Garrett	Tennessee
John E. Garvin	unknown
John E. Gaston	Kentucky
James George	unknown
John Calvin Goodrich	Tennessee
Albert Calvin Grimes	Georgia
Jose Maria Guerrero	Texas
James C. Gwynne	England
James Hannum	unknown
John Harris	Kentucky
Andrew Jackson Harrison	unknown
William B. Harrison	Ohio

NAME	BIRTHPLACE
Charles M. Haskell (Heiskell)	Tennessee
Joseph M. Hawkins	Ireland
John M. Hays	Tennessee
Patrick Henry Herndon	Virginia
William D. Hersee	England
Tapley Holland	Ohio
Samuel Holloway	Pennsylvania
William D. Howell	Massachusetts
William Daniel Jackson	Ireland
Thomas Jackson	Ireland
Green B. Jameson	Kentucky
Gordon C. Jennings	Connecticut
Damacio Jimenes	Texas
Lewis Johnson	Wales
William Johnson	Pennsylvania
John Jones	New York
Johnnie Kellog	unknown
James Kenney	Virginia
Andrew Kent	Kentucky
Joseph Kerr	Louisiana
George C. Kimball (Kimble)	New York
William P. King	unknown
William Irvine Lewis	Virginia
William J. Lightfoot	Virginia
Jonathan L. Lindley	Illinois
William Linn	Massachusetts
Toribio D. Losoya	Texas
George Washington Main	Virginia
William T. Malone	Virginia
William Marshall	Tennessee
Albert Martin	Rhode Island
Edward McCafferty	unknown
Jesse McCoy	Tennessee
William McDowell	Pennsylvania
James McGee	Ireland
John McGregor	Scotland
Robert McKinney	Ireland
Eliel Melton	Georgia
Thomas R. Miller	Tennessee
William Mills	Tennessee

NAME	BIRTHPLACE
Isaac Millsaps	Mississippi
Edward F. Mitchusson	Virginia
Edwin T. Mitchell	Georgia
Napoleon B. Mitchell	unknown
Robert B. Moore	Virginia
Willis Moore	Mississippi
Robert Musselman	Ohio
Andres Nava	Texas
George Neggan	South Carolina
Andrew M. Nelson	Tennessee
Edward Nelson	South Carolina
George Nelson	South Carolina
James Northcross	Virginia
James Nowlan	Ireland
George Pagan	Mississippi
Christopher Parker	Mississippi
William Parks	North Carolina
Richardson Perry	unknown
Amos Pollard	Massachusetts
John Purdy Reynolds	Pennsylvania
Thomas H. Roberts	unknown
James Robertson	Tennessee
Isaac Robinson	Scotland
James M. Rose	Virginia
Jackson J. Rusk	Ireland
Joseph Rutherford	Kentucky
Isaac Ryan	Louisiana
Mial Scurlock	North Carolina
Marcus L. Sewell	England
Manson Shied	Georgia
Cleveland Kinlock Simmons	South Carolina
Andrew H. Smith	Tennessee
Charles S. Smith	Maryland
Joshua G. Smith	North Carolina
William H. Smith	unknown
Richard Starr	England
James E. Stewart	England
Richard L. Stockton	Virginia
A. Spain Summerlin	Tennessee
William E. Summers	Tennessee

NAME	BIRTHPLACE
William D. Sutherland	Alabama
Edward Taylor	Tennessee
George Taylor	Tennessee
James Taylor	Tennessee
William Taylor	Tennessee
B. Archer M. Thomas	Kentucky
Henry Thomas	Germany
Jesse G. Thompson	Arkansas
John W. Thomson	North Carolina
John M. Thruston	Pennsylvania
Burke Trammel	Ireland
William Barret Travis	South Carolina
George W. Tumlinson	Missouri
James Tylee	New York
Asa Walker	Tennessee
Jacob Walker	Tennessee
William B. Ward	Ireland
Henry Warnell	Arkansas
Joseph G. Washington	Tennessee
Thomas Waters	England
William Wells	Georgia
Isaac White	Kentucky
Robert White	unknown
Hiram J. Williamson	Pennsylvania
William Wills	unknown
David L. Wilson	Scotland
John Wilson	Pennsylvania
Anthony Wolfe	England
Claiborne Wright	North Carolina
Charles Zanco	Denmark
Pvt. John, (a volunteer Black)	unknown (probably PA.)

APPENDIX

APPENDIX

THE MANY DEATHS OF BOWIE AND CROCKETT
A collection of various authors' versions
by
George A. McAlister

After twelve years of research and study on the Battle of the Alamo, this author is left with many unanswered questions. Two of these concern David Crockett and James Bowie. The life of each man is well-known, but there are many versions of how each met his death on March 6, 1836. What really happened this day at the Alamo, simply stated is--no one knows. I believe this conclusion is very well illustrated in a 1979 speech to the Texas State Historical Association by Dan Kilgore, author of the book, How Did David Die? The speech is excerpted as follows:

A haze of myth and legend blankets the most memorable event of Texas history, the fall of the Alamo and the slaughter of its heroic defenders. Reuben M. Potter, who wrote the first serious study of the battle, (The Fall of the Alamo, 1860) defined the situation clearly in the opening paragraph of his work published twenty-four years after the battle. He stated.

Details of the final assault have never been fully and correctly narrated, and wild exaggerations have taken their place in popular legend. The reason will be obvious when it is remembered that not a single combatant of the last struggle from within the fort survived to tell the tale, while the official reports of the enemy were neither circumstantial nor reliable. When horror is intensified by mystery, the sure product is romance.

Captain Potter's assessment rings just as true today as when written in 1860, a hundred and nineteen years ago.

Although the Alamo epic yet remains a mass of myth and legend, the public cherishes the story as they know it and will tolerate no changes. Twice in recent years waves of protest greeted publications saying that Davy Crockett either surrendered or was captured and then was immediately executed in the closing moments of the assault. As the author of one of these works, I have a sheaf of letters and newspaper clippings expressing outrage that anyone could even suggest that Crockett did not go down fighting.

If the above needs augmentation, it is found in the words of historian, James Atkins Shackford, (David Crockett: The Man and the Legend, 1956) considered by most to be the definitive author on David Crockett when he wrote, "Except for the date and the fact of its fall, there is almost no single point...upon which testimony of the few survivors does not disagree."

To give interested writers and historians a quick reference source on various authors' versions of the deaths of Bowie and Crockett, I have compiled the following bibliography which may be helpful but admittedly is far from complete. Any further material on this subject which comes to my attention will be added in the future.

George A. McAlister

BOWIE'S DEATH BY VARIOUS AUTHORS

Walter Lord. A Time to Stand, 1961. Page 165.
"Propped in his cot, brace of pistols by his side, pale as the death that faced him, was Jim Bowie. He undoubtedly did the best he could, but it must have been over very soon."

Lon Tinkle. 13 Days to Glory, 1958. Pages 200-201.
"Feeble but armed, Jim Bowie lay on his cot in the southwest corner baptistry of the chapel . . ."

Page 216.
"Rallying with superb effort, he began firing at the enemy, holding his knife in reserve for those who came near. When at last the small room fell silent, it is said that Mexican bodies filled the doorway."

Page 225.
"Sergeant Becerra, hardly knowing Bowie was ill, claimed 'perverse and haughty James Bowie died like a woman, in bed, almost hidden by covers.'"

Page 225.
"Madam Candelaria, whose various accounts are contradictory, testified she was in Bowie's room when the Mexican soldiers found him. She threw her body over his to protect him, she said, but the Mexicans plunged bayonets over her shoulder. When she walked out of the side room into the chapel, she said the blood on the chapel floor flowed into her shoes. Another survivor, Mrs. Alsbury, reported that the Mexicans tossed Bowie's body on their bayonets 'until blood covered their clothes and dyed them red.'"

Page 226.
J Frank Dobie stated: "Knife in hand, back braced against the wall at his head, victims strewn about him."

Martha Anne Turner. William Barret Travis: His Sword & His Pen, 1972. Pages 254-255.
"Fought to the end with pistols and knives."

"Mrs. Alsbury, (Bowie's sister-in-law) told Mrs. Maverick several years later that the Mexicans tossed Bowie's body on their bayonets until blood covered their uniforms."

Felix Nunez. The Gazette, Ft. Worth, Texas, Friday, July 12, 1889.
"There was but one man killed in a room and this was a sick man in the big room on the left of the main entrance. He was bayoneted in his bed."

Phil Rosenthal & Bill Groneman. Roll Call at the Alamo, 1985. Page 27.
"He was bayoneted as he lay helpless on his sick bed."

John Myers Myers. The Alamo, 1948. Page 225.
"Mrs. Dickinson saw Bowie's body tossed on bayonets of a dozen soldiers before it was finally thrown to the floor."

Dr. John Sutherland. Fall of the Alamo, 1936. Page 40.
". . . unable to lift his head from his pillow, he was butchered. He was shot several times through the head, his brains splattering upon the wall near his bedside." He says he was informed by Joe (Travis' slave) and Mrs. Dickinson and had visited the room himself and saw the blood stains on the wall.

Philip Haythornthwaite. The Alamo and the War of Independence, 1986. Page 16.
"---Bowie's body on bayonets---."

Susan Schoelwer. Alamo Images. Page 147.
"Even more mystery surrounds Bowie's actual moment of death. The most popular version holds that he waited in his sickbed in a small interior chamber, weapons at his side as the din outside peaked and then diminished, poised to slay the first Mexicans who burst in upon him. "Bowie, propped on his pillows, shot two soldiers who attempted to bayonnet him as he lay all but helpless and plunged his terrible knife into the throat of another before they could

finish him. "like his comrades on the walls, the dying Bowie was still capable of inflicting fearful casualties, climaxing in a final thrust of his famous knife. (E. Alexander Powell, *The Road to Glory* (New York: Charles Scribener's Sons, 1915, 177)

Other writers liken Bowie's death to martyrdom by emphasizing the sick man's helplessness and the brutality of his assailants. "Colonel Bowie was butchered on his bed and hoisted on the bayonets and his remains savagely mutilated," wrote William Brooker in 1897, echoing the account related years earlier by Bowie's sister-in-law Juana de Navarro Alsbury(Brooker, *Texas*, 64; Sutherland, *Fall*, 40; Maverick, "Fall of the Alamo," 56, Sowell, *Rangers and Pioneers*, 146-49.) And from William Zuber, source of the Moses Rose story, came the most savage version of Bowie's death, which Zuber claimed to have heard from a former Mexican fifer named Apolinano Saldigna. After the funeral pyre had been prepared, Saldigna related, Mexican orderlies carried out the sick Bowie, untouched by the fighting. The Mexican officer in charge then berated Bowie for his betrayal of his Mexican citizenship and family, to which Bowie replied defiantly. The officer consequently "caused four of his minions to hold the sick man, while a fifth, with a sharp knife, split his mouth, cut off his tongue, and threw it upon the pile of dead men." Then, "the four soldiers who held him, lifted the writhing body of the mutilated, bleeding, tortured invalid from his cot, and pitched him alive upon the funeral pyre."(Rohrbough, "How Jim Bowie Died," 48-53.)

Like Travis, Bowie was at first rumored to have committed suicide, and Mexican chroniclers, knowing his reputation as a fighter, scorned to find him in bed. "That perverse and haughty James Bowie died like a woman, in bed, almost hidden by covers," wrote an anonymous Mexican soldier, possible Jose Juan Sanchez Navarro. These contemporary condemnations have had little effect on Bowie's popular image, however, as Dobie explains, "Imagination and patriotic sympathy rebel at the idea of Bowie's dying except in the climax of hand-to-hand combat."(Williams, "Critical Study," 37:35-36; Dobie, "James Bowie,"*Heroes*, 45; Jenkins, *Papers*, 5:71.)

Stephen B. Oates. The Republic of Texas. Page 24.

Walter Lord, "Myths and Realities of the Alamo." '. . . there is less controversy about Jim Bowie, who was desperately ill and out of action. All agree he was slaughtered as he lay in bed.'

Unknown author. San Antonio Express, "Enrique Esparza, the Last Survivor of the Alamo is Dead." December 21, 1917.

". . . his child's eyes were fixed in horror at the sight of the death of Colonel James Bowie. He saw the body of the intrepid soldier-adventurer lifted on the bayonets of the Mexicans and then tossed to the floor."

Francisco Ruiz. "Fall of the Alamo," Texas Almanac, 1860. Page 356-357.

". . . Santa Anna sent one of his aid-de-camps with an order for us to come before. him. He then directed me to call on some of the neighbors to come up with carts to carry the dead to the cemetey, and also to accompany him, as he was desirous to have Col. Travis, Bowie, and Crockett, shown to him.

"On the north battery of the fortress lay the lifeless body of Col. Travis on the gun-carriage, shot only in the forehead. Toward the west and in the small fort opposite the city, we found the body of Col. Crockett. Col. Bowie was found dead in his bed in one of the rooms of the south side."

Esparza, Enrique (eight year-old son of defender, Gregorio Esparza). Interview with Charles Meritt Barnes, San Antonio Express, May 12 and 19, 1907.

"Bowie, although ill and suffering from a fever, fought until he was so severely wounded that he had to be carried to his cot, which was placed in one of the smaller rooms on the north side of the church and some of them got into his room. He loaded and fired his weapons until his foes closed in on him. When they made their final rush upon him, he rose up in his bed and received them. He buried his sharp bowie knife into the breast of one of them as another fired the shot that killed him. He was literally riddle with bullets. I saw his corpse before we were taken out of the building.

CROCKETT'S DEATH BY VARIOUS AUTHORS

Walter Lord. A Time to Stand, 1961. Page 161-162.

"Crockett's Tennesseans, at bay near the palisade, battled with a wild fury that awed even the attackers. Individual names and deeds were lost forever in the seething mass of knives, pistols, fists, and broken gunstocks; but Sergeant Felix Nunez remembered one man who could stand for any of them, including Crockett himself:

He was a tall American of rather dark complexion and had on a long buckskin coat and a round cap without any bill, made out of fox skin with the long tail hanging down his back. This man apparently had a charmed life. Of the many soldiers who took deliberate aim at him and fired, not one ever hit him. On the contrary, he never missed a shot. He killed at least eight of our men, besides wounding several others. This being observed by a lieutenant who had come in over the wall, he sprang at him and dealt him a deadly blow with his sword, just above the right eye, which felled him to the ground, and in an instant he was pierced by not less than 20 bayonets."

Pages 206-207.

"Did David Crockett Surrender? - It's just possible that he did. A surprising number of contemporary sources suggest that Crockett was one of the six Americans who gave up at the end, only to be executed on Santa Anna's orders.

"Colonel Pena flatly said so in his Diario, first published in September, 1836.* Colonel Almonte told a similar story, according to a letter from Sergeant George M. Dolson in the Detroit Democratic Free Press of September 7, 1836. So did an unidentified Mexican officer (who sounds suspiciously like Ramon Caro), according to a letter appearing in the Frankfort, Kentucky Commonwealth of July 27, 1836. A similar account also came from Captain Fernando Urizza after San Jacinto, according to Dr. N. D. Labadie. Urizza said the prisoner's name was 'Cocket,' but Labadie had no doubts whom he meant.

"Nor are all the sources Mexican. Passengers on the schooner, Comanche, arriving in New Orleans on March 27 with first details of the massacre, also reported how Crockett and others had tried to surrender 'but were told there was no mercy for them.' The New Orleans Post-Union picked up the story, and it quickly spread to the

Arkansas Gazette and elsewhere. Even Mary Austin Holley, that most loyal of Texans, finally included it in her 1836 guidebook.

"But it must be stressed that most early Texan accounts declared that Crockett fell in battle. 'Fighting like a tiger,' to use Andrew Briscoe's words. Both Joe and Mrs. Dickinson also believed he was killed in action, although neither saw him till after he was dead.

So there's a good chance Crockett lived up to his legend, and in some circles it remains dangerous even to question the matter. A few years ago when The Columbia Encyclopedia ventured the opinion that Crockett surrendered, an angry retort in the Southwestern Historical Quarterly declared that Texas would need better authority than 'a New York publication.' Next edition, the New York editors meekly changed their copy."

* (Author's note: It should be noted that De la Pena did not record that the seven men, including Crockett, surrendered. His account is given below.)

Jose Enrique de la Pena. With Santa Anna in Texas, 1836. Translated and edited by Carmen Perry, 1975.
"Some seven men had survived the general carnage and, under the protection of General Castrillon, they were brought before Santa Anna. Among them was one of great stature, well proportioned, with regular features, in whose face there was the imprint of adversity, but in whom one also noticed a degree of resignation and nobility that did him honor. He was the naturalist, David Crockett, well known in North America for his unusual adventures, who had undertaken to explore the country and who, finding himself in Bejar at the very moment of surprise, had taken refuge in the Alamo, fearing that his status as a foreigner might not be respected. Santa Anna answered Castrillon's intervention in Crockett's behalf with a gesture of indignation and, addressing himself to the sappers, the troops closest to him, ordered his execution. The commanders and officers were outraged at this action and did not support the order, hoping that once the fury of the moment had blown over these men would be spared; but several officers who were around the president and who, perhaps, had not been present during the moment of danger, became noteworthy by an infamous deed, surpassing the soldiers in cruelty. They thrust themselves forward, in order to flatter their commander, and with swords in hand, fell upon these unfortunate, defenseless men just

as a tiger leaps upon his prey. Though tortured before they were killed, there unfortunates died without complaining and without humiliating themselves before their torturers. It was rumored that General Sesma was one of them; I will not bear witness to this, for though present, I turned away horrified in order not to witness such a barbarous scene."

Lon Tinkle. 13 Days to Glory. Page 206.
"The calmest man, the Mexicans reported, was the Texan in buckskin who wore the peculiar cap. Two Mexican captains, both of whom pronounced his name 'Kwokety,' praised Davy Crockett's composure as well as his skill. Captain Rafael Soldana of the Tampico battalion described him standing up to reload his gun, indifferent to enemy fire, while he poured scorn on the enemy with his great voice before leveling Old Betsy for another kill."

Page 208.
"For Davy Crockett even that was impossible. A Mexican shot had broken his right arm; he began firing with his left till his gun was broken off at the stock and the gun barrel fell on the floor. Crockett drew his knife, and fought with his dirk in the thick of the musket fire, breating the sweetish, sickening odor of burnt gunpowder."

Page 214.
"In mute testimony to a man whose marksmanship was legendary, the greatest concentration of Mexican bodies is said to have been found around Crockett's body. Santa Anna's cook, Ben, said the fifty-year-old frontiersman was surrounded by 'no less than sixteen Mexican corpses' and that one lay across his body with the 'huge knife of Davy buried in the Mexican's bosom to the hilt.' Travis's Joe reported that 'Crockett and a few of his friends were found together with twenty-four of the enemy dead around them.'"

Pages 221.
"Caro, after admitting many previous falsehoods in order to be now believed, claimed that after all the fighting was over, five Texans were discovered hidden away under mattresses in one of the far barracks rooms against the west wall. These men, Caro states, were promptly brought into the presence of Santa Anna, who was outraged that they had not been put to death at once. General Castrillon who had been horrified at the mutilations thus far

committed, bespoke mercy on their behalf. Santa Anna treated this brilliant commander with angry contempt. He turned his back and walked off, leaving the soldier guard which had brought in the Texans to divine his meaning. There was no hesitation. Breaking out of ranks they rushed upon the prisoners and bayoneted them again and again.

"Caro insisted that the whole army could vouch for this episode. But by the time it was published, the Mexican leaders were trying frenziedly to transfer guilt for their later defeat to somebody else, and their testimony, like that of Caro, is hardly objective. Caro himself had a score to settle with Santa Anna."

Martha Anne Turner. William Barret Travis: His Sword & His Pen, 1972. Page 251.

She quotes Sergeant Felix Nunez's account of Crockett's death: "But before Crockett fell, he and his men had piled up more than 25 dead Mexicans around the post they had so nobly defended. While a diversion at the opposite end of the fort gave the enemy a strategic advantage, Crockett and his Tennesseans were put to the bayonet. Contrary to the Mexicans' belief, the palisades had not proved to be the weakest wall.

"Sergeant Felix Nunez had this to say of one of the men defending the low stockade wall, who could very well have been Crockett:

He was a tall American of rather dark complexion and had on a long buckskin coat and a round cap without any bill, made out of fox skin with a long tail hanging down his back. This man apparently had a charmed life. Of the many soldiers who took deliberate aim at him and fired, not one ever hit him. On the contrary, he never missed a shot. He killed at least eight of our men, besides wounding several others. This being observed by a lieutenant who had come in over the wall, he sprang at him and dealt him a deadly blow with his sword, just above the right eye, which felled him to the ground, and in an instant he was pierced by not less than 20 bayonets.

Most sources agree that Crockett fell along the line between the chapel door and the low barracks on the west. Furthermore, both the colored man Ben, the Mexican officers' cook, who remembered Crockett well from his days in Congress; and Mrs. Dickinson, who survived the siege, recognized the body of Crockett. Each also noted his coonskin cap lying by his side. As she was escorted from the smoking ruins of the chapel to face Santa Anna, Mrs. Dickinson recognized the body of the brave sharp-shooter. 'I recognized Colonel Crockett,' she later reported, 'lying dead and mutilated between the church and the two-story barracks; I even remember seeing his peculiar cap by his side.'"

Jesse B. Badgett. *The Arkansas Advocate*. April 15, 1836.

"He fell fighting desperately."
Note: Martha Anne Turner in *William Barret Travis: His Sword & His Pen* also used the above quote.

Phil Rosenthal & Bill Groneman. Roll Call at the Alamo, 1985. Pages 34-35.
". . . died fighting like a tiger," in the words of Andrew Briscoe."

"There were at least seven similar names to Crockett that could have led to misunderstanding by General Urizza and Navarro when they claimed it was Crockett who surrendered. The names were as follows: George Cottle, Henry Courtman, Lemual Crawford, Robert Crossman, Mial Scurloch, Riehind Stockton, and Robert Cochran (sometimes spelled Cocran and possibly Cockat)."

General Miguel Sanchez Lamego. The Siege and Taking of the Alamo, 1968. Pages 50-52.

VERSION I - Crockett went down fighting at the Alamo:

". . . the Texans died fighting, among them Travis, Bowie, Davy Crockett and Bonham. . .: Texas State Almanac, 1953. pgs. 44.

". . . Mrs. Dickinson and the servant of Col. Travis stated that he was killed during the conflict, and that they saw and recognized his person soon after it was over. . .: Letter, Crockett's son to Forsyth, 1840.

". . . Crockett licked the pesky Spanyards. . . but was finally reached by two Mexican musket balls . . . his body was found with his dagger in his hand, surrounded by 17 dead Mexicans. . ." Crockett Almanac, Nashville, 1837.

"Crockett at the Alamo" and "Death of Crockett" in each case shown in battle, with dead Mexicans underfoot, his chest stabbed by a dagger, knife and bayonet. Crcokett Almanac, 1848.

". . . Davy Crockett's right arm was broken by a bullet; he fired with his left until the rifle stock was shattered; he went down, his knife buried to the hilt in the chest of a Mexican soldier, with 15 other corpses around him . . ." Downey: Texas and the War with Mexico, pge. 57.

". . . Among the dead were Col. Travis and Bowie. . . and one of equal rank, Crockett. . ." Santa Ana's victory report, 1836.

These and many other examples conform with Crockett's fighting reputation prior to his arrival in Texas in 1835, which made him the typical Lone Star man, foundation stone of the Texas Tradition.

VERSION II - Crockett captured and then executed:

". . . Seven of them asked for quarter but were refused. They placed their backs to the wall and fell, each upon a pile of fallen foes. . ." Frost: Mexico and Its Wars, page. 168.

". . . Five Texan prisoners were brought out before the victorious army on parade, Mexican bayonets finished the survivors. . ." Downey: Texas. . .

". . . the death of an ancient, whom they called Cocran. . ." Sanchez Navarro, Memorias.

". . . Gen. Castrillon discovered five men hiding in the fort . . . he took the prisoners to Santa Anna . . . who turned his back while soldiers killed them. . ." Martinez Caro: Verdadera Idea . .

". . . Crockett had surrendered . . . when Santa Anna ordered the prisoners' death, Crockett sprung like a tiger at the ruffian, but before he could reach him, a dozen swords were sheathed in his indomitable heart . . ." Penn Smith: Colonel Crockett's Exploits and Adventures in Texas, 1836.

" . . . Gen. Castrillon entered the back room of the Alamo and there found Crockett and five other Americans . . . Col. Crockett was in the rear and appeared bold as the lion, his arms folded. . . Santa Anna replied: 'I do not want to see these men living . . . shoot them and the hell hounds of the tyrant dispatched the six in his presence . . ." Letter by Dolson, according to Almonte testimony.

". . . Gen. Cos told the other Generals it was Travis . . . the other man was Col. Crockett . . . Santa Anna turned and said: 'Soldiers, kill them'. The soldiers opened fire. A shot struck Travis in the back, he stood erect. Crockett had on a coat with capes to it . . ." A Mexican Sergeant's Recollections of the Alamo.

". . . I observed Castrion coming out of one of the quarters, leading a venerable looking old man by the hand; he was grey, his face was red, and he stooped forward as he walked. Castrion said: 'My General, I have spared the life of this venerable old man'. Santa Anna said: 'I want no prisoners. Soldiers, shoot that man', and almost instantly he fell, pierced by a volley. 'What was that old man's name?' I said. 'I believe' said he, 'they called him Coket'. But I haver never had any doubt that Urissa's account gave the fate of Crockett truly . . ." Labadie: Urriza's Account in Texas Almanac, 1889.

". . . While Santa Anna was a prisoner in Texas, he stated that he ordered him to be put to death after it was all over . . ." Lette J. W. Crockett to Forsyth, 1840.

" . . . Some seven men had survived. Among them was one of tall stature, well formed and of regular features . . . It was the naturalist David Crockett, very renowned in North America for his original adventures . . . who had taken refuge in the Alamo, fearing that he would not be spared, because of his status as a foreigner. Santa Anna, turning to the sappers, the troops nearest to him, ordered that they shoot them . . ." Col. de la Pena Diary, 1836.

The discrepancies in these eyewitness accounts are considerable, but admit justified doubts in the accepted versions of Crockett's and even Travis' death in battle.

VERSION III - Crockett survived, and turned up later alive:

"... The mighty backwoodsman, alive and without a scratch, turned up at the battle of San Jacinto ... 'When I fell down, they jumped on me, but before they could ty my hands, I had my thumnale into the eye of 'em ...' Crockett was captured and taken in chains to a salt mine in Mexico ..." Hardin's Crockett Almanac, 1842.

"... I recollected the all-bloody lickin I give him at the Alamo, buckled on my old scythe ... and prepared to start off instantly ..." Squatter's Almanac, 1845.

" ... My name is David Crockett, I am from Tennessee and they think I am dead, and so does every one else, but they are mistaken ... taken at Fort Alamo in Bexar, and sent with two other men to Laredo ... with a part of the army that moved to Monterrey ... sent to Guadalajara and placed in the mine ... at which place they had been ever since ..." Letter Wm. C. White, to editor of Gazette in 1840. This version transfers history into the realm of legend; the folk hero becomes immortal, to ride again when need arises.

Copy of an original newspaper article printed April 19, 1836:

COL. CROCKETT NOT DEAD YET. - We are much gratified in being able to inform our readers that Col. Crockett, the hero and patriot, it is said is not dead. The cheering news is brought by a gentleman now in this city, directly from Texas, and who left the Colonel, as he states, three weeks ago, at the house of his brothe-in-law in Texas, where the Colonel was lying quite ill, but gradually though slowly recovering from his wounds.

The gentleman who brings this news is known to a number of our citizens, who believe him to be a man of veracity. He states that Crockett was left upon the battle ground at St. Antonia covered with wounds, and, as the Mexicans supposed dead. That after the Mexicans had abandoned the place, Crockett was discovered by some of his acquaintances to be lying among the slain, still exhibiting signs of life. He was immediately taken care of, and conveyed to comfortable lodgings, as before state, where his wounds were dressed, and every attention necessary to his recovery paid him. He had received a severe gash with a tomahawk on the upper part of the forehead, a ball in his left arm, and another through one of his thighs, besides several other minor wounds. When the gentleman who brings this intelligence left his brother-in-law's house, Crockett was doing well.

Candor compels us to say that there are many improbabilities in relation to the truth of this report, but the respectable character of the gentleman who says he saw him with his own eyes in the condition and under the circumstances above stated, induces us to give it credit. We have, nevertheless, some doubts of its truth. We give the story, however, as the gentleman represented it, and we sincerely hope it may prove entirely authentic. It is either true, or the man who has detailed to numerous persons in this city the above statements, is a lying villian. It is due to him to say, however, that those persons here who personally know him, give entire credit to his statements.

This is most likely the starting point of the recent argument of the gentlemen that state that David Crockett was left alive after the battle of the Alamo. It may be noted that he was "tomahawked"! Arguments of this type are the most common thing in history when it comes to an outlaw or hero being killed suddenly and without warning. Most are considered "indestructible" by the people who follow their life.

Felix Nunez. The Gazette. Ft. Worth, Texas. Friday, July 12, 1889.
"The peculiarity of his dress and his undaunted courage attracted the attention of several of us, both officers and men. He was a tall American of rather dark complexion and had a long cuera (buckskin coat) and a round cap without any bill and made of fox skin, with a long tail hanging down his back. This man, apparently, had a charmed life and the many soldiers who took deliberate aim and fired, not one even hit him. On the contrary, he never missed a shot. He killed at least eight of our men, besides wounding several others. This fact being observed by a lieutenant that had come in over the wall, he sprang at him and dealt him a deadly blow with his sword, just above the right eye which felled him to the ground and in an instant he was pierced by not less than twenty bayonets."

James Atkins Shackford. David Crockett--The Man The Legend, 1956. Page 233.

"The report states, 'quoting' Madam Candelaria that Crockett had earlier loaded Bowie's rifle and a brace of pistols and laid them by Bowie's side, assuring the sick man that:

He (Crockett) could stop a whole regiment from entering. . . . It looked as though 100 bayonets were thrust into the door at the same time, and a great sheet of flame lit up the Alamo.

Every man at the door fell but Crockett. I could see him struggling at the head of the column, and Bowie raised up and fired his rifle. I saw Crockett fall backward. The enraged Mexicans then streamed into the buildings, firing and yelling like madmen. . . ."

Page 234.

"Whether Senora Candelaria was actually inside the Alamo or not we shall probably never know. But inasmuch as a bit of the testimony of the person who without question was there (Mrs. Dickinson) tends to corroborate her account as reported by Corner (the location of David's body when he fell), her version is the one which seems most acceptable. Even the most meticulous search of the evidence still leaves any final conclusion a matter of probability rather rather than of established fact."

Ann Fears Crawford. The Eagle: The Autobiography of Santa Anna, 1967. Page 51.

[Santa Anna] "I felt that delay would only hinder us, and ordered an immediate attack. The filibusters, as was their plan, defended themselves relentlessly. Not one soldier showed signs of desiring to surrender, and with fierceness and valor, they died fighting. Their determined defense lasted for four hours, and I found it necessary to call in my reserve forces to defeat them. We suffered more than a thousand dead or wounded, but when the battle was over, not a single man in the Alamo was left alive. At the battle's end, the fort was a terrible sight to behold; it would have moved less sensitive men than myself."

Francisco Ruiz.   "Fall of the Alamo," Texas Almanac, 1860. Pages 356-357.

". . . Santa Anna sent one of his aid-de-camps with an order for us to come before him.   He directed me to call on some of the neighbors to come up with carts to carry the dead to the cemetery, and also to accompany him, as he was desirous to have Col. Travis, Bowie, and Crockett, shown to him.

"On the north battery of the fortress lay the lifeless body of Col. Travis on the gun-carriage, shot only in the forehead.   Toward the west and in the small fort opposite the city, we found the body of Col. Crockette.   Col. Bowie was found dead in his bed in one of the rooms of the south side."

Carlos E. Castaneda.   The Mexican Side of the Texas Revolution. 1970.

"On the night of the fifty of March, four columns having been made ready for the assault under the command of their respective officers, they moved forward in the best order and with the greatest silence, but the imprudent huzzas of one of them awakened the sleeping vigilance of the defenders of the fort and their artillery fire caused such disorder among our columns that it was necessary to make use of the reserves. The Alamo was taken, this victory that was so much and so justly celebrated at the time, costing us seventy dead and about three hundred wounded..."

Page 15.
"Let us weep at the tomb of the brave Mexicans who died at the Alamo defending the honor and the rights of their country. They won a lasting claim to fame and the country can never forget their heroic names..."

Page 20.
"The capture of the Alamo, in spite of its attendant disasters, ..gave us a prodigious prestiege."

(Author's note: It is interesting notice that Santa Anna did not mention taking any prisoners at the Alamo. If, as Lt. Col. de La Pena contends, seven were taken and among them Crockett, it raises the question of why Santa Anna did not mention this--after all, David Crockett was an ex-congressman and very famous).

Carlos E. Castaneda. The Mexican Side of the Texas Revolution. 1970.
Ramon Martinez Caro. "A True Account of the First Texas Campaign".

Page 105.

"The enemy die to a man and its loss may be said to have been 183 men, the sum total of their force. Six women who were captured were set at liberty. Among the 183 killed there were five who were discovered by General Castrillon hiding after the assault. He took them immediately to the presence of His Excellency who had come up by this time. When he presented the prisoners, he was severely reprimanded for not having killed them on the spot, after which he turned his back upon Castrillon while the soldiers stepped out of their ranks and set upon the prisoners until they were all killed. (Caro's footnote): We all witnessed this outrage which humanity condemns but which was committed as described. This is a cruel truth, but I cannot omit it.

Urizza, Capt. Fernando. Account given to Dr. N. D. Labadie, "Urriza's Account of the Alamo Massacre," Texas Almanac, 1859. Pages 61-62.

"I observed Castrion coming out on one of the quarters leading a venerable looking old man by the hand: he was grey, his face was red, and he stooped forward as he walked. Castrion said: "My General, I have spared the life of this venerable old man." "Santa Anna said: "I want no prisoners. Soldiers shoot that man," and almost instantly he fell pierced by a volley." When Labadie asked Urriza the old man's name, Urriza answered, "I believe they called him Coket."

Almonte, Colonel Juan Nepomuceno. "Almonte's Journal,", Southwestern Historical Quarterly. Vol. XLVIII.
Pages 10-32.
Almonte set down his facts concisely and in a military fashion. He never mentioned any executions.

Captain Jose Juan Sanchez Navarro. "The War in Texas."
University of Texas Library Journal, Summer 1951.
Pages 71-74.

"Some cruelties horrified me, among them the death of an oldster they called Cocran. . ."

Dickinson, Susanna. J. M. Morphis, History of Texas. 1874.
Pages 174-177.

"I recognized Col. Crockett lying dead and mutilated between the church and the two story barrack building, and even remember seeing his peculiar cap lying by his side."

Esparza, Enrique (eight-year old son of defender, Gregorio Esparza). Interview with Charles Meritt Barnes, San Antonio Express, May 12 and 19, 1907.

"He (Crockett) fought to his last breath. He fell immediately in front of the large double doors which he defended with the force that was by his side."

This Author's Personal Conclusion.

It is apparent from the above conflicting reports that there is no agreement on how James Bowie and David Crockett met their deaths. Until irrefutable evidence comes to light in the future, their deaths will only reflect a particular historian's interpretation.

BIBLIOGRAPHY

Bibliography

The following is the majority of material consulted in the preparation of ALAMO...THE PRICE OF FREEDOM:

PRIMARY SOURCES - ARCHIVAL

Bexar County Archives, Bexar County Courthouse, San Antonio

Daughters of the Republic of Texas Library at the Alamo

Eugene C. Barker History Center, The University of Texas, Austin

Texas State Library Archives, Austin

General Land Office, Records Division, Austin

PRIMARY SOURCES - BOOKS:

Austin, Stephen Fuller. The Austin Papers. Compiled and edited by Eugene C. Barker. Vols. 1 & 2, Washington: Government Printing Office, 1924 & 1928. Vol. III, Austin: University of Texas Press, 1927.

Barnard, Joseph H. A composite of Known Versions of the Journal of Dr. Joseph Barnard, One of the Surgeons of Fannin's Regiment, Covering the Period From December, 1835, to June 5, 1846. Edited by Hobart Huson. Refugio, Texas: n.p., 1949.

Becerra, Francisco. A Mexican Sergeant's Recollections of the Alamo and San Jacinto. As told to John S. Ford in 1875. Austin: Jenkins Publishing Company, 1980.

Binkley, William Campbell, ed. Official Correspondence of the Texas Revolution, 1835-1836. 2 Vols. New York: D. Appleton-Century Company, 1936.

Castaneda, Carlos Eduardo. The Mexican Side of the Texas Revolution by the Chief Participants: General Antonio Lopez de Santa Anna;

D. Ramon Caro, General Vicente Filisola; General Jose Urrea; General Jose Maria Tornel (Secretary of War). Austin: Graphic Designs, Inc., 1970.

De la Pena, Jose Enrique. With Santa Anna in Texas: A Personal Narrative of the Revolution. Translated and edited by Carmen Perry. College Station: Texas A & M Press, 1967.

Duval, John Crittendon. Early Times in Texas. Austin: H.P.N. Gammel & Co., 1892. printed by the author, 1917.

Ehrenberg, Herman. With Milam and Fannin. Dallas: Tardy Publishing Company, 1935.

Jenkins, John H., General Editor. The Papers of the Texan Revolution, 1835-1836. 10 Vols. Austin: Presidial Press, 1973.

Lamar, Mirabeau B. The Papers of M. B. Lamar. Ed. by Charles A. Gulick, et al. 6 vols. 1924-1927. Facimile Reprint, Austin: Pemberton Press, 1968.

Linn, John J. Reminiscences of Fifty Years in Texas. 1883. Austin: State House Publishers, 1986.

Menchaca, Antonio. Menchaca's Memoirs. San Antonio: Yanaguana Society Publications, 1937.

Rodriguez, J. M. Rodriguez Memoirs of Early Texas. 2nd ed. San Antonio: Standard Printing Company, 1961.

Seguin, Juan Nepumuceno. Personal Memoirs of John N. Seguin, From the Year 1834 to the Retreat of General Woll From the City of San Antonio in 1842. San Antonio: Ledger Book and Job Office, 1858.

Smithwick, Noah. The Evolution of a State. 1900. Austin: University of Texas Press, 1983.

Sutherland, John. The Fall of the Alamo. San Antonio: Naylor Company, 1936.

Travis, William Barret. Diary, August 30, 1833 to June 26, 1834. Ed. by Robert E. Davis. Waco: Texian Press, 1972.

SECONDARY SOURCES - BOOKS

Almaraz, Felix D. Jr. Tragic Cavalier: Governor Manuel Salcedo of Texas, 1807-1813. Austin & London: University of Texas Press, 1971.

Barker, Eugene C., Potts, Charles Shinley; Ramschell, Charles W. A School History of Texas. Row, Peterson and Company, Evanston, Illinois. New York.

Baugh, Virgil E. Rendezvous at the Alamo: Highlights in the Lives of Bowie, Crockett, and Travis. Lincoln: University of Nebraska Press, 1985.

Brown, John Henry. History of Texas, From 1685 to 1892. St. Louis: L. E. Daniell, 1892-1893.

Chabot, Frederick C. With the Makers of San Antonio. San Antonio: Artes Graficas, 1937.

Connor, Seymour V. Texas: A History. Arlington Heights, Illinois, AHM Publishing Company, 1971.

Crawford, Ann Fears, ed. The Eagle: The Autobiography of Santa Anna. Austin: Pemberton Press, 1967.

Day, James M., comp. The Texas Almanac, 1857-1873: A Compendium of Texas History. Waco: Texian Press, 1967.

De Zavala, Adina. History and Legends of the Alamo and Other Missions In and Around San Antonio. San Antonio: Privately Printed by the Author, 1917.

Douglas, Claude. Life of a Bravo. Dallas: Banks, Upshaw and Company, 1944.

Driscoll, Clara. In the Shadow of the Alamo. New York: G. P. Putnam's Sons, 1906.

Filisola, General Vincente. History of the War In Texas, Vol. II 1849, Austin: Eakin Press, 1987.

Flynn, Jean. James Butler Bonham. Eakin Press, 1984.

Foote, Henry S. Texas and Texans. Houston: Dillage & Company, 1909.

Ford, John S. Origin and Fall of the Alamo, March 6, 1836. San Antonio: Johnson Brothes Printing Company, 1895.

Gray, William Fairfax. From Virginia to Texas. Houston: Dillage & Company, 1909.

Guerra, Mary Ann. The Alamo. San Antonio: Alamo Press, 1983.

Handbook of Texas. Walter Prescott Webb, Editor-in-Chief. 3 Vols. Austin: Texas State Historical Association, 1952 and 1976.

Haythornthwaite, Philip. The Alamo and the War of Texas Independence, 1835-1836. London: Osprey Publishing Company, 1986.

Houston, Andrew Jackson. Texas Independence. Houston: Anson Jones Press, 1950.

Huson, Hobart. Captain Phillip Dimmitt's Commandancy of Goliad, 1835-1836. Austin: Von-Boeckmann-Jones Company, 1974.

Jackson, Jack. Recuerden El Alamo: The True Story of Juan N. Seguin and His Fight for Independence. Berkeley, Calif: Last Gasp, 1979.

James, Marquis. The Raven. St. Simons Island, Georgia: Mockingbird Book, Inc., 1981.

Kilgore, Dan. How Did Davy Die? College Station: Texas A & M Press, 1978.

Thonhoff, Robert H. The Texas Connection. Austin: Eakin Press, 1981.

King, C. Richard. Susanna Dickinson: Messenger of the Alamo. Austin: Shoal Creek Publishers, 1976.

Knaggs, John R. The Bugles Are Silent: A Novel of the Texas Revolution. Austin: Shoal Creek Publishers, 1977.

Lord, Walter. A Time to Stand. Harper & Brothers, 1961.

McAlister, George A. A Time to Love and a Time to Die: A Tale of the Men - Their Lives and Loves - Who Forged the Republic of Texas. Big Spring, Texas: GAMCO Industries, Inc., 1985.

McDonald, Archie P. Travis. Austin: Jenkins Publishing Company, 1976.

Morphis, J. M. History of Texas. New York: United States Publishing Company, 1875.

Myers, John Meyers. The Alamo. New York: E. P. Dutton and Company, 1948.

Nevin, David. The Texans. New York: Time-Life Books, 1975.

Newcomb W. W. Jr. The Indians of Texas from Prehistoric to Modern Times. University of Texas Press: Austin & London, 1922.

Newton, Lewis W. and Herbert Gambrell. A Social and Political History of Texas. Dallas: Turner Company, 1935.

Potter, Reuben Marmaduke. The Fall of the Alamo. Hillsdale, New Jersey: The Otterden Press, 1977.

Rosenthal, Phil and Bill Groneman. Roll Call at the Alamo. Santa Fe.: Old Army Press, 1985.

Sanchez-Lamego, Miguel A. The Siege and Taking of the Alamo. Santa Fe.: Press of the Territorian, 1968.

Santos, Richard G. Santa Anna's Campaign Against Texas. 2nd ed. Salisbury, N. C.: Documentary Publications, 1981.

Schoelwer, Susan Prendergast. Alamo Images: Changing Perceptions of a Texas Experience. Dallas: DeGolyer Library and Southern Methodist University Press, 1986.

Shackford, James Atkins. David Crockett: The Man and the Legend. Chapel Hill: Univesity of North Carolina Press, 1936.

Tinkle, Lon. Thirteen Days to Glory: The Siege of the Alamo. New York: McGraw-Hill Book Company, Inc., 1958.

Tolbert, Frank X. An Informal History of Texas, 1966, New York: Harper, 1961.

Turner, Martha Anne. William Barret Travis: His Sword and His Pen. Waco: Texian Press, 1971.

Wharton, Clarence. Remember Goliad. 1931. Glorieta, New Mexico: Rio Grande Press, Inc., 1968.

Yoakum, Henderson K. History of Texas From Its First Settlement to Its Annexation to the United States in 1846. 2 Vols. New York: Redfield, 1856.

Zuber, William Physick. My Eighty Years in Texas. Austin: University of Texas Press, 1971.

PRIMARY SOURCES - ARTICLES

Almonte, Juan Nepomuceno. "the Private Journal of Juan Nepomuceno Almonte. Southwestern Historical Quarterly (hereinafter referred to as SHQ) XLVIII, July 1944.

Bacarisse, Charles A. "Baron de Bastrop," Southwester Historical Quarterly 58 (1954): 319:30

Baker, Karle, "Trailing the New Orleans Greys." Southwest Review 22 (April, 1937).

Beretta, John King. "Letters and Documents." SHQ, XLIII (October, 1939).

Brindley, Anne A. "Jane Long," Southwestern Historical Quarterly 54 (1950), pp. 211-238.

Dobie, J. Frank, "The Line Tht Travis Drew," In the Shadow of History, Austin: Texas Folklore Society Publication 15, 1939.

Groneman, Bill, "Charles Zanco - Alamo Defender." American Dane Magazine 49 (August, 1985.)

Hutton, Paul Andrew. "The Alamo: An American Epic," American History Illustrated 20 (March, 1986).

Hutton, Paul Andrew. "Davy Crockett, Still King of the Wild Frontier," Texas Monthly 24 (June, 1986).

Hutton, Paul Andrew. "A Tale of 2 Alamos." SMU Mustang 36 (Spring, 1986).

Lord, Walter. "Myths and Realities of the Alamo." In The Republic of Texas, Stephen B. Oates, General Editor, American West and SHQ, Palo Alto, California: 1968.

Pohl, James W. and Stephen L. Hardin, "The Military History of the Texas Rvolution: An Overview." SHQ LXXXIX (January, 1986).

Ramsdell, Charles. "The Storming of the Alamo." American Heritage (February, 1961).

Ruiz, Francisco Antonio. "Fall of the Alamo," Texas Almanac, 1860.

Schmidt, Eric von. "The Alamo Remembered - From a Painter's Point of View," Smithsonian 16 (March, 1986).

Young, Kevin R. A Family of Rebels. Some notes on the kin of James Butler Bonham on file in the DRT Research Library at the Alamo. Publishing date unknown.

MANUSCRIPT MATERIAL

Leal, John Ogden, trans. "Baptisms of Mission San Francisco de Solano and San Antonio de Valero (Alamo), 1703-1783. Typescript. DRT Library at the Alamo.

Mixon, Ruby. "William Barret Travis: His Life and Letters." M.A. Thesis, University of Texas, 1930.

Strong, Bernice . "Alamo Plaza: Cultural Crossroads of a City, 1724-1900." M. A. Thesis, The University of Texas at San Antonio, 1986.

Williams, Amelia W. "A Critical Study of the Siege of the Alamo and of the Personnel of Its Defenders." PhD. Dissertation, University of Texas, 1931.

PRIMARY SOURCES - CONTEMPORARY NEWSPAPERS

Fort Worth Gazette, July 12, 1889. Interview with Sergeant Felix Nunez.

Frankfort Commonwealth, May 25, 1836. Joe's account of the Battle of the Alamo.

San Antonio Express, May 9 and May 12, 1907. Interview with Enrique Esparza.

San Antonio Express, February 24, 1929. Reprint of interview with Susanna Dickinson.

INDEX

INDEX

replaced Governor Henry Smith 113
unable to raise a quorum 114
vilified Governor Smith 113
vote to impeach Governor Smith 113
Criollos 39, 52
Crockett, David 64, 140, 141
arrived at Nacogdoches 141
Crockett's death-various versions 200
ex-Congressman, bear hunter, story
teller, and "gentleman from the
cane" 140
inspirational words 140
learned delegates from Nacogdoches
already elected to convention 141
no other choice but to stay and die 141
Old Betsy 140
speech 140
the politician 140
Cummins, David 147
Cummings, Rebecca 91, 92, 103
as Travis' sweetheart 92, 93, 103
lived at Mill Creek 92
Darst, Jacob 170
participated in Battle of Gonzales 170
**De Aguauo, Marquis de San Miguel 23,
24, 25**
crossed the Rio Grande 24
governor of Coahuila and Texas 24
leads force back to East Texas 24
recommended two hundred settlers be
brought in 25
relocated Mission San Francisco 24
renamed San Francisco de los Neches 24
De Alarcon, Martin 22
established San Antonio 22
governor of Coahuila 22
selected "half-way station" on Old San
Antonio Road 22
De Arocha, Antonio Cruz 66
De Arredondo, General Joaquin 37
approves Moses Austin petition 44
Battle of Medina 38
force reached the Medina River 38
known for his cruelty 38
pillage, torture, and rape 38
royalist army of 3,000 strong 38
Santa Anna's Mentor 37
De Bastrop, Baron 44, 49
birthplace 44
influential with Governor Martinez 44

intervenes in Austin's behalf 44
man of mystery 44
named land commissioner 49
true name 44
De Coronado, Francisco Vasquez 6
"El Turco" 7
De Vaca's tale of wealth 6
decided to find magnificent city 6
discovered Grand Canyon 6
discovered Palo Duro Canyon 7
Estevanico killed by Indians 6
Estevanico sent with Father Marcus de
Niza 6
Father Marcus reported he had seen the
fabulous city 6
land named Quivera 7
marched eastward into Texas 7
party crossed into present United States
in eastern Arizona 6
reconnaissance party to purported city
of gold 6
Seven Cities of Cibola 7
**De Cos, General Martin Perfecto 96,
133, 173**
agrees all cannon and artillery to
remain at Alamo 111
breaks his pledge 112
brother-in-law of Santa Anna 96
Commandant of Eastern Interior
Provinces 96
commanded the first attack column 174
establishes headquarters at Alamo for
Battle of Bexar 106
fortifies San Antonio 106
left a small detachment at Goliad 105
marches army south in defeat and
disgrace 112
occupies Bexar 106
pledges never again to bear arms
against Texas 111
enters Bexar without opposition 105
surrenders Alamo 111
total Mexican force in Bexar 106
De Escandon, Jose 27
all of the area explored named Nueva
Santander 27
an expedition to settle Seno Mexico 27
Dolores in present Zapata County 27
Laredo founded 27
town of Mier founded 27

Index